THINGS TO COME

JOHN MIDDLETON MURRY

★

THINGS TO COME

Essays

JONATHAN CAPE
THIRTY BEDFORD SQUARE
LONDON

FIRST PUBLISHED MCMXXVIII
NEW EDITION
FIRST PUBLISHED MCMXXXVIII

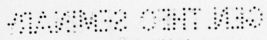

PRINTED IN GREAT BRITAIN BY
BUTLER & TANNER LTD
FROME

CONTENTS

ON LOVE: HUMAN AND DIVINE   Page i

PREFACE TO THE ORIGINAL EDITION   7

THE NEED OF A NEW PSYCHOLOGY   11

NEWMAN AND SIDGWICK   34

KEATS AND TOLSTOY   47

WILLIAM ARCHER AND THE SURVIVAL OF PERSONALITY   64

PERSONALITY AND IMMORTALITY   78

A THEOLOGICAL ENCOUNTER   86

CHRIST OR CHRISTIANITY?   99

RENAN'S DREAM   127

SCIENCE AND KNOWLEDGE   134

'TRUTH TO LIFE'   146

THE PARABLES OF JESUS   157

POETRY AND REALITY   177

THE PHILOSOPHY OF POETRY   187

POETRY AND RELIGION   205

POETRY AND PRAYER   210

THOUGHTS ON PANTHEISM   220

TO BE OR NOT TO BE?   230

THE METHOD OF MICHAEL FARADAY   240

ON READING NOVELS   248

ON BEING A CLASSIC   256

CONCERNING ANGELS   261

PAULINES AND GALILEANS   268

PATRIOTISM   274

A DIVAGATION ON POLITICS   281

THE LORD'S HOUSEKEEPER   292

THE DIVINE PLAIN FACE   301

APPENDIX: T. H. Huxley's translation of Goethe's rhapsody on Nature   313

ON LOVE: HUMAN AND DIVINE

ON LOVE: HUMAN AND DIVINE

I HAD not opened this book since it was written, twelve years ago, until the other day. Then I opened it at the essay on 'Christ and Christianity,' and found these words: 'The choice is between contradictions and silence. Perhaps, if I were older and wiser than I am, I should have chosen silence.'

I am certainly older, less certainly wiser; and it is true that there are very many things in that essay which I should write very differently, or not at all, to-day. Yet I cannot, and do not regret that I wrote them as they stand. I reckon myself as one of those who may claim the benefit of the proverb of William Blake: 'If the fool would persist in his folly, he would become wise.' I have at least been persistent in my folly: outwardly and inwardly. Outwardly, in that the magazine in and for which these essays were written, *The Adelphi*, has been maintained in existence ever since chiefly by my own obstinacy – a shadow or a skeleton of the once prosperous-looking journal, from which some of these essays did as much as anything to frighten readers away. Inwardly, in that I cannot bring myself to regret that I did thus frighten them.

For, although I have become an altogether more orthodox Christian than I was, I have also become a much more revolutionary one. I have come to believe that 'the folly of the fool' is a Christian necessity – perhaps *the* Christian necessity – and that the only way of being foolish enough, or of persisting in one's folly long enough, is to be Christian through and through. I know that is not how most Christians, or any unbelievers, regard the Christian faith: but that is the way I understand it, and that is the path along

i

which I have been drawn, with an inevitability that now appears to have been absolute, towards a full Christian profession. I derive comfort from the fact that William Blake, who uttered the wise word of which I claim the benefit, was the man who first put forward, into a deaf world, a Christian theology, or a restatement of the Christian mystery, which is self-evident and satisfying to me.

'Distinguish therefore States from individuals in those States.
States change, but Individual Identities never change nor cease . . .
Judge then of thy Own Self: thy Eternal Lineaments explore,
What is Eternal and what Changeable and what Annihilable.
The Imagination is not a State: it is the Human Existence itself.
Affection or Love becomes a State when divided from Imagination.
The Memory is a State always, and the Reason is a State,
Created to be Annihilated and a new Ratio created.
Whatever can be Created can be Annihilated: Forms cannot:
The Oak is cut down by the Ax, the Lamb falls by the Knife,
But their Forms Eternal Exist For-ever. Amen. Hallelujah.'

But when these essays were written, Blake was virtually unknown to me; as, I think, he still is to the majority even of educated men, even of educated Christian men. Nor is it reasonable to expect that anyone but a born 'fool' should wrestle with him, saying: 'Except thou bless me, I will not let thee go.' And God forbid that I should imply that a knowledge of William Blake is necessary to salvation. But I think he is a very great teacher for those men of to-day who have, finally and ruefully, to acknowledge that they belong to the tribe of 'fools.'

Whether the 'fools' are many or few – and I believe their number is increasing faster to-day than it has for many years, perhaps even for centuries – what seems to me certain is that the path to the Christian faith cannot be an easy one to-day, simply because it is the only path to a future not fatal to humanity. I believe, just as strongly as I believed when I wrote this book, that the possibility of a not inhuman future for mankind lies wholly in the determination of individual men and women to achieve their own reality. What I did not understand, when I wrote this book, was the difficulty of this apparently simple thing – the achievement of his own reality by the individual. Yet, even so far as I had gone, mine had not been a particularly easy road. Those who care to check my assertion may do so by reading the story of my life in *Between Two Worlds* – a narrative which ends eight years before even this book was written. Those ensuing eight years were, themselves, no easier than those which had gone before. But in them was contained the one entirely revolutionary happening of my life – which supervened upon the death of the one creature whom with all my heart and mind and soul I *loved*, and the consequent snapping of the one bond that maintained me in some living connection with Life, or the Universe, or God.

Then, through complete dereliction, isolation and desolation, I learned the only thing I have ever learned in life: by which I mean the only knowledge that has changed me perdurably, and made of me a different creature, who thenceforward received experience in an entirely new way. Because this change was so simple, so immediate and so complete, I have never found a satisfying way of describing it. It was no more than the immediate knowledge that it is no use 'hanging on.' Yet how can that convey anything? When, at the same time, and the same moment, I learned that the only thing worth doing, the only thing that could be done, was to 'hang on'? Evidently, 'the choice is between contradictions and silence,' still. Indeed, I have to admit that I am, in this matter, as the Ethiopian who cannot change his skin. The choice will always be, as regards the things that most concern me, between 'contradictions and silence.' What I have learned since is that the Christian faith is the most thorough-going admission that the nature of reality, as it discovers itself in naked human experience, is such that it can be expressed only by contradictions or silence.

But to return to my revolutionary happening – the sudden realization that it is no use hanging on, yet the only thing to do is to hang on: or, to put them both together, that the only thing to hang on to is the discovery that it is no use hanging on – the advent of this knowledge is, as I say, the only revolutionary happening of my life. I date the reality of my existence from that moment. Although even I, who have no fault to find with my existence since then, could not by the wildest licence speak of it as a happy one, I have had a clue: I would call it a faith, were it not so squarely and firmly based on my experience. The clue is simply this: that one *can* hang on to the knowledge that it's no use hanging on – to anything.

In other words, that apparently negative attitude does become very positive. The words I naturally turn to in order to describe it, and make it live again within me, are those of William Blake: 'All that can be annihilated must be annihilated.' Perhaps – I cannot tell – there has been a streak of perversity in my nature, whereby I have exposed myself to more and more intimate annihilations than come to most people. It almost appears to be so when I try to make a map of my life, as it were on Mer-

iv

cator's projection. Nevertheless, that is not how I have experienced it, any more than Mercator's squares are like the reality they represent. I verily believe I am incapable of conducting my life on the principle: This, or that, will be good for me. Although it is true enough that for very many years now I have known that annihilation was good for me, I have never been able to seek out the occasion for it. Furthermore, I have the stubborn feeling that it is impossible to do so; or at least that to do so would not bring one any nearer at all to what I mean, and what I believe Blake meant, by annihilation. I suspect that there is a difference, so deep as to be almost absolute, between self-mortification and self-annihilation. The former is something which you do to yourself, the latter is something which happens to you.

I am – it is one of the few definitions of myself to which I answer – emphatically a man to whom things happen. By that I do not mean that I am a centre of important happenings: the opposite is the case. I am the last conceivable subject for the gossip-monger or the newspaper story. The most paradoxical destiny I can imagine for myself would be to become a headline, if for no other reason – though other reasons are legion – than that I essentially am a man to whom experience happens: my entity resides in a peculiar faculty – I had almost said gift – of non-entity. Were I a poet, I should be tempted to claim for myself a (very modest) share in the 'poetical character' as Keats describes it: 'It is not itself – it has no self – it is everything and nothing – it has no character.' But I am not a poet; neither have I any desire to be one. So that it is sufficient to register myself as one who, having come to believe that 'all that can be annihilated must be annihilated' has, nevertheless, never sought annihilation. Neither have I avoided it.

By my standards and in the perspective of my experience

– that is the important thing: not to avoid annihilation. Yet, since I cannot help wondering whether that sentence would have had any effective meaning at all for me before I was thirty-three years old, I am disinclined to thrust it at the world as wisdom. It is recorded rather as an indication of an idiosyncrasy, or as 'a result that is whispered': I have learned not to avoid annihilation.

About much of it that comes our way, neither I nor, I imagine, anyone else has much choice. Yet I have often asked myself whether there are not some great primary differences between human beings in the quality of their 'experiencing natures.' [1] My own experience may not be very comprehensive, but I have come to suspect that it is abnormally intense. Again, were I a poet, I should be tempted to shelter behind Keats's use of the word 'intensity,' and excuse my nature by his. As things are, I merely confess that when the wave goes over me, I am engulfed. I have nothing to cling to, and now no desire to cling. And as it is with the primary and elemental happenings of life, so it is with the secondary. In the realm of thought, I appear to myself to be simply a place in which such thoughts as can, find lodgment; they seem to be anybody's thoughts, or everybody's thoughts, or perhaps even more truly nobody's thoughts, which have attached them-

[1] In the short space between the first writing and the revision of this essay, I have discovered that Maine de Biran had asked himself exactly this question and answered more positively than I had dared to do. 'Each individual,' he says in a note to his *Mémoire sur les perceptions obscures*, 'is distinguished from another of his species by the fundamental manner in which he feels his life, and consequently in which he feels – I do not say judges – his relations to other things, in so far as they can favour or menace his existence. The difference in this respect is perhaps stronger even than that which exists between people's features or the external formation of their bodies.' Quoted, by way of my friend M. Charles Du Bos, by Mr. P. Mansell Jones in *French Introspectives*.

selves to me. I am not so much 'a lodge for solitary thinkings,' as for homeless thoughts – thoughts without visible means of subsistence. I have no proprietary interest in them. If others come along and dislodge the present inhabitants from the caravanserai, that is an affair which they must settle between themselves. I am not identified with any of them – not even those which are dearest to me. That is not to say it does not hurt me terribly to let them go. It does. But somehow I feel that precisely *because* it does hurt me terribly to let them go, I must not cling to them. If they must be evicted, evicted they must be; but I take no hand in expelling or defending them. I feel that I am merely passive to any thought that can take possession of me.

Only I find, by experience, that there are not many thoughts which can take possession of me. The truth appears to be that the condition of my thinking any thought is that it does take possession of me, in the simple and literal meaning of those words. First of all, of *me*: not of my mind merely. A thought, to gain a permanent abode in me, must take possession not merely of my mind, but of my heart as well; and it must take possession of both at the same moment. Secondly, it takes possession of me; I do not take possession of it. And if, as sometimes happens, I have to struggle hard and for a long while to enter the thoughts of another man, what appears to me to happen is paradoxical. The more I struggle, the less I am; as though the very struggle itself were only an effort to make myself more 'passive and receptive,' to work myself to such a condition that the thoughts can enter me.

Again, I invoke Keats. My mind – or what serves me in place of one – is 'a thoroughfare for all thoughts: not a select party.' That is no doing of mine; it is not an ideal condition after which I strive: neither have I a professionally 'open mind.' This receptivity is my natural

vii

condition. My peculiarity is that a thought which is not somehow related to the act of living has very little reality for me: for abstract speculations I have neither taste nor capacity. Between the thoughts my mind alone can entertain and those my being also can embrace, there is a gulf: and only the latter sort can really find lodgment in me.

Indeed, I have almost a horror of abstraction, if it remains abstract. Somewhere, somehow, every abstract thought must be capable of undergoing the test of living experience, of being tried out in the action or the attitude of the individual man. What I live by, or can live by, is the ultimate court of appeal. But I do not pretend to know beforehand what I can live by. That, it seems to me, is my business to discover; and in the last resort the meaning and purpose of life, as I have experienced it, is simply that I may discover in myself that whereby I can live. To live means something quite different from existing merely – in my perspective – though I am quite willing to admit that what I mean by 'living' is only my individual mode of existing. But so soon as this word 'individual' enters, we have changed the category. Individual existence is life. As D. H. Lawrence said in his neglected masterpiece, *Fantasia of the Unconscious*, 'Life manifests only in the individual.'

So that the meaning and purpose of life, or my share of it, is to discover the necessary conditions of my own individual existence. That, it seems to me, can only be done by actual living. It is not to be discovered beforehand by taking thought. Thought can never determine what is necessary or intolerable to the being. 'Experience will decide,' as the hymn says. And experience is something which comes to one in the act of living. The sensation, as I have to record it, is that of being flung, time after time, into the ocean of life to swim or drown. And every time the ocean is a different ocean. As with living, so with the thinking that is consubstantial or homogeneous with the act of living. Every *new* thought that finds lodgment in one's being convulses the whole of the inward world: everything is upheaved, nothing is the same after the upheaval – except one's sense of the inscrutable power that is manifest in this never-ending destruction and creation of the personality. There is the mystery. For the more one is destroyed and created, the more certain grows within one the assurance that it is not for nothing; the more incessant is the process of annihilation, the more intensely glows the conviction of a sustaining power – of a divine and loving concern that 'all that can be annihilated shall be annihilated.'

In this perhaps very personal sense it appears to me that the meaning and purpose of life, which is first revealed as to discover the conditions of one's own individual existence, is finally revealed to be to know God – and to know a God of love, whose love indeed is not the same as our human love – how could it be? – but whose love is not *essentially* other than our human love at its highest. For, in my experience of human love – and I have a little – it attains its own purity only in the simple acknowledgment that one must let the loved one be. 'Let the loved one be': that, first in its plain negative and then in its more delicate positive, is the purity of human love, when refined from the crude ore. First, not to demand, not to interfere, not to possess – to *let* be; second, to cherish, to liberate, to suffer to unfold – to let *be*. Of a God moved by a love not essentially other than this, it seems to me my whole life is witness – a God who has 'let me be': a love against which I have cried out many times in agony and desolation, and shall (I fear) cry out again: but a love which in my utter extremity has burned me up as in a furnace, raised me up from nothingness, created me anew, and set me once again rejoicing on the road to the unknown future. I could not love my loved ones as God has loved me. I should not dare to; I have not a fragment of the strength. But neither am I required to do so. God will do that to them. But I can and do recognize, with an uplifted heart, that His love to me is not *other* than the love I feel for them. That this is so, I acknowledge finally, when I discover that I have nothing more to ask of life for them than that God should love them as He has loved me.

So, in my peculiar pilgrimage of discovery, I finally reach the conclusion that all I can do for the children whom I love is to see to it that they grow up with the capacity of being loved by God. I speak as a fool: I say 'see to it,' although I know well that I cannot *see* to it. What they absorb of this capacity lies not in my power to determine. It is like the sunlight or the lively air: circumambient and unwilled. They will absorb it, only as I have absorbed it – by being loved and cherished as a child, so that with a blind and delicate insistence, my nature craved for love as the only atmosphere in which it could breathe and expand. The finding of this love, the terror of its being taken away, its being taken away by death; its returning to me as something which I no longer sought to take, but sought to give; the finding of one to give it to, her being taken away by the same death; yet a third time, seeking a loved one who would not die – asking no more than that, and finding it, and being torn to pieces, and discovering, through my love of a child, that such love can compel our waking and deliberate selves to an annihilation that is absolute; and the returning of love again, through my dying this death, richer and simpler and fuller, made new – such is the outline of my life. 'Behold, I make all things new.'

That to me is the mark of the finger of the loving God:

that He makes all things new. He takes everything away
– everything; and, if only we can let go, He gives it back
again, in a new world; always in a new world.

'I in Six Thousand Years walk up and down; for not one
    Moment
Of Time is loſt, nor one Event of Space unpermanent,
But all remain: every fabric of Six Thousand Years
Remains permanent, tho' on the Earth where Satan
Fell and was cut off, all things vanish and are seen no
    more,
They vanish not from me and mine, we guard them firſt
    and laſt.
The generations of men run on in the tide of Time
But leave their deſtin'd lineaments permanent for ever
    and ever.

The myſtery, in so far as it has apprehended itself through
me, is that the wisdom and the love of God are revealed
in our lives, in the measure that we, by submitting to
our own annihilation, become the vehicles through which
is manifeſt the eternity of Love. Nothing that we have
made our own by love can ever be deſtroyed; because
we held it not in time, but hold it in eternity. And into
that order we can transfigure our exiſtence, in the measure
to which our hearts are ready to let go the creatures and
the things we love, or dream that we love. We cannot
love them until we have let them go. We may be required
– so hard it is for us to learn our lesson of love – to let
them go in death; it is because we could not let them go
before. Only that loved creature is taken from us, whom
we cannot let go, because only thus could we learn to love
her or love him. Our jealous, possessive, ſtrangling arms
muſt be torn away, in order that the creature of eternity
may be manifeſt, and life be victorious over death. For
not to be able to let the loved creature go, is to kill its

life in the clutches of our death. So we can love ourselves (as we must, for we are created by God) only by letting go of our Selves: only in Self-annihilation and the readiness for it. The only self we can love is the self that is surrendered to God.

Love is in its pure essence eternal. It *is* only when there is Self-annihilation: it is the operation and the mark of love to annihilate the Self. Love annihilates the Self, and thereby opens the gate of Eternity, which can never be barred against our entrance again. Thereafter, we have but to pause in an eternal moment, to behold the angels ascending and descending on its ladder, 'like singing masons building roofs of gold,' busy at their task of making all things new, redeeming and creating existence. For these moments, thereafter, there is no need to search: perhaps we had better not search for them lest we forget our business, which is our Master's. But we shall never forget that the work of the angels from which we turn our eyes away and the work to which we turn our eyes instead are the same work.

Thus, as it seems to me, the meaning of history lies in the redemption of human love by divine love: the painful ascent of human love towards divine love, towards which it must struggle onward or die. The nature of human love is that it is possessive: by seeking to possess that which is eternal, it sinks back into Satan's world from the divine spark which kindled it. For the nature of human love is that it is also divine. Most men and most women have seen the gleam once in their lives; most have felt, for a rapt eternal moment, that they themselves were not and only the loved man, or woman, or friend, or child, was. And how innumerable the times I have seen a young man or a maiden, simple and unknown, *transfigured* by the radiance of love! The annihilation whereby human love becomes divine is not a recondite or unknown thing: no privilege of the eccentric, such as I confess myself to be. It is the common and universal spark whereby the life of men is kindled, continued and sustained. It sets life in motion. But afterwards men and women lose the thread; they seek to possess each other, or seek possessions, in order to be secure. They pass under the dominion of fear. Instead of growing unafraid, they become more afraid. And fear is the enemy of love, and the destroyer of life.

I look upon myself as one in whom fear and love reached an extremity. That, if I have any, is my significance. All the fear that is eating the life out of the world to-day found in me its symbolic victim. If ever a child was born to experience a destiny of insecurity it was I. Snatched as a little boy from the class into which I was born, transmuted by education into a gentleman, yet carrying with me the blind hunger for that tender protective love which (I sometimes and perhaps unjustly feel) has become a rarity in any but simple folk: an only child, doomed as a boy to the appalling conflict between the values of his mind and the impulse of his heart; intolerably sensitive and afraid, shrinking from the absence of warmth in the new society he entered, drifting like a naked ghost to and fro over the solid landscape of social security, which he envied and yet despised – I could write an Odyssey of that timid wanderer. Yet, at the last, what would the story be? Simply this: how he sought love as an escape from fear – his only refuge from fear; how the one refuge was taken from him; how in spite of all terror he was naked and alone and afraid, without any refuge at all; how he knew that there was no refuge and that this was his destiny; how he found a courage not his own to endure to the end and be saved. 'We, in our Selves, are nothing.'

Truly, I know something about Fear; and it is simply because I have known so much about Fear that I have been taught a little about the perfect love that casts it out.

Would to God I could say that that was how I cast it out.
It was not so. Fear was cast out of me, simply because
my last and my only refuge from it was taken away. Fear
was cast out of me because I was wholly afraid, wholly
alone, wholly helpless. There was nothing I could do,
any more. I was taken out of my own hands, and I let
myself be taken; and I have never been in them since.
Yes, perfect love casteth out fear. I know that that is
true. But that is not how the knowledge came to me.
What I experienced was that perfect fear casteth out the
Self.

And yet – 'contradictions or silence' – I ask myself why,
in that strange crucial moment of my life, I could not even
seek to escape my fear any more; why all desire and dream
of escape abandoned me then; why this inverted courage
had come to me? and the only answer I can find is that
my extremity of fear had wrought in me an extremity
of love. The woman I had loved, and whose death worked
so upon me, I had loved even to anguish: she was verily
all I had – my very life of very life. By my love for her and
by nothing else I was saved from the sterility and barrenness of absolute fear. The thin-spun thread of her life
was my sole link with eternity. 'I believe,' she wrote in
a letter to be opened only when she was dead, 'no truer
lovers ever walked the earth than we were – in spite of
all, in spite of all.' And it was true.

They may tell me, I may tell myself, that I gave to her
and she gave to me, the love that is for God alone. That
also is true. But let us not be over-wise. I will not, because
I dare not, condemn that young man. For I still believe
that the one thing needful is that we should love – not
wisely, but too well. No matter though we give this love
to a creature, if only the love be extreme, it has God in
it. In the love that touches self-annihilation, there is
always God – both visible and invisible, both manifest

and hidden. The visible and manifest God, the unearthly purity and delicacy and tenderness and beauty, is obscured by death. The invisible and hidden God abides, waiting to reveal Himself.

The thread of life that bound my earth to heaven was snapped, the navel-string that brought me blood and made my heart beat in some kind of tune with the beyond was severed; all I had, and had because I only loved without consuming desire to possess, was gone. There was now no refuge from my fear, because I knew that love was the only refuge for me. And my loved one was gone. It was the memory of that love that forbade me to seek refuge in the love of a creature. The only creature I could love was she; or her child. And we had no child. So that there was nothing for me to do but to surrender to my fear – to face it.

To surrender to a fear is, in common language, a very different thing from facing it. But it may be there is a meaning in my reluctance to depart from this notion that, in some sort, I surrendered to my fear. Perhaps the contradiction is reconciled in the knowledge of what it was I feared – for what I feared was everything that was not united to me by love. That may sound a vainglorious manner of speech: but I am striving after the truth of my experience, and must choose my foolish words to fit it. Except where it was softened and changed by love, the vast otherness of the world, I felt, would crush me, or petrify me. And – such was my poverty – I could love only where I was loved. Then the icy fingers of mistrust which gripped at my heart were loosened, and I could breathe. Something warm and tender was interposed between my shrinking spirit and the world's hard otherness. Of a love that could flow out from me, and soften and irradiate the world, I knew nothing, save in the surmise of my intellectual imagination. There had been moments of intense and self-destroying contemplation when it seemed to me that in some strange fashion I verily did love all the world, and my own bitter destiny – for they came to me at a time when I knew that my loved creature must die. But I knew it, and did not know it. Intellectual knowledge is not, nor ever has been, living knowledge to me. To know a thing, in the matters which deeply concern me, is to have 'proved it on my pulses.' But, so far as the knowledge of the mind is knowledge, I knew that the loved creature must die; and the world I had to contemplate was the fearful world of war become a final and personal desolation by her death. And somehow it would appear to me terribly beautiful – with a beauty that blinded and illuminated me, in whose light I seemed half to understand that our love, by its very extremity, must inevitably be destroyed. There was in it that which could not *live*. My thoughts dashed themselves against the bars, asking: Why, then, was it born, if now in some sort I understood that it *must* be destroyed? It seemed to me, in some of these moments, that to understand, as I did, that it *must* be destroyed was also to understand why it was born. It was born in order to be destroyed by its own exceeding beauty.

Perhaps I was mad. I know that I wanted to die; and I walked about the streets during the air-raids in the hope of kindly death. But I do not think I was mad, because I had no thought of suicide. Death would come to me by destiny; or not at all. In this order also, I neither sought nor avoided annihilation. I wanted to die, but it was not in my hands. And, as I say, after a fashion I loved this world in which I longed to die, but in which it was not in my hands to die when I would. But this was not a love which flowed out from me to soften and irradiate the world, it was a terrible beauty which streamed in upon me from the world and killed my heart – 'a

spear-swift star.' With all my mind, and with all my soul,
I loved what I saw: but with all my heart, I could not.
For what I loved was a world, a destiny which involved
the killing of my heart. That was what I was summoned
to love, and I did.

What 'great ministering reason shall sort out the mysteries
of souls to clear conceiving?' Even the mystery of a
little soul like mine? It is clean beyond my power. But
I must struggle on, in my attempt to show that even in
my own case, though I knew it not, it was in some sense
love which cast out fear; that because love of the heart
was my only refuge from the otherness, I had to surrender,
to face the otherness when the sole object of my heart's
love was gone. For this contemplative love of mine, of
which I have spoken, sprang from the effort of my mind
to accept a world in which my heart could not love at all,
in which there would be, and by anticipation was, no
refuge from the otherness. But in that contemplative
love I could not live; I became a living death. My moments
of living were my moments of loving her with all my
mind and with all my soul and all my heart. And then,
as by fatal necessity, my heart would strain and burst
with the desire that she might live, and we somewhere,
somehow, be simply happy. Nothing, nothing mattered
but that; and that was to be denied. So whenever the
invincible love of the heart stirred again, it surely ended
in a new agony of desolation, and a new ecstasy of deathly
love for the terrible beauty of Necessity.

When she died, there was no love in my heart any more.
There was nothing for it to love. I found, with a sort of
cold despair, that I loved nobody. I had not known how
completely my poor loving of others had depended on
my love for her; nor did I know it then. It is only at this
moment, fifteen years afterwards, that I have understood
this simple thing. To me at that moment it was simply as

though a sudden abyss had opened between my friends and me, or as though we were separated by some invisible and transparent medium, on the other side of which I saw them, but only saw them, spoke to them, but only spoke to them. There was no warmth of life uniting us; they had passed into the otherness.

Therefore, I faced the otherness. There was nothing else for me to do. Wherever I turned it stared at me; it was as my own shadow. Ah, these words. If indeed it stared at me, must I not be facing it all the while? If it was everywhere, could I not surrender to it anywhere? 'They are shallow minds which take things literally.' I knew what I had to do. I had to be alone; I had to *be*, alone. I took myself in my own two hands and made myself to be completely alone. I cast out fear from the last extremity of my body. And *I* did nothing at all. In that it is the pattern and archetype of the few decisive actions of my life. Shrinking, cowardly, in the very anguish of fear, I am compelled along a strange road into the unknown. In an even more intimate sense than Blake meant it, 'I, in my Self, am nothing.' For Blake, in his Self, was a magnificent and splendid thing – a rebel angel. Not a shred of such splendour clings about me. I, in myself, *am* nothing – the very purity of nonentity.

That is why I have so little sense of sin. It is as though I were too insignificant to sin, or too weak, or I know not what. To do evil! What courage! What superhuman energy! My trouble has been to *do* anything, to *will* anything. Envy, I should say, was the sin I was inclined to – envy of those who did, or willed, or had. I seem to have got rid of that long ago, or most of it. What remains is but 'a mote to trouble the mind's eye.' My other sin *is* cowardice, for I shall never be rid of that. But when a thing has to be done by me, it will be done – that I know:

xviii

because I was taken out of my own hands long ago, when something took possession of me and cast out fear, when some power unknown and unimaginable to me took hold of me and whispered, as I am told the psychiatrists do to their patients, and said, 'Look at your fear.'

But there was no psychiatrist for me: neither was any conceivable. Who could heal my soul but myself? For precisely that relation of love and trust which is surely presupposed in seeking the help of a soul-healer was now impossible to me. Neither, for the same reason, could I have gone to a priest who, in his true function, is the healer of souls, indeed. (The labourer is worthy of his hire; but can souls be healed *for a fee?*) I knew that in order to seek out any human instrument of my healing, there must be a motion of love towards him in my heart: and there was none in my heart, towards any man. Love there was still, an anguish of love for my darling, with whose beauty all things on earth seemed incommensurable now. But to speak of this love to any human creature – how could that be? To speak of this love to another meant to love him with the same love. (May not the final paradox, the ultimate barrenness, of psychiatry without God lie even there?)

'Look at your fear.' Ah me! There is indeed the solution. But who shall give us courage to look at our fear? Surely not they who carry it on their faces that they have never dared to look at their own. Just as surely, not we ourselves. For our fear, the deep and universal fear, is of everything, and of ourselves. The very unwritten law of this civilization in which we live to-day is that we must not look at our fear. We must not look into the nature of this fear of insecurity which now, like a panic fear, runs through the human herd, as though the whole spiritual outcome of our becoming materially united had been to make us infinitely more liable to fear and infinitely more afraid. In such a world it is not for the man who clings to material security, in a suppressed frenzy of fear, or enjoys it in ignorance that there is anything to be afraid of, to bid 'Look at their fear' the poor devils who, in the like frenzy or the like ignorance, are the more sensitive victims of the universal fear.

No, I do not believe that the psychiatrist or the priest to-day has the authority to bid men 'Look at their fear!' Unless he is a very exceptional man, he has not faced his own. But I am quite certain that of the two the priest is in the right of it, if he truly believes in his own doctrine that, in order to look at our fear, we must verily die in our Selves. *We* cannot look at our fear: and so long as we imagine that we can, so long will our fear be transformed into new fear, and hatred, and despair. We cannot look at our fear ourselves, neither can any other human creature look at it for us. And if, by the generosity and grace of God, we should meet with a human creature who is to us the instrument of our being able to look at our fear, then there is one infallible sign by which we may tell that he has been an angel of light and not of darkness – namely, that he, in himself, was nothing, and knew himself to be nothing, but a humble instrument of the love of God. That such men are, I know; and perhaps if I could have turned to one of them in those days, I should have suffered less. But I understand now why it was impossible that I should turn to one of them. To utter my trouble to any man, to tell of my love turned to the ashes of lack of love, would have meant that the lack of love had turned to love again. Thus I understand the strange paradox by which I, who could speak my trouble to no man – not a word to the dearest of my friends: but now no friend was dear – when the trouble was overpast, and the death had been undergone, should seek to speak it to all the world.

xx

That problem has sometimes troubled my mind. Troubled, do I say? Nay, flitted across it, for truly I believe no problem has troubled me less. But I have often half-idly wondered why I, an exceptionally timid and reticent man, should from a certain definite moment of my life have become, by a sudden transmutation, one compelled to self-exposure. I have been accused not once, but many times, of spiritual exhibitionism; and there have been moments when I have been deeply hurt, even to a sense of outrage, by what seemed to me a malignant caricature of my purpose and myself. Nevertheless, somehow it has appeared to me, after a little while, completely unimportant. Nay, more, I have understood that what excited my critics to contempt was an inevitable appearance; it seemed to them that in truth I was exhibiting and exploiting my Self.

Yet, I should be dishonest, and worse – lacking in loyalty to those who have been loyal to me – were I not to avow that I believe that what has moved me has been the very opposite of this. It is simply because my Self has become, in a peculiar sense, not *my* Self at all, that I have been so free with it to the world. This I cannot explain except in words which, I know, will appear to many to be steeped in presumption. It is, I think, both a terrible and a joyous thing to be forced, as I was, through the very perfection of my own nonentity, into a position where there is no *possible* intermediary between oneself and God. I knew, at first, only the terror; the joy was unknown and undreamed of. As it was a terrible and joyous thing in the experience, so its consequences have been terrible and joyous too. In some strange way, my Self has been taken out of my keeping: it is not my private possession, any more. It is assuredly not by my own desire that I have handed so much of my intimate history to the world, or come to wear my heart upon my sleeve for daws to peck at. My self-exposure has been to me one incessant self-annihilation.

So my first annihilation was only the beginning. Maybe, the first was the worst: for then I had no faith at all. All I knew was the absolute necessity of blind surrender to death, or to the absolutely unknown which is death. To be taken once, finally and for ever, out of one's own hands, into the hands of no mortal power; to be conscious all the time while this thing was happening: that can happen but once in a man's life. It happens again, but it can never be the same – never quite the same. For, although I too can say, like William Blake, that I have 'died many times' since that first death, always thereafter in such a dying I have had, far away in some remote region of my being, the spark of a faith that I should be born anew. It is as though, having once been moved to surrender myself to the unknown God, thereafter I had only to surrender to the God whom in part I knew. With every subsequent surrender, came more knowledge of God, and a more certain faith in the working of His will upon me.

I speak as a child: there is no other way to speak of this thing. Yet I must not pretend that some at least of those ensuing deaths have not been more grievous to me than the painful first; I know full well that in some of them I have suffered more, felt a far fiercer pang of pain than I did then. Then I was stunned and numb with grief; but in other dyings I have felt the agony in a condition of exquisite and intolerable consciousness. That first sorrow happened to me; I was the passive victim. But I have lived to know what it is to be compelled to inflict the sorrow on myself, to tear myself away, as it were, by the living flesh, from a little creature whom I loved and who loved me; I have known what it is to break the heart of innocence, because there was nothing else to do. Not destiny, not

God, but *I* was responsible. I have learned the pain of having to inflict an incomprehensible pain upon a child. I speak as a fool; but I do not believe a man can suffer worse than that.

It is nothing less than the truth to say that in my subsequent dyings I have come to feel pains that are quite incommensurable with that first numb grief, and the terror of surrender which followed it. But what I have never felt again is the same fear; the fear that was so perfect that it cast out pain. Thereafter, as the years have followed, I have become slowly and steadily less afraid of my dyings; and it may be that as my fear of annihilation has diminished so my capacity to experience the pain of it has increased. I cannot tell. Or it may be that I have passed the absolute of pain. For no pain that I can dream of, or imagine, could be worse than the one I have spoken of.

I speak as a fool: for I can imagine one that is quite incommensurable with that one – that is to betray the God who has forged out of me the capacity to know and love Him. Yet, at one and the same moment, I can and cannot imagine that. Nevertheless, that imagination, which is of fairly recent birth in me, has opened the gates of my soul to a new fear – a fear unknown to me before: a fear of another order than that which God by His mercy slowly drove out from me. This new fear I am glad to have as my companion. It is a fear for which I am thankful: it does not disturb, or terrify me, but it chastens me. It is something which I lacked. Because of this new fear I have been compelled to pray again, as I cannot remember praying for forty years: and perhaps even more simply than I prayed as a child. It is not that I am afraid that God will not love me: that I know He will. But I am afraid, sometimes, that I may not love Him enough: that, although the spirit may be willing, the flesh may be weak.

For, as I have learned, through the little spark of human love that was transmitted to me as a child, to know as a man the manifest and unfathomable love of God, so at the last it has been simply revealed to me that the only way I can love Him enough is the way declared to mankind by His Son, Jesus Christ: that we resist not evil. It is not that I fear that I personally shall be moved to resist evil any more. I have tried to do so, and I know that to resist evil creates more evil; I know, perfectly well, that for myself love is the only way.

What I fear, in this grim modern world whose nature we gloze over, is that the time may come, even in this country which is so dear to me, when love will be deliberately used to kill love. Let me make my meaning plain. There are in this civilized Europe of ours such things as concentration camps. We do not know them yet in this country, and God grant we never shall. But it seems to me not impossible that we may. Let only the panic fear, the panic hatred, the panic degradation, which remains my grimmest and least delible memory of the last war, take demoniac possession of this country, and those of my conviction – whether or not they be Christian by profession – will be herded into concentration camps. That, in itself, has no terrors for me; and I believe that, God helping me, I can endure any direct physical pain. But if, in order to break my spirit, suffering is deliberately inflicted upon my loved ones – and is this unknown in the civilized Europe of 1937? – then, verily, I am afraid that I may not be able to endure.

' Ah,' my reader will say: 'but these things will never happen in this country.' I have no such confidence in Christian England, though I wince to say it. I can only hope and pray it will not be so, and that by the mercy of God the spark of Christian imagination will not perish from among us, but even now be blown into a fire – the fire of the love that casts out fear. That is my hope, as the former is my fear, for my country: therefore for it, and for myself, I pray the only prayer that comes natural to me:

'Our Father, which art in Heaven, hallowed be thy Name. Thy Kingdom come; Thy will be done on earth as it is in Heaven. Give us this day our daily bread, and forgive us our trespasses as we forgive them that trespass against us. And lead us not into temptation, but deliver us from evil.'

'Lead us not into temptation, but deliver us from evil!'

I have not attempted in the foregoing to deal in detail with the many positions taken up in this book which further experience has forced me to relinquish: it seemed to me better to give an independent account of the position I have reached to-day, and of one part of the road by which I reached it. In order not to cramp my style I decided to write a new preface of this kind, before allowing myself seriously to re-read my book.

I am probably prejudiced; but it seems to me to have this in its favour, that it is alive and not dead. It is the expression of a crude, imperfect and clumsy, but nevertheless a living thought. And I cannot help smiling, rather joyfully, at some of its peremptory expressions. In particular I have enjoyed the dictum: 'Therefore, it follows that the writer who slips back into the bosom of the Church to-day is, quite simply, an insignificant writer. It is a summary test, but quite infallible' (p. 154). I have an odd feeling that it may be true; and a still odder feeling of relief because it may be true. But better still are the words, descriptive of such as myself:

'They rebel against orthodoxy because their minds cannot reconcile the pain of the world with the omnipotence of a personal and loving God. They have proved upon their pulses that "the world is full of heartbreak, misery, pain and oppression": upon their pulses also must be proved the reality of a personal and loving God.

'I do not say it cannot be done; I believe, on the contrary, that it has been done: but I do not believe it will be done again save by minds more simple than the rest. The personality and the love of God are, for the grown mind, only metaphors.'

That was veritably prophetic. I gladly acknowledge that my mind is become 'more simple than the rest,' and that I am thereby become an insignificant writer. I am.

Indeed, the story of my journeying since this book was written, which I have briefly told above, has been precisely the story of the discovery of my own insignificance. Perhaps, at some time, I may be able to tell that story not summarily but in living detail: at present it is beyond my powers. But there was one stage in my discovery of my own insignificance concerning which a word must be said.

That was my adherence (or more truly my conversion) to Marxist Socialism. Of that conversion there is a record in my little book: *The Necessity of Communism*, and of its aftermath in another little book: *The Necessity of Pacifism*. But I may say here that I reckon my acceptance of Marxism among my major and beneficent 'annihilations' – one for which I can never be sufficiently thankful. I had become a Christian – that is, I had returned to the communion of the Church of England – a little while before I became a Marxist Socialist. Marxism did more than anything to make my Christianity a real and intimate purgation, 'trying the reins and the heart.' By its drastic illumination I realized how completely, and with how complete an un-consciousness, I was a creature of 'this world': how entirely I was surrendered to unwitting participation in an economic process that was not merely un-Christian, but anti-Christian. Marx suddenly showed me that the old Christian summons that we should be ready 'to leave wife and children and houses and lands' was not remote and obsolete, but terribly real. It was very grievous to me, but I managed to acknowledge the summons. And it is characteristic of me that when, by Marx's vision, I recognized the impending and righteous doom of capitalist society, and of myself as an unconscious participant in it, I prayed spontaneously and with a bursting heart that I might not be required to leave my children.

I do not suppose that many men of to-day, and certainly not many Christians, know the experience of being consumed even to tears by the reading of *Das Kapital*. Yet I do not for one moment believe that I was a fool to be such a fool. I am quite unrepentant; and I am inclined rather to say that not until Christians can experience that book as what it is – a denunciation by a great Jewish prophet of the radical corruption and inevitable catastrophe of the modern world – will Christianity be adequate to the real experience of modern man. A Christianity which ignores Marxism, or dismisses it as mere 'atheism' or 'material-ism,' is not merely a religion which cannot speak to our condition, but one which will necessarily become the ac-complice and the slave of Fascism. By that I do not imply that all Christians must become Marxists, any more than I implied before that all Christians must become adepts of William Blake. But I do unhesitatingly assert that a Christianity which is not avowedly revolutionary, in the social as well as the spiritual sense, as was the religion of Christ, will finally be found doing the Devil's work to-day.

Therefore, I beg that no Christian who may have read this preface will misrepresent it to himself, or to others, as the recantation of a Marxist. I was a Christian before I was a Marxist; I never ceased to be a Christian while I was a Marxist; and I am in some sense a Marxist to-day. Marxism has deepened and strengthened and purified my Christian faith; and Karl Marx remains for me the great modern prophet of the wrath and love of God – of the approaching Judgment in the world of time. He is the new John the Baptist of the revolutionary Christ, who is the same to-day, yesterday and for ever, bidding us flee the judgment of wrath by the revolution of love.

LARLING,
November 30, 1937.

PREFACE TO THE ORIGINAL EDITION

I HOPE that these essays, which form a sequel to a previous volume, 'To the Unknown God,' will be found to possess an inward unity, in spite of an occasional outward appearance of inconsistency. This outward inconsistency, which is particularly marked in the essay 'Christ or Christianity,' I have no desire to mitigate, for it belongs to the centre of my position that there is no absolute truth to be had in things spiritual. What man can attain is glimpses of the ineffable through many perspectives, and I try accordingly to make as many perspectives as possible temporarily my own. I regard revealed religion as a means towards an end that is, and will always be, the goal of humanity: an integration of the personality and an enrichment of the consciousness. But it is only one among other means, themselves as valid. With these other means I am equally concerned.

I find myself assailed, as was inevitable, from two sides – from the side of orthodoxy and the side of rationalism. It cannot be helped, and I do not suppose this book will be more kindly handled by either side than its predecessor. The Christian perspective is precious to me, and I am not going to surrender my right to use and profit by it simply because I am told by the one party that it is the only perspective, and by the other that it does not exist. In spite of the Church (or *The Church Times*) and in spite of the rationalists, I claim to be, in my own peculiar way, a Christian. I am as fully entitled to my share of the Christian heritage as any believer. On the other hand, I am not a heretic, nor even a Pantheist, but simply a believer in humanity in its finest manifestations. In other words, I am a great believer in heroes, and the greatest of my heroes is Jesus.

That, I fear, is a very unfashionable thing to say. Nowadays you can be orthodox and fashionable, or sceptical and fashionable. You cannot be what I am and be fashionable. I am rather sorry about that, for I have my living to earn. But since I find that the man of Nazareth gives point and focus to all my experience and my thinking, in ways which I hope will be apparent to any sympathetic reader of these essays, it would be less than honest in me not to declare the same and take the consequences.

Most of these essays originally appeared in *The Adelphi*; one was published in *The Hibbert Journal*, another in *The New Criterion*, a third, 'The Need of a New Psychology,' is an unpublished lecture.

ABBOTSBURY
January 28, 1928.

THINGS TO COME

THE NEED OF A NEW
PSYCHOLOGY

I CAN imagine anyone who happens to read the title of this lecture, saying impatiently:

'A new psychology indeed! But what earthly need have we of a new *psychology*? Surely we need a thousand new things other than that – a new education, for instance, or a new religion, or a new social conscience, or a new science of medicine, or a new ductless gland.' You know better than I do all the new things we are supposed to need, and by obtaining them we shall be a whole giant stride nearer the millennium.

I want the millennium as much as anybody; yet I am tired of the short-cuts to it that are offered me. I have lost faith in them. There was the great nineteenth century with all its energies focused on taking the shortest cut to the millennium, and it landed a whole generation of us in the bloodiest war in history. Obviously, something had been left out of the calculations. It doesn't seem to me the faintest use blaming other people for that ghastly episode. In so far as we had reached years of discretion when the crash came, we were all responsible, and the simplest and truest explanation of the catastrophe I have been able to find is that something very important had been left out of the beautiful sum which the nineteenth century worked out for us, and which I for one took for granted, the sum which proved conclusively that the greater the advance of mechanical civilization, the greater the progress of humanity.

It seems strange to me that so few people should really be concerned to discover what was left out of the sum – and that so many are satisfied with obvious and superficial answers. Some say more education would have saved us. But would it? The highly educated people, so far as I could observe, didn't behave any better than anybody else anywhere – and when it really came to the sticking-point, and there was nothing to do *but* stick it, it was the simple-minded ones who did most of the sticking. More education of the old style is a very poor solution. I cannot imagine that anyone really believes in it. 'Education' is become a catch-word like any other; like all the rest of the panaceas, it is empty at the core. Who will tell us what kind of man education should educe?

Or, we are told, more religion will do the business. Again, it was not apparent that the more religious behaved any better than the less, and I think it *was* apparent that modern religion chiefly consisted in supplying exalted excuses for debased desires. More religion, of the old kind at any rate, is not a safeguard one would care to rely on.

For the fact is that in time of stress or alarm, a nation behaves as a close-packed crowd. Those refinements of mechanical civilization, which seemed to the nineteenth century to be at once the evidence and the guarantee of Progress, have chiefly served to pack the crowd closer still. We have gone a good way towards annihilating space; at a moment of excitement there is no elbow-room between Land's End and John o' Groats, or between Los Angeles and New York City. A modern nation is become a crowd, and a crowd is swayed by Highest Common Factor of the desires of the people within it. Once the crowd is in action, good-bye education, good-bye religion, good-bye everything that primarily appertains to the individual man.

The crowd was the element that was left out of our nineteenth-century calculations; it was left out because no one had firmly realized that a modern nation, simply because it is modern, is infinitely more of a crowd than the old ones were. Man is a thinly varnished savage at the best; lump him together in millions and the varnish melts at the touch.

What is to be done about it? It is pretty clear to me that more education, more religion, more prohibition, more birth-control, or more vitamines – excellent as some of these things may be in themselves – will not touch the root of the evil. They are doubtless admirable things; I have a respect for the people who pursue them, but I cannot work up any enthusiasm about them myself. I may be called a political indifferentist. But there is some justification for me. I have been scared out of my life, by my own behaviour and the behaviour of all other men and women; I have learned that when the trouble comes, we all forget that we are little gentlemen and what not and become in the twinkling of an eye about as morally exalted, and a great deal less beautiful than the beasts that perish. I feel that I am living in a house which may catch fire at any moment, and it seems to me that I am not unreasonable when I am unable to get excited over the designs for the wall-paper or the colour of the curtains. What I want is some small guarantee that the house will not catch fire again. For the sake of that certainty I will do without many conveniences and improvements. I may be wrong in this, but I cannot help thinking that it is not I who am wrong, but the people who think me wrong.

So the fundamental problem of modern life presents itself to me in simple terms – terms so simple that I am afraid they would have little interest for the politician. I cannot imagine an election being fought on this issue, although, as I say, it seems to me by far the most important of all. It seems to me that until we have settled this problem, we cannot really settle any problem; all we can do is simply to tinker with the questions that come to hand day by day. Our tinkerings may be good; they may be bad; at the best the chances are even. We build more schools, more hospitals, train more doctors – what for? In order that there shall be healthy men and women. But *why* should there be healthy men and women? What a stupid question! But is it really so stupid? I cannot see that mere health will prevent a nation from once more stampeding like the Gadarene swine down a steep place into the sea. And when I am told by the Dean of St. Paul's or some lesser luminary, that eugenics will save us, I want to know what we are to breed for. We know what we want of a sheep – good mutton and fine wool – what do we want of a man?

It seems to me that the war, if it taught us anything (which I sometimes doubt) taught us this: that if man is not to be perpetually in danger of self-destruction by his own barbarism, he must be able to resist the elemental pull of the crowd. There are crowds of all kinds – little crowds and big crowds, crowds of the majority, crowds of the minority. The little crowd (which is the sect) is as vicious as the big one (which is the nation). The man to be bred, to be educated, to be legislated for – is the man who will resist this elemental pull of the crowd. So stated, the problem seems almost childishly obvious. And yet, I wonder.

What *is* obvious, painfully obvious, is that it is appallingly difficult to resist this elemental pull. 'Oh, I can't do that; think of my position,' is the commonest of all cries, and it is one of the most tragic, for you know immediately that if that man *were* to lose his position, he would lose himself – quite literally. He cannot stand alone; he needs the tacit approbation of his fellows to be convinced of his own self-existence. And the same profound impulse is at work in every province of society: men and women must attach themselves to some body or church, without such an anchorage they feel unsafe. We are up against a deep and aboriginal instinct of gregariousness. And this aboriginal instinct, instead of being checked or sublimated, is simply reinforced by the catch-words of modern civilization. 'Organize! Combine! You can do nothing without organization.' Surely, it depends upon *what* you are trying to do. If advances in the mechanics of civilization are indeed ends in themselves, then it is probably true that you can *do* nothing without organization and combination. But if they are not, if the basic assumption that mechanical advances in civilization correspond with moral and spiritual progress is unsound, then there is at least a chance that the converse of the parrot-cry is true. 'Resist organization! Stand alone! – you can *be* nothing without disorganization.'

Let us distinguish, and let us distinguish absolutely. As far as the mechanics of civilization are concerned organization is a necessity. But there is another department of life – let us call it the dynamics of civilization, and in this department I make bold to say organization is a delusion and a snare. The question is: Are the dynamics to be sacrificed to the mechanics? If they are to be sacrificed, I see nothing ahead but more catastrophe.

And I can see no way of maintaining the organics alive except by a new individualism – somehow men must make themselves capable of resisting the elemental pull of the crowd. We have to try to unlearn the habit of hunting in packs, where not what we are or may be decides our destiny, but what we have in common with a million similars. I speak absolutely, under compulsion of brevity. Some one may say: 'But are we not all members of a society?' Of course we are; it is impossible for any of us to live in utter isolation, and as undesirable as it is impossible. But do not let us mistake mechanics for essentials any more. What is essential is that each one of us should be an individual, able in time of stress – and times of stress are far more frequent than national catastrophes – to resist the pull of the crowd, to follow his own star, to obey his own soul.

This is where the need of a new psychology comes in. Here am I, talking about the necessity of becoming an individual – but how is it done? The very possibility of answering that question obviously depends upon an answer to the question: 'What are we?' Well, what *are* we? The old answer was 'an animal with reason.' Aristotle said: 'A political animal.' Whatever we may think of these bald answers of the old psychologies, they were emphatic on the point of man's animality. For the last few centuries – above all since Rousseau – we have been inclined to shun that part of it, until the war insisted that we should remember it. And I am afraid those ancient realists when they declared that man was a rational animal did not mean that he was an animal who behaved rationally – they knew too much about him – but simply that he was an animal who differed from the rest of his fellow animals by having somehow developed a queer rational faculty, which he sometimes used and seldom obeyed, and used principally as a convenient instrument for his instinctive and animal ends. He was, in fact, an ape who could invent the rifle.

He invented other and more mysterious things: he invented art, and poetry, and goodness and God, for example: but it was a very small section of mankind which invented these things, at least in the sense of lifting them out of the common rank of instruments to animal ends. For the average man God was the unknown power he tried to cajole or bludgeon into helping him to defeat his enemy; poetry the howl he raised over the dead body of his foe while he kicked it through the dust. On the whole neither God nor poetry have changed very much in the general conception. Mr.

NEED OF A NEW PSYCHOLOGY

Horatio Bottomley invoked God once a week during the war, and he led a campaign against the Poet Laureate for not writing a war-chant. Nevertheless, it is true that 2,500 years ago one small people, in spite of spending most of its time in fighting itself, had refined art and poetry and the idea of God into essences with virtue to resist the corrosion of time. The Greek world perished, but it left behind an immortal spirit.

The rational animal had achieved something which survived him, and could emerge from a thousand years of rank oblivion with its power to enchant and allure men utterly undimmed. But one of the reasons why that secular oblivion had overwhelmed it was that yet another psychology had been launched upon the world. There had appeared one who said: man is not merely a rational animal, he is a creature with an eternal soul. It was an astonishing thing to say, and we, whenever we really think about it and the man who said it – which is not so very often – are always astonished by it. If that word had been spoken in Plato's Academy, strange things might have happened. But destiny ruled otherwise; it was spoken to simple fishermen in an obscure corner of the Roman Empire. The fishermen could not understand it; but they saw the man who said it, and perceived that he was indeed a man apart. He called himself the son of man; he spoke of God as a father; he said all manner of mysterious things which he tried to make simple to their understandings – but the essence of it all was this – that man was a creature who had an eternal soul, if he could only find it; that it was his business in life to find it; that it was worth taking all manner of risks to find it, even the last great risk of death; that the man who did find it entered into a scarcely imaginable happiness which he called the Kingdom of Heaven; but the Kingdom of Heaven was within men.

I will not try to describe the strange perversions that simple and mysterious message had to endure – of which the chief and the most inevitable, it seems to me, was the growth of a belief that the man who discovered it and brought it was himself a god. What other thing could those simple fishermen have believed? There was perhaps only one place in the world in those days where they would not have believed that. The place was Athens – a shadow of herself, but still supreme. Had Christ gone to the Areopagus, he too would have passed by the altar to the Unknown God, and he too would have said like Paul: 'Whom therefore ye ignorantly worship, him declare I unto you'; but he would not have said: 'I am he.' What he would have to say to the men of Athens would have been far different from what Paul said to them, and far more intelligible. It would not, like Paul's message, have been 'foolishness to the Greek.'

But let me not indulge my imagination of what might have been, except so far as to imagine him saying to Plato, something of which the great Greek himself had more than an inkling: 'Man is an animal endowed with reason; but he is something more; he is a creature who has it in him to become an eternal soul.'

As I say, I think Plato would have glimpsed his meaning, and I think it was inevitable that the Galilean peasants should have been blind to it, for it is not at all simple, this notion that man has an eternal soul, which he can only make his own by a very painful process, to which the pains of death itself are the nearest analogy. This necessity of dying in life and into life, which Christ discovered, and which many other saints and geniuses were to discover after him, some helped by the great captain of Nazareth, but most, like him, in utter loneliness, was too subtle for simple minds. It was in truth one of the profoundest, nay, I would say absolutely *the* profoundest psychological discovery ever made. It was no wonder that the peasants and the fishermen simplified it. They turned that eternal life of the eternal soul which man was to touch here on earth into something that he would get only after death. Who shall blame them? When they were told: Whosoever loseth his life shall save it, how could they imagine that it was possible to lose one's life and yet still live, how should they understand that Christ had really done it, how should they know what the temptation in the Wilderness really meant? No, they read those parables literally, and they placed the Kingdom of Heaven, which was in man, outside him; they made what was, and is, a religion of life, into a religion of death.

Whereas the old Greeks had said: Man is an animal with reason, the Christian Church said: Man is an animal with a soul. But of course no one could say how he got it. If that had been learned from Jesus, there would have been no Christian Church. Obviously he got it by some divine miracle. Man was an unworthy creature who by God's grace had been distinguished from the brute creation by this fantastic adjunct, of which he knew nothing save that he was supposed to have it. Of himself this poor creature could do nothing; he certainly could not call his soul his own; it was merely a mysterious channel through which the divine agency was poured when he did something that was not utterly base. So the Church frowned heavily upon the works of man; all his great inventions were lost – art and poetry, and perhaps God himself.

I am telling the story summarily. There is another side to it. This Church came to include within it the whole of the Western world; it became the sole refuge of whatever had remained alive in the great Greek tradition. Its great men tried, and not in vain, to reconcile what they could learn of Greek thought with a strangely but rightly elastic interpretation of their own theology. The thought of an Eckhart and a Dante is of the same order as the thought of a Plato; it is, indeed, essentially the same thought. But I am not concerned with the mighty men of genius, who could relive the experience of Christ and rethink the thought of Plato, and as often as not be excommunicated for their pains; I am concerned simply with the two great psychologies which shaped the ordinary man's attitude to life – the Greek, that man was an animal with reason, the Christian that man was an animal with a soul. The Greek tried to trust man with the slender curb of reason: Greece flourished for an incredibly short space of time in consequence – two hundred years at most. The Christian Church did not trust man; it allowed him an immortal soul as it were on express condition that he did not try to find out what it was or to make use of it, and in consequence the Christian Church flourished exceedingly for 1,500 years. For the fact was that the Church psychology was an eminently practical psychology. Man *is* an animal, and he has to be treated like an animal, governed and ruled and driven like one, and for these practical purposes it is obviously better to tell him that he is endowed with a soul, than that he is endowed with reason. A soul is a mysterious thing which he cannot use; reason is apparently a simple thing which he can use, and if he uses it, he is bound to use it badly. Much better for the practical purposes of life to tell him what is right and what is wrong and threaten him with eternal torment if he does not obey, than allow him to make up his own mind which is which, for the chances are ninety-nine in a hundred that he will not really choose; he will only use his reason to make excuses for the choice of his instinctive and animal nature.

That in the simplest terms is the reason why the Church lasted so much longer than Greece.

Still, whether man is an animal with reason or an animal with a soul, it is certain he is a queer beast. Humanity is for ever throwing out odd sports – saints and men of genius and heroes, not too many of them – and a larger number of the middling sort – men with a touch of saintliness, or genius, or heroism, men who are not content with what their fathers have declared unto them, but want to know it for themselves. After the Church had been in complete control for fully a thousand years, men arose who declared once more that man was after all a rational animal with the right to decide his own destiny. Naturally, inevitably, they turned for support to those who had trodden this way before them – they rummaged out of the caverns of oblivion all that the Greeks had written in books or carved in stone, and as they looked back on these golden remains through the dark alleys of time, it seemed that a glory and a gleam hung about them – an enchanted whisper seemed to murmur among them like the sound of the sea in a shell, saying that the free man's life was beautiful beyond all dream.

Ever since that time man has been pursuing this ideal, or this will-o'-the-wisp, of freedom. He has thought, he still thinks, that freedom can be gained by throwing off external restraints. Democracy was to bring freedom; it has not brought it. The Socialist State would bring freedom; it has not brought it. But neither the French Revolution of 1789 nor the Russian Revolution of 1917 – object-lessons big enough to strike the world, one would have thought – have yet really convinced the mass of men that a violent change of political institutions will not bring the lovely thing to birth. But men are less certain than they were.

But see where we have got to. Our search through European history for an answer to the question: What is man? has brought us to the point at which we started. Man is a rational animal – that belief has brought disaster. Man is an animal with a soul – that belief has compelled revolution. The first is the psychology of the old individualism; it believes that man has the power to decide by the free use of his intellect what is good for himself and his fellows, and to pursue it. For the best part of the time man does nothing of the kind; he decides nothing for himself, he follows his leader who follows his, like sheep through a hedge. The psychology of the old individualism collapses on the fact of the crowd. It did so 2,300 years ago in the Peloponnesian War; it collapsed again in the European War. That man is an animal with a soul is the psychology of the crowd; it maintains that man is essentially a creature of base impulses, from the consequences of which he can be saved only by the miracle of a vicarious sacrifice. It collapses, has collapsed on the fact of individualism; man in the long run does insist on trying to be master of his fate.

All psychologies which are true enough to become current among men belong to one or the other of these kinds. Take the newest – the psychologies of psycho-analysis. They are new versions of the old Church psychology. The primal urge in man, says Freud, is the sexual urge; it is the will-to-power, says Adler; the Church agreed, but it insisted that man had sundry other wicked urges. The Church said that these things must be repressed. The Freudian says that repression is the root of all evil. Who is right? Surely, the Church in the main, at least. Control there must be. Freud suggests none, Adler suggests the control of a Socialist Utopia. Jung, who is the wisest of them all, believes that the primary urge is ineffable – the mystery of life itself. But still, even he has no answer to the problem of control. We are to set life free within ourselves – but freedom, for its own sake, is meaningless. Psycho-analysis, even in its subtlest and wisest forms, leaves the fundamental problem of human life untouched. It is, essentially, a technique of self-liberation; it has nothing to say, and of its famous doctors only Jung has really thought, about the ultimate goal of the liberated self.

But can we reach no conclusion from our glimpse at the history of the Western world? Must we see it all as culminating in the War and throw up the sponge in despair if we think about it, or if not, promptly forget about it and glide towards the next catastrophe?

I think we can reach a conclusion. There is nothing startling about it, yet it gives food for thought. Man is an animal with reason – as a description it may do, as a psychology for life it will not work. Man is an animal with a soul will not work either. Try to shape man's life according to the one, and sooner or later he will cleave to the other. That seems to me to be the lesson of history. I conclude from it that both have elements of truth, and that either, alone, is partial and disastrous. If we are to have a psychology that will save us, it must be a combination of these two – not a mere mechanical compound, for what truth can a mechanical compound possess concerning a living organism? – but a dynamic combination. That is the first datum.

The second is the fact from which we started. Our immediate problem is somehow to produce men and women who are capable of resisting the elemental pull of the crowd. We have to grope our way towards some new kind of individualism, not an individualism of the old kind, which proclaimed individuals where none existed, but one that will create them.

How are we to find a psychology that will create individuals, or help to create them? That is to me the chief problem of to-day. Perhaps it will be said: How can a psychology create anything, much less an individual? To such an objector, we reply that it is of the utmost importance for all that we may think and do and be, whether as separate persons or members of the body politic, for us to decide what man is. What we believe man is, if it is a true belief, that in the long run he will become. Mankind is a potentiality. To ask what he is, is to ask of what is he potential. That seems the simplest commonsense. Yet what do we find when we look into the psychologies that are offered us as an account of what man is. Not one of them but is static. Tacitly they all assume that man is unchangeable. Not one is dynamic. If we want a psychology that is really dynamic, one that declares that man's true being has to be *achieved* — we must go to religion. And even then we must go to religion as individual seekers, determined to exclude nine-tenths of what is offered us, resolute above all to refuse all element of miracle and all recourse to divine interposition. We must translate all that theology back into the dynamic process of which it is the awkward symbol. Our task is to become individuals; by the very terms of our own commission we are bound to refuse to be saved in our own despite. The salvation we need is the salvation we can achieve for ourselves.

Still, we are on the right track; everywhere in the Christian religion we find traces of the dynamic psychology we seek. But those traces all lead us back to the great individuals who have achieved themselves within the elastic framework of the Christian tradition, and through them they lead back, back always to the same figure of Christ himself, and we begin to see him as he was, before he was shaped to the pattern of a god, and to hear his words as they were spoken, before they were changed into scriptures. Like John Keats we cry: 'The pity of it, that his life was written by those interested in the pious frauds of religion — *yet through all this I see his splendour.*'

It is the splendour of the great individual — the lovely and wonderful man: The hero who has made heroes.

The truth, the fundamental truth, behind and within all religion that still has meaning for our lives, is this: that a hero makes heroes, a man makes men. And behind that fundamental truth lies yet another: that these men who make men, first made themselves.

That is the point. What they were, man is. Potentially, no doubt. But man is what he is potentially; he is that more truly than he is anything else. That may seem non-sense to some minds, but let us ask them quite simply how are we to describe, in what terms can we define, a living and evolving creature, save in terms of what it may become. We do not know what it may become, says the unimaginative rationalist. But we *do* know. Take all the heroes of human-ity; choose from among them those who have made the deepest and most permanent appeal to men; try to discover what those men really were; if you can discover it, that is what man *is*. He is not some poor devil of a beer-swilling factory-hand who kills what remains of his faculties by waiting for the result of the four o'clock race. Man *is* the man who appeals, not in this month or year, but year after year, century after century, to the secret soul of man.

From such men we must set ourselves to learn our new psychology; in such men we can discern a reconciliation, a harmonious reconciliation, of the two psychologies that have dominated the western world, and separately failed. In them we see that man is a rational animal, and at the same time something more – a creature with a soul.

But, as I anticipated long ago, some one will say: There is nothing new in this. I agree: there is nothing new in it. It is as old as the heroes themselves – and as new. But what, I think, would be wholly new would be a general or at least a growing realization that it is to them that we have to go for a psychology that will be of real value to our living lives;

that to learn the truth about man we have to study him in his highest forms. To study is the wrong word; there is no word for the science I have in mind; it is, above all else, a science of life. What is to be studied must evade all formulation and schematism; it is the process of growth of a harmonious and single being out of its discordant elements. It can be apprehended only by imaginative insight and our sympathetic power of re-living, according to our capacity, the profound experience of our great fore-runners.

It must sound vague and misty in the form in which I put it before you; but I think you will agree that a truly dynamic psychology, one that regards the inward growth and spiritual development of man as its central problem, one that differs from all the so-called scientific psychologies in this – that it does not and never will regard man as a mechanism, *must* at first sight seem vague and misty. Exact definition is only possible in a mechanical universe. That is why scientific psychology has got us nowhere – either it is physiology or bio-chemistry, or it is nothing, as it was bound to be. You cannot impose mechanical formulation on the dynamic; with your first definition you have excluded the thing you hope to discover.

We must get it firmly into our heads that dynamic psychology is not amenable to what is called the scientific method, and that it must primarily depend upon fine and delicate intuitions of quality and value. The man who can see no fundamental difference between Christ and Paul, or between Shakespeare and Milton, is simply like a Hottentot in the Parthenon; he is in the presence of things which he has not even begun to understand. But that does not mean that this dynamic psychology will depend upon individual caprice. The silent judgment of the centuries has decided who *are* the heroes of humanity; the difficulty begins when

26

we try to understand them, or if we do in a measure understand them, when we try to explain how and what we understand.

It is, I admit, a vast and terrifying difficulty. But we have to face it. We have to approach the heroes fearlessly and try to wrest their secret from them. We have to regard them as real beings, in the firm persuasion that what man has done, man can do again. There are no miracles, except the one incessant miracle of life itself. You cannot *understand* that any more than you can understand an apple-tree, any more than you can understand yourself; but you can know an apple-tree, and you can know yourself. Just so the heroes can be known.

But that will not be enough. Obviously I can claim to know my hero, and the world will laugh at me; some may be patient and inclined to believe that I am struggling with something which I cannot wholly grasp; but most will charge me with vanity and presumption. And I shall be hurt or angry. But it will not do. In such a quest one has no right to look for sympathy. I must be able to prove what I say. How can that be done?

I think that I begin to see a way in which it might be done. Let us suppose that as we wrestle with our heroes for their secret, one after another, we begin to discern that they all are shaped after the same pattern; that they all pass through strange experiences which they describe, each in his own language, but in such a way that we cannot fail to be aware that what they are describing is fundamentally the same experience. Let us suppose – to take a single example – that we find that some of the most mysterious utterances of Jesus concerning that Kingdom of Heaven that is within us prove to be faithful descriptions of what other lonely heroes have had to endure in their living lives; let us suppose we find that at the crucial moment when the man becomes a saint, or the poet a great poet, we find them all with the same sense of utter isolation and abandonment, of an annihilation that they can describe only as the darkness of a veritable death, from which they are as it were reborn; – then, I think, we can fairly claim to have proved something that is of importance to men.

I do not say that all this is proved. But I have come to believe that it can be proved. With whatever heroes I have wrestled for their secret, I have found them all obey the same pattern, pass through the same wilderness, plunge in the same darkness, and emerge in the same rebirth; so that I have come to believe that what has proved to be true of them so far, will prove to be true of them all without exception.

But who are *they*? I have called them the heroes of humanity; I have in passing spoken of some of them by name – of Christ, and Plato, of Eckhart and Dante, of Shakespeare and Keats. There are many more, some of whom I know well, some of whom I may know, some of whom I shall never know. I think I can know the saint and the poet, whoever he may be; I do not think I shall ever be able to know the painter or the musician. Yet I believe that, in so far as they are great, they will be one day found to obey the same pattern, to have achieved themselves in the same way.

But again, who *are* they? They are simply the men who, throughout the ages, have spoken to the soul. That is why they are never forgotten. Man's soul, in spite of himself, insists upon remembering them. But why speak of the soul, when there is no such entity known to modern psychology? That is one very good reason for insisting upon it. But the more cogent reason is that we must speak of the soul.[1] It is

[1] This lecture was delivered in February, 1925, more than two years before the publication of General Smuts' *Holism and Evolu-*

not man's mind these men speak to, for man's mind can make nothing of what they say; it fumbles helplessly among their paradoxes, and cannot grasp their creations. Yet something in man declares again and again as it hears them: 'This is true.' True, mark you; yes, and truer than anything else, true with some different kind of truth than any our intellect can take hold of.

From that alone it seems to me that it must be the soul of man to which they speak, and which listens to them, or wakes to life on hearing them. But that is not all. I find that these men themselves spoke of the soul with no uncertain voice. I find that they regarded the strange process, by which they attained to a condition out of which they could speak to the soul of man, as a process of winning their own souls. Will you tell me that is a mere coincidence? You could repeat the word Coincidence a thousand times, and I should not believe you. No, no; what gives these men the power to speak to the souls of men is the fact that they had achieved their own. Then they begin to utter a language which the highest, and because the highest the unawakened part of us, claims for its native speech. We are like men distraught with the memory of a dream; this is indeed our speech, but we have forgotten how to speak it. And, alas, there seems to be no way of learning it any more.

Nevertheless, these men, who fought for and conquered their own souls, keep our souls alive. Our souls are alive, but we cannot get at them; they are us, but we cannot make them ours. We are like the inhabitants of a house of many

tion. The fact that his appeal for a science of 'Personology' is fundamentally the same as my appeal for a new psychology is happy coincidence. General Smuts, for reasons with which I sympathize, rejects the word 'soul' for the word 'personality.' The word is indifferent to me.

rooms of which all are in darkness save one, and we are not in that; we can see the light gleaming there, but we cannot find the way to the door. If we could, we could enter and kindle the taper we have in our hands, and go through the rest of the house lighting up every room; we should see and know all that we are. If only we could find the way!

For, after all, though it is hidden, the soul to which these men speak and out of which they speak is not something utterly mysterious, some strange and angelic visitant to sinful clay. Whatever it is, it is something which made these heroes more completely human than other men. They were different from other men, because they were more *men*. They were not ascetics; they ate with harlots and publicans and sinners; they could freely do all manner of things that the merely righteous man is afraid or ashamed to do. What the possession of their own soul meant to them was that first and foremost they had the courage of themselves. They *were* themselves, and in this process of becoming themselves (for which they paid the full price) they advanced a full stage in the evolution of humanity. They became in a precise sense a new kind of men. We feel it in them, but we do not know how to describe it: words fail us, as they must before a new thing. But the word to which we find ourselves compelled is the word 'natural'; they were more natural than other men; the words they spoke are more natural than the words of other men. They are strange words, rich with beauty and laden with truth, yet they are uttered with some consummate ease and naturalness; completely without effort; for all their mysterious content they are simple. We feel that they looked on the world with different eyes. And, perhaps above all else, that they were so spontaneous that they could not betray themselves. Whatever they did had the whole of themselves behind it; they could not act from a part of themselves alone.

That is what, so far as my poor words can describe the impression, is achieved when a man has achieved his soul. He becomes real in a way that other men are not real; he is, in the truest and highest sense, an individual, able to stand utterly alone, but not avoiding his fellow-men, nor despising them; moving freely among them, but with his tower of refuge, his self, inviolable in their midst.

Such are the men and women we need, and this is what men and women truly are, for this is what they are meant to be.

Is it an impossible and fantastic ideal? I do not believe it is; though I believe the process will be slow indeed. Those who are impatient for results will get no satisfaction. But one thing we shall have learnt from our dynamic psychology is the unreality of time. The man who achieves his soul lives for ever; his influence is undying. If we could bring even a little of the miracle to pass in ourselves, we too might be living a thousand years from now.

How we shall do it, I do not presume to say. I do not set up to be a prophet or teacher. I am merely, in my own small way, an investigator in a realm where, at present, collaborators are few, and from what I have learned I make bold to say that there is a way by which men can make themselves into true individuals. Whether this way can ever be explained and expounded, in the ordinary sense of those words, I do not know; I doubt it. By no stretch of the imagination can I conceive a textbook of this new psychology – its only textbooks could be imaginative biographies of the heroes of the past. But it lies in the very nature of the science itself that it cannot be apprehended by the mere intellect; but neither can it be apprehended without the intellect. The intellect is necessary to guard against superſtition; it is insufficient to carry us to the living truth. What we need is not an abnegation of the reason – man *is* a rational animal – but a reason conscious of its own limitations – man is a rational animal with a soul. To possess his soul, he has to fight for it.

And there I leave it. I do not pretend to have proved anything to you; indeed, if I felt that I had proved anything, I should know I was wrong. I have been simply contending for the obvious, yet always forgotten truth, that a true psychology muſt be dynamic. I shall sum up in the simpleſt terms if I say that the words of Jesus contain more, infinitely more true psychology, than all the scientific inveſtigation of the laſt hundred years; but the words of Jesus do not ſtand alone, they ſtand with the words of the truly wise in all the ages; they have the same myſtery and the same message as Shakespeare's.

Finally, leſt I be accused of being a mere crank, and of presenting to you as psychology the mere vaticination of my own brain, let me quote some words which came to my hand by accident; they were written by one of the greateſt of modern scientific psychologiſts – Professor James Ward of Cambridge. You will find them in the firſt essay in the current *Hibbert Journal*.

'On the whole we are led, even as psychologiſts, to the Greco-Pauline doctrine of the threefold nature of man as body, mind, and spirit. It is at the laſt or higheſt level that we all find the eternal values, and that the Chriſtian's faith finds God, and enjoys *already* "the peace which passeth all understanding," the beginning of eternal life. It is true that all this is beyond the reach of the natural man. But that no more proves its unreality than the inability of the brute to reach to our common intellectual world is any argument for denying the reality of that.'

There, indeed, is my case in a nutshell. As the brutes are

to us, so are we to what we may become, and the psychology we need is one that will accept the fact, and make it its chief aim to point the way, through the study of the heroes of humanity, to what humanity may be.

February, 1925.

NEWMAN AND SIDGWICK

IT lately chanced that, in an endeavour to investigate for myself some characteristics of the Christian mind, I read more or less simultaneously Newman's *Apologia pro Vitâ Suâ* and a little treatise by J. M. Lloyd Thomas: *A Free Catholic Church*. The comparison of these books in themselves was illuminating, for it showed the extraordinary difference of ultimate conviction in which a kindred, one might almost say, an identical, primary certitude can be manifested in the sincere Christian. I do not compare the powers of these two men; but the contrast between the movement of their minds, the ground of initial certitude once left, is astonishing. In Newman the movement becomes ever more narrow and exclusive: his immediate conviction of the existence of God instantly becomes a cause of anxiety and profound misgiving: he is tortured, his soul is pierced to the quick, by the terror lest he should be cast out from the grace of that God whom he knows to exist: and the terror does not abate until he finds refuge, where so fearful, though so noble, a soul must needs find refuge – in the Church which gathers under its wing the greater part of Christendom. It was a small shock, indeed, to realize that Newman was one who must be with the majority. But in no ignoble sense. He believed in God, but he did not trust Him: he was afraid of Him. Where but in the largest cavern should he hide him from the wrath to come ?

In a Lloyd Thomas the fear does not exist. The movement is not narrow and exclusive: on the contrary, trusting in the God in whom he believes, he longs to unite in his 'Free Catholic Church' all truly religious-minded men. He is never for one moment perturbed about the possibility of

34

his own damnation: probably the very idea of damnation never entered his head in any shape or form. He does not even demand of the members of his ideal Church that they should believe in God in any dogmatic sense: they might perfectly well be Deists or Pantheists or Agnostics. So long as they are men of good will, he is confident that the grace of God – of which he probably has no very definite idea – will be vouchsafed to them.

This incidental contrast is remarkable enough: two transparently sincere and deeply religious men march from an identical premiss to antipodal conclusions. Yet an even more striking comparison is suggested by those same two books. Among those whom Lloyd Thomas most eagerly seeks to include in the new Church are those who hold 'a not un-Christian agnosticism which is too full of faith and spirituality to tolerate so mean a thing as a theological dogma.' As a type of the attitude, he quotes the words of the Cambridge philosopher, Henry Sidgwick:

'If I am asked whether I believe in a God, I should really have to say I do not know, that is, I do not know whether I *believe* or *merely hope* that there is a moral order in the universe that we know, a supreme principle of Wisdom and Benevolence guiding all things to good ends, and to the happiness of the good. I certainly *hope* that this is so, but I do not think it capable of being *proved*. All I can say is that no opposed explanation of the origin of the cosmos . . . seems to me even plausible, and that I cannot accept life on any other terms, or construct a rational system of my own conduct except on the basis of this faith. . . . Duty is to me as real a thing as the physical world, though it is not apprehended in the same way; but all my apparent knowledge of duty falls into chaos if my belief in the moral government of the world is conceived to be withdrawn.

Well, I cannot resign myself to disbelief in duty: in fact if I did, I should feel that the last barrier between me and complete philosophical scepticism, or disbelief in truth altogether, was broken down. Therefore I sometimes say to myself, "I believe in God," while sometimes again, I can say no more than I *hope* this belief is true, and I must and will act as if it was.'

That is deeply interesting, as are all sincere statements of belief by men capable of making them; but what is peculiarly striking is a very marked resemblance between Sidgwick's profession and Newman's own in the *Apologia*:

'I am a Catholic by virtue of my believing in God; and if I am asked why I believe in a God, I answer that it is because I believe in myself, for I feel it impossible to believe in my own existence (and of that fact I am quite sure) without believing in the existence of Him who lives as a Personal, All-seeing, All-judging Being in my conscience. I dare say I have not expressed myself with philosophical correctness, because I have not given myself to the study of what others have said on the subject: but I think I have a strong, true meaning in what I say, which will bear examination.'

What Newman says is this: 'I know that I exist, and by the same act of knowledge I know that my conscience exists. This conscience sees all, judges all, my acts: it is a personal God living in me.' And Sidgwick says: 'Duty is to me as real a thing as the physical world, though it is not to be apprehended in the same way. . . . I cannot resign myself to disbelief in duty.' Is it not clear that the basic experience is the same in both men? And if we require a yet closer link of connection than the accepted bond between duty and conscience, it is supplied by Wordsworth's invocation of Duty as the 'stern daughter of the Voice of God.'

NEWMAN AND SIDGWICK

The fundamental fact on which Newman and Sidgwick build their so different edifices of faith or agnosticism is the same: it is the reality of conscience, which is for Sidgwick as real as the physical world, and for Newman as real as his own self-existence; it is the same basic and primary experience as that which was the cause of the conversion of the French poet, Paul Claudel:

'J'ai fui partout: partout j'ai retrouvé la Loi:
Quelquechose en moi qui soit plus moi-même que moi.'

The French poet in these words goes perhaps farther than Newman, in that he declares that the inward Law – Duty or Conscience – from which he cannot flee, is more truly himself than he. This reality, of whose enduring existence he has immediate knowledge, Newman declares to be God himself 'living as a Personal, All-seeing, All-judging Being' in his conscience. Claudel would agree with him: so also, manifestly, would Wordsworth have done.

At this further step, if it be indeed a further step, Sidgwick seems to hesitate. The nature of his apparent hesitation deserves to be studied. Duty is to him as real a thing as the physical world, though it is not apprehended in the same way. Concerning this knowledge of Duty, Sidgwick says: 'But all my apparent knowledge of Duty falls into chaos if my belief in the moral government of the world is conceived to be withdrawn.' Why he should now call his knowledge of Duty (which was as real as his knowledge of the physical world, though of a different kind) 'apparent' knowledge is not clear. Either he was prejudiced as a logician in favour of confining the term 'knowledge' to intellectual knowledge; or the fact that the knowledge of Duty either necessitated or depended upon a belief in 'the moral government of the world' made the burden of belief in his knowledge of Duty at times too onerous.

37

But in truth Sidgwick, in spite of his seeming clarity, is very difficult to follow at this all-important point. Seeing, however, that the primary and original fact is his knowledge of Duty, which is as certain as his knowledge of the physical world, it seems that the relation between this knowledge of Duty and the knowledge of 'the moral government of the world' must be the relation of cause to effect. That is to say, knowledge of Duty necessitates, not depends upon, knowledge of the moral government of the world. Yet, apparently, this knowledge of the moral government of the world can be conceived to be withdrawn; and, if it is withdrawn his knowledge of Duty also fails: it becomes merely 'apparent.' Beneath this evident vacillation lurks a real uncertainty, which is perhaps impossible to define precisely. Probably it is this. Knowledge of Duty is primary and really unintermittent. But it necessitates knowledge of the moral government of the world. This knowledge, however, is intermittent, and when it fails, it reacts on the felt certainty of the knowledge of duty. In simpler words: belief in duty which is no effort, necessitates belief in the moral government of the world, which is an effort. Sometimes this effort is unsuccessful. When it was successful Sidgwick could say 'I believe in God'; when it was unsuccessful he could only say he hoped the belief in God was true, but that he must and would act as if it was.

That may be a tedious, perhaps an obvious, piece of analysis. But I cannot help thinking that there is but little chance of making a real advance in psychology, or rather of establishing it as a true science, unless we are prepared to dig new foundations (or excavate old ones) for it. We must use the self-recorded experiences of highly conscious men as our data. Newman describing the origins of Newman's faith, Henry Sidgwick describing the foundations of Henry Sidgwick's belief, – a faith and belief which actually did

38

shape their lives – are surely of more real importance as data for a true (and therefore a dynamic and creative) psychology than the external observations of others by experimentalists and physicians. It is time, high time, a serious beginning was made with the work of co-ordinating the inward experiences of that great body of men in whom the human consciousness came nearest to perfection – the great priests and prophets, the great philosophers and the great artists. Perhaps the question may appear to be begged by saying that in them the human consciousness came nearest to perfection. But, in that matter, we have the consensus of centuries to approve the choice. And, again, if it be said by the 'scientific' psychologist, that the data thus used are selected, uncharacteristic, and abnormal, the conclusive reply is that it needs something approaching a great man even to attempt to tell the truth about himself. It may be objected, finally, that great men are prone to deceive themselves, that they do not, because they cannot, tell the truth about themselves. That is an easy form of scepticism. The fact is that, whether or not a great man can tell the whole of the truth about his inward experience, he knows and can tell infinitely more of it than any outside observer. Take Newman, for example: his acts and utterances disturbed, perplexed and scandalized the most part of his contemporaries, he seemed to them casuistical, shifty and treacherous. When he gave to the world the story of his own life as he himself knew it, his obvious sincerity instantly prevailed. His *Apologia* was manifestly the truth concerning a rare human soul. That Newman deceived himself, as all men do, does not diminish the truth of his record by a single scruple. It is because his record is true that we can detect the self-deception.

The sooner a systematic and concerted effort is made to co-ordinate the most intimate and fateful experiences of men whom we know to have touched the reality of themselves a little (or a great deal) more closely than the ruck of mankind, the better for us all. We might begin to economize something of that enormous waste of spiritual effort which is entailed upon those who are engaged in a perforce lonely struggle for a meaning, a purpose, and a truth; they might no longer need to begin everything, every time, all over again from zero. And this new psychology which we venture to adumbrate might indeed eventually possess that characteristic of science which is most to be envied by those who practise in more lonely provinces – its real collaboration. The scientific novice begins where the mightiest of his predecessors ended: the investigator of the human soul begins from nothing, generation after generation.[1]

Though this has the appearance of a digression, it is not: for this comparison and contrast between two men ostensibly so opposed as Newman and Sidgwick was begun solely with the purpose of showing by example how the new 'psychologist' might set to work. It would not be difficult, though it might be delicate, to show not merely how, but why these two men, starting from the same initial certainty, reach in the end positions so widely sundered; but even in this elementary stage of the inquiry it has become clear that the *sine quâ non* of such an inquiry is a new terminology if we are to avoid vagueness and waste of effort. That the one word 'knowledge' should have to be used, even by a philosopher like Sidgwick, to cover two utterly different kinds of apprehension, equally certain, and equally real, is obviously intolerable. Not only does it make advance in this realm difficult by impeding the communication of results; it also gives every scope to the wilful obscurantism of the pure rationalist.

[1] In his *Holism and Evolution* General Smuts puts forward a powerful plea for a psychology of precisely the kind which I suggest here. He calls it Personology.

For it is pathetically easy for the rationalist to object to any investigator in this realm that he is using the word 'knowledge' in a sense which he does not understand; and yet I do not suppose that the average rationalist is really possessed of greater sincerity or dialectical ability than either Newman or Sidgwick. Both these men were compelled to use the word 'knowledge' to cover two modes of apprehension which they recognized as generically different. The rationalist may object that one of these modes of apprehension is 'faith.' 'Faith' it may appear to those who have no experience of it; but to those who have it is not faith at all. Sidgwick declares that Duty is *as real to him as the physical world*. An element which can properly be called 'faith' enters only when Sidgwick tries to believe in the moral order of the universe.

The point is that the rationalist begs the whole question, and begs it in a rather puerile way. He is manifestly false to his own primary experience. For though it goes without saying that he has no experience of that 'knowledge' of which Newman and Sidgwick speak, he undoubtedly knows that he exists. Are we to believe that when the rationalist says: 'I know that I exist' he means simply that he concludes that he exists because other people tell him so, or behave as though he did? Or are we to understand that he never says or thinks: 'I know that I exist,' but merely 'I believe that I exist'? The truth is that this elementary act of non-rational knowledge – 'I know that I exist' – is made by every conscious being.

But in order to explore further this domain of non-rational knowledge, we need a new terminology. Every one who is not a professional obscurantist attaches a real meaning (though perhaps not a definable one) to the statement 'I know that I exist'; and only the professional obscurantist would say it was an illegitimate use of the word 'to know.'

And there is a real objection to the rationalist's demand that the word 'knowledge' should be restricted to intellectual knowledge. He begs the question. 'Knowledge' does, in fact, include more than that. In the language of the Bible it includes even the act 'to know a woman' – and that, however fantastic it may sound to the rationalist, is a very real knowledge indeed. Knowledge cannot be restricted to the knowledge of concept and proposition. It is very important to the rationalist that it should be thus restricted, because he thereby creates odium and prejudice against non-intellectual knowledge. But we are concerned not with theories but with the truth. So that it should be our task to distinguish between kinds of knowledge, retaining the same root-word for all, but adding various prefixes to them, as for instance body-knowledge, mind-knowledge, soul-knowledge. These faculties, and the various entities which supply their prefixes, cannot indeed be defined; but by a honest co-ordination of the mass of significant data which we have we could, I believe, give to them a fairly definite and unmistakable content. We cannot expect mathematical rigour in the new psychology; but we can fairly expect to achieve a rigour as great as, if not surpassing that of the biological sciences.

With these difficulties and these possibilities in mind, let us return to the case of Newman and Sidgwick. Both start from the acceptance of the voice of conscience as a primary reality: but whereas for Newman this voice becomes immediately the voice of a personal, all-seeing and all-judging God, Sidgwick hesitates. He does not care to make the perilous leap. He might make it, however, if he could be sure 'that there is a moral order in the universe we know.' But he does not know whether 'he believes or merely hopes' that this is so. He 'certainly hopes' that it is so, but he 'does not think it capable of being *proved*.' His language suggests that in order that his 'hope' should become 'belief,' it would have to be proved (in the sense of a downright logical demon-stration) that there is a moral order in the universe. It is doubtful whether Sidgwick really meant that, if only because it is doubtful whether the proposition itself has any mean-ing; more probably he was struggling against the bias of his own vocabulary to express the fact that a moral order in the universe (if it existed) was not an unintermittent reality to him, as was the voice of conscience.

We return to Newman, who curiously enough is far clearer and more explicit than the Cambridge philosopher concerning this phase in the genesis of religious belief. Newman writes:

'Starting then with the being of a God (which, as I have said, is as certain to me as the certainty of my own existence, though when I try to put the grounds of that certainty into logical shape I find a difficulty in doing so in mood and figure to my satisfaction), I look out of myself into the world of men, and there I see a sight which fills me with unspeak-able distress. The world seems simply to give the lie to that great truth of which my whole being is so full; and the effect upon me is, in consequence, as a matter of necessity, as con-fusing as if it denied that I am in existence myself. If I looked into a mirror, and did not see my face, I should have the sort of feeling which actually comes upon me, when I look into this living busy world and see no reflection of its Creator. This is, to me, one of the great difficulties of this absolute primary truth, to which I referred just now. Were it not for this voice, speaking so clearly in my conscience and my heart, I should be an atheist, or a pantheist, or a polytheist when I looked into the world. I am speaking for myself only; and I am far from denying the real force of the arguments in proof of a God, drawn from the general facts of human society, but these do not warm me or enlighten me; they do not take away the winter of my desolation, or make the buds unfold or the leaves grow within me, and my moral being rejoice. The sight of the world is nothing else than the prophet's scroll, full of "lamentations, and mourning, and woe." '

There follows the famous and perhaps familiar passage: 'To consider the world in its length and breadth, its various history . . .' and Newman continues:

'What shall be said to this heart-piercing, reason-bewildering fact? I can only answer, that either there is no Creator, or this living society of men is in a true sense discarded from His presence. . . . I argue about the world; — if there be a God, *since* there is a God, the human race is implicated in some terrible aboriginal calamity. It is out of joint with the purposes of its Creator. This is a fact, a fact as true as the fact of its existence; and thus the doctrine of what is theologically called original sin becomes to me almost as certain as that the world exists and as the existence of God.'

That is remarkable, both for its substance and its passionate sincerity. Newman looks on the world of men and finds no vestige of moral order, no trace of the finger of God. What Sidgwick can find sometimes, Newman finds never. The difference between them emerges with greater clarity: just as, in regard to the inner world, Newman's sense of the reality of conscience is more intense than Sidgwick's, so, in regard to the outer world, his sense of the absence of any moral order, is more intense than Sidgwick's. And these two intensities seem to be interdependent. It is — to speak metaphorically — because of the whiteness of the light in the world within that the world without appears to Newman as 'irrecoverably dark, total eclipse.' For both men alike, the acceptance of the fact of conscience necessitates the existence of a moral order in the universe; but the kind of moral order necessitated varies with the intensity and the manner in which the fact of conscience is accepted. To speak metaphorically again: Newman, for whom the voice of conscience became immediately the unquestioned voice of God and the manifest evidence of His personal existence (just as the voice of a man is evidence for a normal mind of his personal existence), because of this certainty of God's existence, expects a world of pure white; and because of his expectation of pure white, the world appears pure black. His eyes are God-bedazzled, and the world is utterly dark. With Sidgwick quite otherwise: the voice of conscience does not immediately become the voice of a personal God. But it leads him also to expect, though with a less intense and exacting expectation, a moral order in the world. His eyes are not dazzled, and the world seems grey and neutral. Sometimes he can find vestiges of moral order – a gleam, as it were, whose real existence cannot be proven – and sometimes he cannot find it. When he finds it the voice of conscience is corroborated and he can say, 'I believe in God'; when he does not find it the voice of conscience receives no reinforcement, and he can say only: 'I hope that God exists.'

But whereas Sidgwick evidently finds the gleam of 'moral order,' when he finds it, in the world of men that is, as it is, Newman can find it only by an intellectual sleight – if one may use the phrase for definition's sake, with no nuance of contempt, for an act so fearful in its consequences. He has to reconcile intense white and deepest black; he can do it only by supposing that black is the conscious and deliberate negation of white. It cannot be merely the absence of white, it can be only the intentional withholding of white. The world of men as it is can be made to present a moral order to Newman's vision only if he supposes that it has been deliberately outcast by God.

Once that supposition became a certainty the rest of Newman's progress was inevitable. So terrible a God was terribly to be feared. What pardon would He have for courage or sanctity or goodness without the mark of election? The one narrow and scarce decipherable way of salvation which He had darkly indicated must be found? Let us hope that Newman found it, and with it, if not peace, some respite from the terror of the ultimate wrath of God – a wrath whose vehemence could be dimly conjectured from the savage fury of His punishment of generation after generation of men for an offence committed by their first parents in the dark backward and abysm of Time.

KEATS AND TOLSTOY

THE recent re-publication of Tolstoy's *What is Art?* has been the occasion of a more serious critical discussion of that remarkable book than it has received before. Yet it has not been apparent that the more serious discussion has brought us any nearer to settling the fundamental question which it raises; the impression is rather that now, for the first time, it has been realized that the question is fundamental. Previously the correct attitude was to laugh at Tolstoy for a barbarian; now there seems to be an uneasy feeling that something more cogent is necessary. The old-fashioned appeal, still made in circles where nothing is learned and nothing forgotten, to that mysterious æsthetic sense which is the privilege of one in a hundred thousand, begins to tinkle a little wearily, like the bells on a démodé buffoon, who made his faded reputation by replying to this question of 'What is art?' – *Je ne sais quoi, mais je sais ce que tu ne sais point qu'est-ce que c'est ce je ne sais quoi.* It was a good old joke, in the good old days.

As well try to derail an express-train by putting a half-penny on the line, as to counter Tolstoy's attack with such forlorn impertinences. That Tolstoy's attack is wrong, we all feel. But, how to repel it is another matter. To declare that art is a *je ne sais quoi* is a dangerous weapon against a giant who can reinforce his *mais, je sais, moi* by dropping *Anna Karenina* and *War and Peace* upon our diminished heads. We need less flimsy defences.

It is not easy to summarize Tolstoy's position with fidelity. He is not always consistent with himself, and his inconsistencies are not always negligible. In one place he declares that the function of art lies just in this: to make that understood

47

and felt which in the form of an argument might be incomprehensible and inaccessible'; in another that 'an artist's work cannot be interpreted. Had it been possible to explain in words what he wished to convey, the artist would have expressed himself in words. He expressed it by his art, only because the feeling he experienced could not be otherwise transmitted.' The positions are obviously irreconcilable, and we must be content with assuming, from the main trend of his argument, that the latter was more truly his own position.

Indeed his fundamental proposition is that art consists in the communication of feelings, as opposed to thoughts. This absolute dichotomy underlies the whole of his argument. From it he concludes that the best art is that which communicates the best feelings. The judgment which are the best feelings depends upon the religious perception of the age; those are the best feelings which most approximate to the feelings inculcated by the common religion. Since this attitude may appear strange and almost barbarian, it may be worth recalling that it is the Greek attitude. Plato and Aristotle – as Tolstoy himself was perfectly aware – both insisted on the finality of the moral judgment in deciding the question what is good and what is bad art. Tolstoy emphatically reasserts their position. There are, he says, two acts of judgment: the first, whether a work is a work of art or not, is decided by the judgment whether the work does in fact communicate feelings; the second, whether it is good or bad art, is decided by the judgment whether the feelings communicated are good or bad. This judgment depends on the religious perception shared by society.

From this brief outline it will be obvious that to call such an æsthetic provincial is itself provincial; it is both traditional and formidable; in a word, it is classical. And this quality in it is ignored partly because it is taken at second-hand, and partly because it is forgotten that Classicism is a principle more profound than the Palladianism of the eighteenth century. The principle of the autonomy of art, in whose name the Tolstoyan æsthetic is rejected as barbarian, is a wholly romantic conception. Again, Tolstoy is perfectly aware of the situation. He says that the modern principle that artistic beauty is an end in itself, sovereign in its own right, only arose at the Renaissance, with the decay of a common religious perception. There was no longer a generally accepted tribunal to which the judgment, whether the feelings communicated by a work of art were bad or good, could be referred. The fact that feelings were communicated, irrespective of what the feelings were, alone decided the goodness or badness of a work of art.

But, in fact – and here Tolstoy makes an important and characteristic advance – the common religious perception, although ignored by the privileged classes, does still exist. The moral law of Christianity is recognized by the greater part of Western humanity. The Renaissance, which meant to the privileged few the abrogation of a common religion, meant to the many the purification of that religion from accretions and perversions. The many do know, by virtue of their active Christianity, what are good feelings and what are bad. And their judgment, that the feelings communicated by most modern [1] art are bad, is final.

It is important to be clear as to the indictment which Tolstoy brings against modern art. He does not deny that works of art are produced, though he is scornful of the inability of the educated public to distinguish between a true work of art, which does communicate feelings, and a false one, which does not communicate anything. But he declares that the further and necessary distinction among the works of art –

---

[1] 'Modern' art, in Tolstoy's argument, means post-Renaissance art. I have used the epithet in the same sense.

which are good and which are bad – is not made at all. The very necessity of making the distinction has been forgotten. A particular example of his attitude appears in his essay on Maupassant. All Maupassant's works are true works of art; they communicate feelings. But a few are very good, some a mixture of good and bad, and others wholly bad, judged by the morality of true Christianity.

It is essential (Tolstoy continues) to a true religion that its perceptions and moral feelings are capable of being shared by all. A good work of true art will therefore be universally appreciated – or at any rate appreciated by all those whose religious and moral perceptions are not atrophied. The demand for an educated taste as a preliminary condition of appreciation is unnecessary and irrelevant, for by hypothesis the work of art communicates feelings, and man's emotional nature is independent of education. 'Art is differentiated from activity of the understanding . . . by the fact that it acts on people independently of their state of development and education, that the charm of a picture, of sounds or of forms, infects any man, whatever the plane of development.' Therefore, the question what are good and what are bad works of art, resolves into the question: who in modern society have their religious perceptions still unobscured, and their capacity for absolute moral judgment uncontaminated, for they are the final court of appeal. To this Tolstoy answers unhesitatingly: the simple-minded, the peasants.

That is, I believe, a fair statement of Tolstoy's argument. There are two weak, or at least doubtful, links in the chain. Is it true, or is it wholly true, that art consists in the communication of feelings in Tolstoy's sense of the word 'feelings,' a sense in which they are utterly distinct from thoughts. Secondly, is it true, or is it wholly true, that the highest religious perception which exists in modern society is the

Christian perception? Some may consider that Tolstoy's contention that the judgment, whether a work of true art is good or bad, must be made, and must be a moral judgment is also wrong. I do not; moreover I regard it as indubitable that this necessary moral judgment must, as Tolstoy contends, be based on a religious conception.

The problem – to take the second doubtful link first – is to determine where the religious conception is to be sought and found at the present time. Or, to translate into historical terms, was the religious significance of the Renaissance really contained, as Tolstoy asserts, in the Reformation; or was it something outside the Reformation? Tolstoy decides the question simply. At the Renaissance, he maintains, the educated classes abandoned Christianity for atheism, while the simpler folk restored and purified it. But it is not so simple. The finest minds at and after the Renaissance, once the first flush of rebellion was over, were not atheistical. They had bidden a long farewell to dogmatism and form-alism: Church Christianity, as Tolstoy calls it, was no longer for them the embodiment of 'the highest life-conception' of which they were capable. They embarked on the search for a higher one. It is strange that Tolstoy, the artist, should not have recognized the nature of the effort and the achieve-ment of the greatest post-Renaissance artists, for they fully satisfy the conditions which, he said, 'must be fulfilled to enable a man to produce a real work of art.'

'It is necessary that he should stand on the level of the highest life-conception of his time, that he should experi-ence feeling and have the desire and capacity to transmit it, and that he should moreover have a talent for some one of the forms of art.'

But Tolstoy, who was apparently insensible to the nature of Shakespeare's achievement, could not see (or would not admit) that the greatest post-Renaissance artists had stood head and shoulders above 'the level of the highest life-conception of their time.' To account for Tolstoy's blindness in this respect would take us far: we should need to search for its causes deep in his elemental nature. But a glimpse of them is given in his curious *Confession* of 1879.

'Art, poetry? . . . Under the influence of success and the praise of men I had long assured myself that this was a thing one could do though death was drawing near – death, which destroys all things, including my work and its remembrance, but soon I saw that that too was a fraud. It was plain to me that art was an adornment of life, an allurement to life. But life has lost its attraction for me; so how could I attract others? As long as I was not living my own life but was borne on the waves of some other life – as long as I believed that life had a meaning, though one I could not express – the reflection of life in poetry and art of all kinds afforded me pleasure: it was pleasant to look at life in the mirror of art. But when I began to seek the meaning of life, and felt the necessity of living my own life, that mirror became for me unnecessary, superfluous, ridiculous or painful. I could no longer soothe myself into what I now saw in the mirror, namely, that my position was stupid and desperate. It was all very well to enjoy the sight when in the depth of my soul I believed that life had a meaning. Then the play of lights – comic, tragic, touching, beautiful and terrible – in life amused me. But when I knew life to be meaningless and terrible, the play in the mirror could no longer amuse me.'

The importance of that confession is as manifest as its sincerity; it marks the climacteric in Tolstoy's spiritual evolution. But we are here concerned only with the light it incidentally throws upon Tolstoy's conception of art before what has been called his 'conversion.' Art was to him a faithful representation of life, which ceased to have meaning when life ceased to have meaning. And, in truth, after this point life never regained a meaning for Tolstoy. For some inscrutable reason the realization of the fact of death, which came late to him, was never overcome; he could not accept it. He turned to Christianity in its most paradoxical form as an escape from the inevitability of death; it was a gamble which henceforward continually allured him, but which he never really risked until that famous 'going-out' a few days before his actual death.

The immense, the overwhelming fact of death was precisely the one with which Shakespeare was pre-eminently concerned; and Shakespeare overcame it. That, I think, could be shown, though not, of course, by logical demonstration; it must suffice here to declare a conviction that the author of *Lear*, of *Antony and Cleopatra*, and *The Tempest* had achieved by successive stages a victory over death, in the sense that he had reasserted, rediscovered in the depths of his own being, without recourse to any revealed religion, the meaning of life which had been destroyed for him momentarily, as for Tolstoy permanently, by the realization of death. The great difference between these great men is that Shakespeare fought out the desperate battle in his art. To his growing despairs and his painfully won triumphs he compelled his art to be adequate, and thereby he expanded the very fabric of art. Tolstoy, on the other hand, definitely and finally abandoned art at the clutch of despair. He was like a Shakespeare who should have written *Hamlet* and thrown in his hand. It was not surprising that his most flagrant critical injustice should have been done towards Shakespeare; nor can one help suspecting that behind the insensibility to Shakespeare, which he so freely displayed, lay concealed something more radical – a profound and perhaps unconscious resentment against one who had achieved a victory where he himself had confessed and even proclaimed defeat.

Tolstoy denied that the artist, who should elect to remain an artist, could achieve a higher life-conception than that contained in Christianity. There are many life-conceptions contained in Christianity, and I believe it would be true to say that one of them – the most essential, the one held by the founder of the Christian religion – cannot be and has not been surpassed. But, in the first place, that life-conception was not the life-conception of Tolstoy's own version of Christianity: his Christianity was shaped according to the pattern of his own secret despair – a religion of asceticism and abnegation. And, secondly, the revelation of the great artist is not of the same kind as the revelation of the great prophet. It may be akin and complementary to it, but it is not the same. The artist and the prophet, in their highest forms, do share that 'belief in an integral unity' which Baudelaire declared to be the necessary condition of a sound art; but the artist does not assert it, he reveals it in his representation of particulars.

The claim that post-Renaissance art should be judged good or bad by reference to the life-conception inculcated by Christianity is invalidated if it can be met by the counter-claim that not Christianity (Church or Tolstoyan) but post-Renaissance art itself contains and communicates the highest life-conception of which Western humanity has so far proved itself capable. And that is precisely the claim which, I believe, can be made for the highest achievements of post-Renaissance art. In these man faces, without the adventitious aid of revealed religion, the 'burden of the mystery'; and the feelings which they communicate are not, as Tolstoy asserts, mere feelings of pleasure at beauty (the 'æsthetic emotions' of modern theory), but feelings of a different and higher order. It would be a derogation, or at least a falsification, of these feelings to call them specifically 'religious'; but it would be worse to deny the truth that they are allied to the 'religious' emotion. These feelings are hard, if not impossible, to define; but certainly they have never been better *described* than by Keats in the famous definition which he deduced from the effect produced upon him by *Lear*. 'The excellence of every art is its intensity, capable of making all disagreeables evaporate from their being in close relationship with Beauty and Truth. Examine *King Lear* and you will find this exemplified throughout.' This mysterious identity of Beauty and Truth in the representation of life, and the equally mysterious power of seeing and then revealing that they are identical, are the real basis of the principle of the autonomy of art; by virtue of attaining this power the artist moves beyond the province of the moral and religious judgment – *if* he can attain it. For then he has fulfilled his final purpose, of revealing what the most exalted religion can only assert – that there is a 'meaning' in life. And we, to whom he communicates his knowledge and his revelation, are no mere blind accepters of an oracle: we

> 'take upon us the mystery of things
> As if we were God's spies.'

Thus Tolstoy's claim that the feelings communicated by modern art must be judged good or bad by reference to the feelings inculcated by Christianity, because Christianity contains the highest life conception of which man is capable, falls to the ground because modern art, in its highest forms, itself contains the highest life-conception of which man is at present capable. If criticism would resolutely insist on a hierarchy of artistic achievement, and show reason for the order it established, it would quickly be evident that art is indeed autonomous, furnished with both the right and the power to judge its own unworthy members, and able to protect by a sort of benefit of clergy its less exalted forms against the presumptions of the moral judgment. For it could fairly be claimed for the art of literature at least, that in its elementary acts of perception – the seizing of a true and revealing metaphor, for example – it is, however unconsciously, prophetic of a belief in that 'integral unity' which at its highest it consciously perceives and deliberately reveals. 'Every true metaphor,' said Baudelaire, 'is drawn from the inexhaustible riches of the analogy of the universe.'

But it is evident that these feelings – above all the supreme feelings of the identity of Beauty and Truth in the particularity of the world – which modern art does at its highest communicate, are not feelings which 'infect' every man 'independently of his state of development or education.' Never to have felt 'the burden of the mystery' at least is to be, as it were, disqualified from responding to such feelings, or recognizing that they have been expressed. And from this we see the falsity of Tolstoy's main dilemma.

'If art is an important matter, a spiritual blessing essential for all men, then it should be accessible to every one; if, as in our day, it is not accessible to all men, then one of two things: either art is not the vital matter it is represented to be, or that art which we call art is not the real thing.'

Art *is* accessible to all men. That all men do not accede to it does not affect the fact of its universal accessibility. Certainly, if the feelings communicated by art were mere feelings, as Tolstoy believed or desired to believe, we should expect all men, irrespective of their development, to be affected by them. But they are not thus affected, and the conclusion is not 'that the art which we call art is not the real thing,' but that the feelings communicated by art are not simply feelings. And indeed they manifestly are more than feelings. They partake of the nature of feelings, they partake of the nature of thoughts; yet they are neither the one nor the other. What are they?

About this vital point Tolstoy gropes. 'The function of art,' he says, 'lies just in this: to make that understood and felt which in the form of an argument would be incomprehensible and inaccessible. Usually it seems to the recipient of a truly artistic impression that he knew the thing before but had been unable to express it.' The second sentence is a true description of the 'artistic impression,' the first a manifestly false conclusion from it. Take a simple example:

'We must endure
Our going hence, even as our coming hither:
Ripeness in all.'

These limpid lines achieve and reveal an identity of truth and beauty. Try to express what they say in the language of discourse; with your utmost efforts you will not avoid translating them into a declaration of Stoic indifferentism. What they actually convey is something totally different – a sense of acceptance of human destiny. They may be said to contain a thought; but not what they contain, but what they are, is of importance. They are of another nature than any *thought*.

Yet it would be true to say that it seems to the reader of those lines 'that he knew the thing before, but had been unable to express it.' This is indeed a mark of 'the truly artistic impression.' And Tolstoy is in this description remarkably at one with Keats in the first of his famous axioms on poetry.

'First. I think poetry should surprise by a fine excess and not by singularity; it should strike the reader as a wording of his own highest thoughts, and appear almost a remembrance.'

From this singular characteristic of the true artistic impression Tolstoy makes two chief deductions. Both are false. One, that art supplies a comprehensible equivalent of what would be incomprehensible as an argument, he himself, as we have seen, elsewhere disowns. The other, that art should be comprehensible to any man whatever his level of development, depends on the assumption that art is an affair of mere emotion. That is manifestly wrong. The lines from *Lear*, which have been used as an example, do not communicate a mere feeling, any more than they convey a mere thought. What they communicate is something of a third kind, in which feeling and thought are inextricably blended.

By thus falsifying the peculiar and unique nature of the true artistic impression, and simplifying it to a mere emotion, Tolstoy was enabled to deduce what he desired to deduce in order to justify his own despair of art: namely, that art was comprehensible to, and amenable to judgment by, 'the natural man.' Here the contrast between Tolstoy and Keats is in the highest degree illuminating: for Keats, who, as we have seen, agreed with Tolstoy in his description of 'the true artistic impression', was also preoccupied with this question of the 'naturalness' of art. Witness his second and third axioms:

'Second. The touches of beauty should never be half-way, thereby making the reader breathless instead of content. The rise, the progress, the setting of Imagery should, like the sun, come natural to him, shine over him, and set soberly, although in magnificence, leaving him in the luxury of twilight. But it is easier to think what poetry should be than to write it. And this leads me to

Another axiom – 'That if poetry comes not as naturally as the leaves to a tree, it had better not come at all.'

KEATS AND TOLSTOY

Underlying all these *aperçus* of Keats is some conception or intuition of the 'naturalness' of poetry. Poetry comes naturally to the reader, its own internal progress is natural, and it comes from the poet himself as naturally as the leaves to a tree. But, unlike Tolstoy, Keats insists that what comes naturally to the reader is not what comes easy to him; it is 'his own highest thoughts.' Moreover, what comes naturally from the poet is not what comes easy from him. 'It is easier to think what poetry should be than to write it.'

Visibly Keats and Tolstoy have parted company. Where – as Tolstoy has persuaded himself that art, which is natural to man, is also easy to him – 'it infects any man, whatever his plane of development' – Keats is instinctively proof against the false suggestion both as regards the reader and the writer. And Keats had to contend with the Tolstoyan æsthetic in his own time. The two contemporaries who for a time most influenced him, Leigh Hunt and Wordsworth, had both fallen into the ditch: they had both convinced themselves that poetry should employ 'the real language of real people.' Moreover, only a month before, the enunciation of his axioms, Keats had had to counter Leigh Hunt's criticism that the first book of *Endymion* was 'unnatural.' 'He must first prove,' said Keats to his brother, 'that Caliban's poetry is unnatural. This with me completely overturns his objections.' One can hardly conceive a briefer or a better answer.

At this point the æsthetic question: 'What is the universality of art?' has manifestly resolved into the ethical question: 'What is natural to man?' And Tolstoy and Keats are making widely different answers. Tolstoy's is the simpler; it is Rousseau's answer. What is natural to man is what he approves 'independently of his state of development and education.' Keats' answer makes no such simple text for revolutionaries or *surréalistes*. What is natural to man is 'his own *highest* thoughts.'

One would not contend that Keats' answer, in these terms, is conclusive or even satisfactory. It would be easy to turn its point by pressing for an answer to the question: 'What are these high thoughts?' But we are already on ground where dialectic will not greatly avail to advance or discredit Keats' intuition. What is natural, for man and poet, according to Keats, is what is natural to them in a condition which both may achieve: of this condition poetry is to the reader as it were premonitory. He makes contact through it with his own highest thoughts, and it appears to him almost a remembrance.

The difference between this and the Rousseau-Tolstoy conception is vast. For Rousseau and for Tolstoy man becomes natural by becoming a barbarian. For Keats he becomes natural by advancing in some simple and mysterious way. What is this way of progress?

Keats' fundamental positions may be called intuitive, but they have commanded the assent of subsequent generations. Pure poetry comes naturally from the poet; and comes naturally to the reader. What does he mean by *naturally*? Most probably, at the moment of enouncing his 'axioms' he did not know. Does *naturally* mean the same in both cases? Obviously the poet differs from the man, in that he is a poet. He *naturally* gives expression to something, and the something expressed comes *naturally* to his reader. This something is the reader's own 'highest thoughts.' The problem of poetic expression as such does not greatly concern Keats. For him, when true poetic expression comes, it comes naturally. But the essential poetic achievement is, in some sort independent of the gift of poetic expression. This may seem a curious position for a poet and particularly for a poet like Keats to have taken; but that he did take it is incontrovertible. In the second *Hyperion*, the last of his long poems, in which he concentrated all his agonized speculations on the

worth and destiny of the poet, he asserted the position
unequivocally.

'Who alive can say
"Thou art no poet, mayst not tell thy dreams"?
Since every man whose soul is not a clod
Hath visions and would speak, if he had loved
And been well-nurtured in his mother tongue. . . .'

It remained from first to last central to all Keats' thinking
on the poetic faculty (which is the deepest of any known
to me) that the poetic condition is attainable by all men –
at a price. The price is that which he hints at in the strange
lines above, which can only be interpreted in terms of his
own biography. The soul of the man who would attain to
the poetic condition must not be a clod; and he must have
loved.

What Keats meant by love will be known to those familiar
with his letters to Fanny Brawne: it was a complete self-
surrender. What he meant by the soul, he had tried to
explain some months before, at the moment when the agony
of his love took hold of him, in a letter to his brother (April,
1819). His conception of the soul, as might be expected, is
exceedingly pertinent to his conception of the poetic condition as one attainable by all men. The soul is for Keats
something which exists only potentially in man. In the
natural man the division is twofold – into Heart, which he
defines as 'the seat of the Human passions', and Mind. All
direct sensational contact with the world of experience is
made by the Heart; the true function of the Mind is to make
this directly apprehended experience conscious. A man
becomes natural by refusing to allow his Mind to become
dominant and self-sufficient. If he can keep his Mind loyal
to the experience of his Heart, then somehow the Soul is
created. For a man to possess his Soul is to possess his Self,

in the deepest sense of the word, and, mysteriously, at the moment of this Soul-possession, he sees the necessity and the beauty of the process by which he has come to achieve it. 'Do you not see,' cries Keats to his brother in the middle of this letter on the world as a Vale of Soul-making, 'how necessary a world of pains and troubles is to school an Intelligence and make it a Soul?'

Much could be written, and much in vain, on this strange letter of Keats. No mere analytical acumen will extract sustenance, or perhaps even a meaning, from it. It is obviously the record of a profound personal experience, an attempted statement of a process of self-creation which Keats had undergone. Therefore an intellectual criticism of it is condemned to futility. But its relevance to his conception of the poetic condition as *natural* to man is striking. It is, in Keats' belief, natural to man that he should come to possess his soul; but this natural process is the very reverse of easy: it is, on the contrary, the hardest thing in the world, for it depends on the maintenance of the heroic effort to keep the consciousness loyal to the unconsciousness. Out of this condition, if he can achieve it, the poet speaks, and the reader responds to his utterance as to a wording of his own highest thoughts, because he feels that the condition which underlies the poet's utterance is premonitory of a condition to which he himself may attain. This condition is at once a condition of being and a condition of knowing. Only by having achieved his soul can the poet see the necessity and the beauty of the process by which he attained it. Keats' letter is indeed a fuller enunciation of Baudelaire's disconcerting (and therefore neglected) proposition: 'La première condition pour faire un art sain est la croyance à l'unité intégrale.'

The relevance of Keats' transcendental conception of the self-created soul (which, it must be emphasized, is not a speculation, but an attempted statement of an actual experience) to the problem what are the strange 'thought-feelings' communicated by a supreme work of literary art, is not far to seek. Here is a condition of being, natural to man in the sense that its attainment is the final end of a natural effort to harmonize the discrepant elements of heart and mind – a condition of being in which thought and feeling are united to form a third and distinct faculty of perception. And what is perceived by this self-created faculty is that 'integral unity,' of which Baudelaire spoke. 'Do you not see that a world of pains and trouble is necessary to school an intelligence and make it a soul?' That is one, and perhaps the highest object of the new faculty. Not 'Do you not understand?' not 'Do you not feel?' but 'Do you not *see*?' But the true expression of this condition is not argument but art. Keats moved a great step nearer to it in the sonnet which he wrote immediately after his letter:

'How fevered is the man who cannot look
Upon his mortal days with temperate blood!
Who vexes all the leaves of his life's book
And robs his fair name of its maidenhood. . . .'

And he advanced another and a still greater stride, in the days immediately following, when he found in the Grecian urn the perfect symbol of that identity of Beauty and Truth he had struggled to discern, and by the searching sincerity of his effort, created the faculty to discern it.

'Thou still unravished bride of quietness,
Thou foster-child of silence and slow time. . . .'

WILLIAM ARCHER AND THE
SURVIVAL OF PERSONALITY

On December 20th, 1924, I received quite unexpectedly a long letter from William Archer, which singularly impressed me, since I was almost a total stranger to him. When, on re-reading the letter, the full significance of the time and place of his writing came home to me, I said to myself: 'William Archer is going to die: this is his spiritual testament.'

I hastened to reply to the letter before it was too late. Hurriedly and incompletely I tried to tell him that my rejection of *personal* immortality was different, altogether different, from an acceptance of annihilation. This hasty letter of mine I have also reprinted below. Though I cannot prove the fact, I am reasonably certain that William Archer received my letter while he was still able to read it, for by the kindness of his brother, Mr. Joseph Archer, I received an empty envelope addressed to myself in a handwriting notably less firm than that of his original letter. I shall always believe that this envelope was intended to contain a reply to my reply.

William Archer's letter speaks for itself. I have added by way of explanation the passage from my book to which he refers.

'27, Fitzroy Square, W.1.,
'*December* 19*th*, 1924.

'Dear Mr. Murry, –
'I am really writing from a nursing home, where I am awaiting an operation to-morrow. This is my excuse for troubling you with a letter about your book *To the Unknown God* before I have had time to finish it. I shall scarcely

64

finish it before the time fixed for the operation; and when I may be able to write after that, who can say?

'The book interests me greatly, though it deals with an order of experience to which I am a total stranger. For instance, on p. 75, the whole passage from "What one feels to be true . . ." to the end of the paragraph conveys practically no meaning to me.[1] "Truth," as I understand it, means the correspondence between an inward conception and an outward reality, and I cannot be satisfied with what may be called intuitional evidence, or evidence from desire or satis-

---

[1] The passage in question is the following:

'That, it seems to me, is the obligation I have undertaken: to write and to publish what I feel to be true. Not what I *think* is true: I can make mistakes about that, without any consciousness of wrong. And where a mistake is a matter of indifference, at worst no more than a prick to an intellectual vanity, there the assertion is not worth making. What one feels to be true is quite another affair. Now the whole man is involved. If he is mistaken in his feeling for truth, the very roots of his being are troubled and torn. When through his whole being there comes a flash of sudden awareness of unity within him, and from some place that he scarcely knew leaps up a sense of knowledge and a sense of oneness in that which knows; when his deepest, unfamiliar self rises and takes possession of all that he is, body and mind and soul, and declares: *This is true*, – then, if he is wrong, it is disaster and dismay.

'Yet perhaps the man to whom that truly happens never can be mistaken. If his deepest, unfamiliar self has risen and taken possession and pronounced: *This is true*, perhaps indeed it *is* true, for ever and ever. For this mysterious judgment is pronounced first and foremost upon a man's own acts. Of a man's acts many are indifferent – even this also may be a mark of imperfection: were we more truly living, perhaps our smallest acts, having the self in its oneness directly behind them would be no longer indifferent but vital – but as we are, many, nay most of our acts are indifferent. But a moment comes when the whole being is awakened and on the alert: a crucial act is coming to birth. And on this judgment is pronounced. *This is right*, or *That is wrong*; and from that judgment there is no appeal.'

faction. What reason have I for believing that the nature of things, if I could arrive at it, would be satisfactory to me? 'My purpose in writing, however, is not to raise such questions. I might or might not wish to raise them after having finished your book; but as yet I am only at the before-mentioned p. 75. My real wish is to suggest to you a sort of *caveat*.

'I understand from what I have read, and still more explicitly from the review in the *Times Literary Supplement*, that you totally and rather emphatically reject the idea of the survival of personality, of individual consciousness, after death. Now, I am myself very far from being convinced of any such survival; but my mental constitution forbids me to reject positive evidence on *a priori* grounds; and I hold the evidence on this point to be such as to leave it a *very* open question. If it is so, I suggest that any philosophy which builds on the idea of annihilation is necessarily incomplete and over-hasty. A grub who should construct a religion on the assumption that he could never be anything but a grub, would be rather nonplussed when he found himself a butterfly.

'If there is one thing I am certain of in this world, it is that there is *something* which we do not begin to understand behind the phenomena which we loosely describe as spirit-ualistic. Of course, there is often trickery, fraud and hysteri-cal delusion behind them – I make every allowance for this element. I further admit the extremely unsatisfactory nature of the alleged "communications" which "come through." They are trivial, commonplace, futile – they seem to rob death of its dignity, and discount the very idea of a future state. (I speak, of course, of ordinary communica-tions alleged to come from recently deceased people. The outpourings of great men, from Socrates downwards, are manifest bunkum – mostly fraud, I fancy, though partly perhaps, due to sincere delusion.) Both on account of the poverty of the communications, and of the enormous antecedent difficulty of conceiving at what point of the evolutionary process the power of surviving the death of the body came into being, I am myself, as I said before, quite unconvinced of survival. But at the same time I am absolutely convinced, from repeated experience and observation, of the genuineness of a very great number of the phenomena, and of the crass stupidity of the men of science and others who simply denounce and refuse to study them. There is *something* there which science must, so to speak, fathom and assimilate, on pain of wilfully living in an incomplete universe. And a complete outline-picture of the universe is, I take it, as essential to the man of science as to the philosopher.

'It would take far too long to go into the nature of the evidence on which I base this opinion. You will, of course, suspect me of absurd credulity – but why should I be credulous? I have no strong desire for a survival which I cannot conceive, and which seems, on the evidence, to be most unalluring; and I have no shrinking, physical or sentimental, from the idea of annihilation. Only I have an instinct which impels me to include in my mental vision of the world whatever I believe to be *fact*, and to disregard *a priori* objections to things of which the evidence seems to me convincing. Now I have had many communications from a dead relative, under circumstances *absolutely* excluding trickery or fraud, which can be explained, I think, only on one or other of three hypotheses:

'(1) That some part, at any rate, of his memory and intelligence survives.

'(2) That some more or less mischievous intelligences, of an order inconceivable to us, are able imperfectly to simulate the characters of the dead.

'(3) That certain living people have the most marvellous powers of getting at, and so to speak pumping, not only the supraliminal, but also the profoundly subliminal, memories of other living people.

'Now if either one of these hypotheses could be established it must enormously change our picture of the world.

'Hypothesis (2) I take to be the most difficult, not to say the absurdest of the three. It could be accepted only by a man violently prejudiced against the other two.

'Hypothesis (3) is the least upsetting to our preconceptions, for I suppose we all admit the reality of a certain measure of thought-reading. But to make the hypothesis work, we should have to conceive an almost *in*conceivable extension of the power; and even then many of the phenomena would, I think, remain unaccounted for. If, however, this should ultimately prove to be the right hypothesis, it would point to the possibility of methods of communication between mind and mind, which, if developed, would revolutionize life.

'The reasons against Hypothesis (1) – some of them at any rate – I have stated above. But there is no denying that this is by far the simplest, most obvious hypothesis. The other two are to be regarded rather as last-resort methods of escape from it. And if Hypothesis (1) should establish itself – not necessarily as implying immortality, but at all events the survival (perhaps temporary) of certain elements in the human personality – I presume that the bases of your philosophy, or religion, would be seriously disturbed.

'Forgive me if I touch upon matters that are painful to you. There are obviously very wide differences between our points of view and habits of thought; but in writing this letter I have assumed that we have in common a desire to be loyal to things-as-they-are, which I take to be synonymous with intellectual honesty.

'Should I emerge all right from to-morrow's ceremonies, I should be glad to meet you, and to tell you in some detail the facts on which I base my conviction that there is *something there*, and something of importance. Of course I am not going only on my own experiences, but on hundreds of others, which my own enable me (not uncritically) to accept.

'Yours sincerely,

'WILLIAM ARCHER.

'Written in bed.'

To this letter I replied:

'DEAR MR. ARCHER,

'I sincerely hope that all has gone well with the operation.

'It is difficult for me to answer your letter fully in writing; a long conversation (which I hope we shall have) would be necessary. But on the point with which your letter is chiefly concerned, I would say this.

'You have been compelled to take my views on this matter of survival at second-hand. Unfortunately such questions as these are precisely those on which the "reporter" (critic or not) invariably plays one false. It is true that I do not believe in *personal* immortality; but I do most strongly believe that something survives, and is immortal. . . .

'I most emphatically do not believe in annihilation. I have no fear of it, and for many years I did believe in it; but now I do not. But with equal emphasis I do not believe in the immortality of this personality. You will find something of my belief if you read the essay at the end of my book called *Lost Secrets*. What precisely I do believe is very, very hard to express: but I think I could convey it to you in conversation.

'With regard to your difficulty concerning my criterion of

truth, I can say only this. To me there are at least two kinds of certainty. For instance, the voice of conscience is just as *real* to me as the existence of the physical world. It is, for me, just as *true* that conscience exists, as that this paper on which I am writing exists. But these two existences are apprehended in a different way. So I conclude and firmly believe that there are two kinds of knowledge. I cannot escape this conclusion. If I try to avoid it, I find that, in spite of myself, my whole life is shaped by it. Therefore, in any final truth I must be able to include both these kinds of truth. The temptation is to neglect one for the other: I have tried to resist the temptation. That has led me into positions, and at last into a sort of certainties, which I find it extraordinarily difficult to express without becoming unintelligible or being misunderstood.

'Once more with every sincere wish for your speedy recovery,

'Yours very sincerely,

'J. MIDDLETON MURRY.'

That letter was written in great haste, and its language in part is not my own. I used a sentence of Henry Sidgwick which corresponded very closely with my own experience. To be more precise would have taken time which could not be wasted. That William Archer should receive my letter while he was able to read it was to me a matter almost of life and death. As I have said, I believe he received it, and read it, and prepared to reply.

Now I will try to say what I should have tried to say to William Archer if the meeting had taken place.

Murry: I believe in, I am convinced of, the immortality of the *soul*.

William Archer: But what *is* the soul? Does such a thing indeed exist?

70

WILLIAM ARCHER

Murry: I believe that it does exist, but I do not believe that its existence can be proved.

I can only try to show you what I mean by the soul, and why I believe in its reality.

For a long while, for many years, I did not believe that it existed. I knew nothing whatever about it. I had a body, I had a mind, but I had (so far as I could tell) nothing besides. Somehow that body and that mind co-existed, but in growing discord; and this discordant co-existence of two elements was all that I meant when I used the word 'I.' I said I knew this or that; it was my mind that knew: I said I did this or that; it was my body that did it. I had no self. I was conscious that I had no self. Therefore in nearly all things I took the line of least resistance. In nearly all I did I tacitly sought the approval of others, and lacking that I did not know whether what I was doing was right or wrong: it reached such a pass that I can truly say I needed the recognition of others to be secure of my own existence. And when I had reached this extreme condition of not-being, I remained there for many months.

William Archer: I am not sure that I know what you are talking about, but I think I have been in something of the same condition: it is painful.

Murry: It is terrible: it is a waste and stony place; it is the dark night of the soul.

William Archer: But can you speak of the soul? Its very existence is what you are going to persuade me of.

Murry: You are right. I must not speak of the soul. In this waste and stony place I knew nothing, except that what I desired was not. I desired to be myself, and my self was not. I longed for truth, and all I knew was that the truth was not here or there. I did not long for a soul (though, perhaps, indeed I did, though I did not know it), because I did not know that such a thing could be. What I desired above all

71

else, what I desired in all things that I desired, was to *be*. Simply that.

William Archer: I do not understand. But wait a moment: let me say I am not sure that I understand. How did you know that you were not?

Murry: That I cannot say: for it had taken me many years to learn, and I learned it as one grows, unconsciously. I found at length that I did not believe in myself, but in others' belief in me. That came to me very slowly; but when it came to me, it was an agony. On some days it seemed to me that I was struggling – and in vain – to be born, and that until I was born I could know nothing.

William Archer: But you knew a good deal, surely? Self or no self, that could make no difference to your knowledge.

Murry: It made all the difference in the world. 'Though I have *all* knowledge and have not charity, I am nothing.'

William Archer: I do not understand. What difference would 'charity' make?

Murry: In the Greek, you remember, charity is love. I was like a man who is an infinitesimal part of a great process. I knew the process; there were moments when I could see that it was a wonderful and beautiful process and I worshipped it (yes, worshipped it) in awestruck adoration. Yet something in me was frozen. It was my mind which adored; but in my heart I rebelled against this monstrous and lovely tyranny to whose beauty must be sacrificed all that I prized and dreamed. I adored the beauty, but I did not love it.

William Archer: Do not be mystical. I shrink from mysticism.

Murry: I am simply trying to describe what I felt and was. Many men had felt it before me. I think that Spinoza called this condition the *amor intellectualis dei* – the intellectual love of God.

William Archer: Of God?

Murry: So he said. But he was wrong. His was but a love of the outward and visible garment of God. His *amor intellectualis dei* had yet to become an *amor spiritualis dei* – that is what 'charity' means.

William Archer: Can we not leave God out of it? Remember I have yet to be persuaded of his existence also.

Murry: I will try to leave God out; but do not misunderstand me: I did not say and do not believe that *he* exists.

William Archer: But surely you spoke of an 'intellectual love of God,' which, you said, had to be somehow changed into a 'spiritual love of God.' I can understand an attitude which could be called 'an intellectual love' of a God who is not a person, although, as I say, I do not believe such a God exists; but I cannot attach any meaning to 'a spiritual love' of a God who is not a person.

Murry: Perhaps it is only a word that troubles you: there is love of the body, as a man's for a woman, or a mother's for her son; there is love of the mind, as love of beauty or of justice or of truth; and there is love of the soul; but for the love of the soul there is no object but God, and there can be no love of the soul for any person. Indeed love can be predicated of the soul only by metaphor. That may be seen if we consider by what means the soul is born.

You will remember where and what I was: a mind and a body in a waste and stony place. This mind and body were not me: there was no *me*. I was now one, now the other, never a single and certain thing – save perhaps at fleeting moments when I was as it were possessed by the strange beauty of words I could not understand, or moved beyond myself by the sight or sound of some harmony I could not grasp.

William Archer: That was ecstasy: you should have known it for what it was.

Murry: I did; nevertheless it haunted me. It seemed to whisper that there was indeed a condition – a something – that could be attained.

William Archer: A condition, *not* a something.

Murry: A condition, *and* a something. If I were to *be*, if that incessant discord within me were resolved, I should have attained *something*. Would not being itself be something?

William Archer: Why not an illusion?

Murry: If it were an illusion, it would not last. Illusions do not last. But I do not believe that I thought these things at that time. It is hard in remembering oneself not to interpret what was in terms of what is. I can vouch only for desolation, for longing, for a profound sense that I was not. I longed to be. I remember that I said those actual words to myself many times; but I can scarcely have known what I meant by them.

I had come to a point when I no longer believed in others' belief in me. What did it matter to me that they should believe in me, when I did not? Or of what profit that they should believe in my existence, when mere existence was worthless to me? But there was one person remaining who believed in me in a different way. I felt that she saw something in me that I could not see. I mean exactly what I say: I felt that she verily did see a *me* of whom I knew nothing. To him she spoke, and sometimes he answered. Am I becoming mystical? If so, I cannot help it, for I am trying faithfully to describe what was.

William Archer: Not more, and perhaps not less, than you have been hitherto.

Murry: It does not matter. I had come to the point when all the *self* which I knew was simply this woman's belief that such a self existed. Nothing more – nothing. The woman died.

Then I was alone, and there was no going back. The last straw at which I could clutch was gone, and I knew this had to be. I had to be stripped naked, and I was. I do not know how to describe this nakedness. You drown, and I cannot describe this drowning. All I know is that there is a point at which you do not struggle against it: you do not fight for life: you go down, down, with a sense of gladness and relief. The struggle is over. You go back, back into the dark from which you sprang.

William Archer: And then?

Murry: Then a spark is born, which is, and knows, and is your self and is something quite other than yourself. At the moment you are not, you are; and that which you are not, you are. That is the birth of the soul; and in knowing itself, it knows I AM THAT I AM, which is the name of the nameless God.

You shake your head. Is it indeed incomprehensible?

William Archer: I fear so: it means nothing to me.

Murry: But wait. Forget all that I have said, save only this: that the soul verily exists, that it is other than mind and body, that it is as it were the hidden meaning of them both, that it is man's purpose here on earth to attain his soul, that at the moment he attains his soul he knows that the soul exists out of time and space and belongs to another order of reality than any our body feels or our mind knows. Can you conceive that this should be true?

William Archer: Yes, I can conceive it.

Murry: Suppose it were true. Then it would be wrong, somehow vulgar and belittling, to speak of personal survival. The soul which is out of time and space eternally is, and therefore is impersonal. There is the eternal soul; there is that in which the eternal soul eternally exists, in another mode of being, which neither our senses nor our mind but our soul alone can comprehend. To seek to reimpose per-

sonality upon the soul which is the triumph over personality
– that would be strange, would it not? Strange and futile
and unworthy.

William Archer: If the truth were as you say, it would be
so.

Murry: I put it before you as a hypothesis – to explain
that 'something there' of which you speak – that this may
indeed be the goal and purpose of human life: to achieve a
soul, here and now, but that this purpose is not always attained before death. (It can be attained before, I believe,
only through a death in life.) But mortal death must come,
and then it is attained. Suppose that mortal death is indeed
such a nakedness and such a drowning as I have described –
suppose that the spark of the soul is born in that darkness
from which we sprang and to which we return, and that we
do indeed put on this incorruptible – inevitably, without
distinction of saint or sinner, wise man or fool, by the very
fact of death – then would not your sense of 'something
there' be explained?

William Archer: Not explained, perhaps – yet perhaps indeed explained.

Murry: And if this should be true, as I believe it is true,
then would not our business here on earth be to conquer the
last enemy death through a death here in life, and not by
seeking communication with the dead? They live indeed,
but not with our life: they have paid the price for their souls,
and for their entry into that incomprehensible mode of
being which mankind has sometimes called God. Something
is there. I believe it more strongly than you, but because I
believe it, I believe that to seek to compel that eternal and
timeless being to re-enter this world once more is mistaken.

'We do it wrong, being so majestical,
To offer it the show of violence.'

William Archer: So you condemn effort at communication with the beyond.

Murry: I condemn nothing. I simply say that our effort should be to attain a condition and a knowledge whereby we should not even desire such communication, because we should know that it was impossible by such means. We shall conquer death only by dying; and if we die, whether in this life or at the end of it, we shall need no communication with the dead.

William Archer: But I have had such communication.

Murry: So have I, though I did not seek it. And it told me, as it told you, that there is 'something there.' But what more could it tell? What would you have it tell? That all is well? Would that be enough? And if it were not enough, would all indeed be well?

The knowledge that 'something is there' may come to a man by many ways; but to know the something that is there – to that, I believe, there is but a single way.

PERSONALITY AND
IMMORTALITY

I HAVE received a number of communications concerning William Archer's letter and my imaginary conversation with him. The statement of my position was as clear as I could make it at the time. In writing of such matters one is hampered by the intuitive and immediate nature of one's own convictions; one does not know where the main difficulty for others will lie. Where all is a chain of personal and indemonstrable beliefs, it is not apparent which will be the weakest, or the most perplexing link in others' eyes. The letters make this clear.

There is a paradox, or a contradiction, for other minds in the simultaneous assertion of a disbelief in personal immortality and a disbelief in annihilation. Immortality, for others, is the immortality of this personality; if this personality is not immortal, then the condition after death must be one of annihilation. Or it is a condition of virtual annihilation: an immortality that is not an immortality of this personality, with all its faiths and fears and fallibilities, is empty and worthless. These are the two main objections, or the two difficulties. One is logical and of fact; the other ethical, and of value: one declares that an immortality not of this personality is meaningless, the other that it is valueless.

The crux of the question, as ever in such discussion, lies in a word. The word is 'personality.' It is a vague word, one of the vaguest. I have neither the desire nor the authority to pin it to a meaning. But obviously in this context 'personality' must be an attribute of all human beings. We are not discussing that still vaguer attribute which we award to some and deny to others when we say that 'X has personality, and Y has not.' Personality, in the sense in which we can argue whether it is or is not immortal, must belong to all men alike. It is the answer to the universal question. 'What am I?'

That question can be answered by any individual in a thousand ways, on a thousand levels. The introspective intellect will find no term to its investigations. The skins of this onion are infinite. 'I am this and that,' I say. But I am the I which says 'I am this and that.' And again, more truly, I am the I which says I am the I which says, 'I am this and that,' and so *ad infinitum*. The intellect can define an organic reality only as an infinite series. The intellect was not made for the work. Whatever I am, I am not an infinite series. I know that, quite simply; and if the intellect insists that I am, then I promptly conclude that the intellect has taken in hand a problem of which it is incapable. We cannot measure beauty in a pint pot.

There is, at this first check, a choice. We may once for all discard introspection, as certain of the modern psychologists affect to do. We can look on men as we look on animals – automata that behave after a certain describable fashion. The idea is to me nonsensical, and I mention it only to indicate that it is held. For those who hold it, of course, the whole conception of personality is an illusion. Therefore, we need waste no time over it.

My personality in the widest sense exists; I may describe it as the organic whole of my attributes as a living being. But to require or to desire that this personality shall be immortal seems to me inordinate. My cardinal attribute as a living being is my mortality. All that I am grows up out of, is fundamentally based upon, the fact that this body dies, and its functions wither up and cease. If we begin to talk of personality as something independent of this living body, unaffected by its change and decay, we are already plunged full into transcendental realms. To talk of that personality, whatever it may be, and however it may be conceived or imagined, as 'this personality,' is a mere juggling with words. If any personality can be immortal, it is obviously not 'this personality'; and if a personality is not 'this personality,' why call it a personality at all?

Why indeed? Except for the profound and ineradicable belief of humanity that there is, as it were, a core of living reality hidden somewhere in the swaddlings of 'this personality.' At moments it seems to emerge; memories of things that have never happened, nor could ever have been happenings at all, premonitions of what will never be, of conditions untranslatable into terms of the life we know, — these strange inward tremors of the human psyche can be ascribed only to something which we at once are and are not. For some inscrutable reason we set a value on these moments; they are precious to us. In them, it seems, we were on the brink of an understanding that slips wholly from the grasp of our searching mind. They are the poet's 'moments of vision'; they are common to all men.

But few men would claim these tremors, or that which is moved by them, as part of their personality. Their personality is their own, these things are not; and when they visit a man, all that he knows as his personality is in abeyance. Something slips out of those swaddling bands and for a brief instant takes possession. Looking back upon them, striving to retain the memory of them, a man will say: 'Then I was not myself,' or he will say: 'Then I was indeed myself.' And, strangely enough, the propositions are interchangeable. For these moments warrant the belief, which doubtless they first inspired, that a man has a self that is beyond and hidden from his self of every-day. It depends upon himself to which side the scale of speech inclines. 'Then I was indeed myself' is the word of the idealist; 'Then

I was not myself' is the word of the materialist. But the fact is the same; and it is a fact of common experience.

These are 'the intimations of immortality' concerning which Wordsworth wrote his ode. They are not rare, they are not the privilege of peculiar men: it is simply that some men attach more significance to them than others. To one man they are the key to the mystery: to another they themselves are the real mystery, best left unplumbed, incalculable and inexplicable disturbances of the tenor of existence. But to neither are these tremors a function of their ordinary personality. That is, as it were, suspended, and this suspension is welcomed by one man, and resented by another. Whatever it is that a man is, and whatever it is that he touches, in such a moment, it is not himself in any ordinary sense of the word.

If we put resolutely aside the dogmas of theologians, and refuse to accept anything but the immediate experience of mankind before it has suffered metamorphosis at the hands of the doctors, it is to these 'intimations of immortality' that we are reduced for the basis of a faith concerning the spiritual reality of man. Doubtless Wordsworth begged the question to some extent when he gave these moments of vision that splendid title. But he had to account for them; he dared not ignore them; they were supremely real to him. They had been supremely real to many men through many centuries before him; and out of their felt reality had grown the tenacious faith of man that he possessed a soul, and that it was immortal. This faith, superbly expressed by the founder of the Christian religion, had been vulgarized. The notion of the soul as a hidden and a higher self was too mysterious or too mystical. The ordinary mind fastened upon the concrete elements in its symbolic expression; it insisted on reading in the letter and not in the spirit, and the doctrine of the immortality of the soul became degraded into something

scarcely distinguishable from the immortality of the body.
It was not surprising, for those who spoke with most authority
concerning the soul and its immortality used words that
were difficult and strange. They said that the soul could
only be found by a hard and mysterious process of death
and rebirth. There seemed to be no straight road to the soul.
It was remote and inaccessible.

This process of death and rebirth which was, quite evidently, an actual and lived experience for those who autho-
ritatively proclaimed it, was changed into a mere ritual act
in religion. A ceremony was performed over the would-be or
unconscious initiate; and he was told that he was dead and
reborn into the possession of his soul. And, of course, he
remained precisely what he was before. He had to take the
existence of his soul on trust. He knew nothing about it,
and very few of his teachers knew more than he: and those
who did know had to face the old difficulty of explaining a
new order of experience to those who had not experienced it.
'Even a proverb is not a proverb to you,' said Keats, 'until
your life has illustrated it.' It was very much as though a
man should try to explain to a cow the nature of *homo
sapiens*. The instructed cow would imagine him as a very
superior kind of cow – everything, in fact, that she as a cow
would desire to be in the cow-paradise. The condition of
being something profoundly other than cow would be in
itself unintelligible, and very undesirable.

So – if the crudeness of the comparison may be forgiven
for the sake of its clarity – those who demand the immortality of this personality find the doctrine of the immortality of
something other than this personality not only undesirable
but positively repellent. They forget, first, that they are demanding a rank impossibility. The immortality of this personality is a contradiction in terms: the mere fact of immortality would make this personality quite unrecognizable

They forget, again, that the conception of this personality is vague and unsatisfactory. Every deep-searching effort to disengage a solid core of reality from the superficies of this personality leads straight to conditions of being that are not personal at all. When we touch most nearly the sources of our being, or the heights of understanding, this personal and phenomenal 'I' dissolves away, and 'personality' is discovered to be not the essence, but a veil, of our own reality. And those others who object not to the possibility, but to the valuelessness, of an immortality not of this personality, forget that the conjecture we make, or the conviction we hold, concerning the nature of the soul derives from those moments of earthly existence when men, and those the greatest, have seemed to themselves to come nearest to the hidden reality of themselves and of the universe. The soul is that of which they are aware at their moments of profoundest comprehension. That this comprehension is of another kind than any our quotidian faculties allow is indubitable. But that it should therefore be valueless, or of less value than our mundane impotencies before all ultimate problems, is a strange position indeed.

In this matter we must hold fast to the spiritual perceptions of the great men before us. They are the highest wisdom we know. Of course, it is open to any man to reject them absolutely as the utterances of delusion. But even the realist must take count of the fact that these utterances of the poet and the saint have remained indelible from the hearts of generations of men. They may not have understood them; but they have been so moved by them that they have never forgotten them. The utterance of the great poet and the great prophet is compulsive; what they declare and reveal may be mysterious, but they speak to us as having authority and not as the scribes. If their wisdom was an illusion, it is curious, to say the least, that this illusion should retain an undiminished power over men, while the so-called truths pass incessantly into desuetude and decay.

But it may be said that what we call their wisdom was only flashes of illumination, momentary and bewildering; they came to them through no effort of their own, and they were beyond their interpretation, as they were beyond their control. There is no help in them. The presumption will not hold water for a moment. The more diligently we examine the great spiritual heroes of the past, the more evident it becomes that they indeed struggled for the possession of their souls. The ultimate wisdom which they touched was the just reward of what they endured in their loyalty to the truth. Their progress to a consummation was, for all its pains and loneliness, a natural progress; they received deep into themselves all the suffering that life gave them for their portion; when the great ninth wave bore up against them they faced it and plunged into its depths. Thus they emerged. It is no accident that the men who have uttered what seems to us the highest wisdom are those who have most greatly suffered, or that the highest faith is wrung out of the deepest despair. When Shakespeare in *The Tempest* declares his belief that this world of appearances will fade and his faith in a generation yet to come with a new vision of the human universe, we know by the dark horrors of the great tragedies out of what an abyss of desolation he had wrung his knowledge. It is the old knowledge, won by the old ways, which are for ever new to the man who has the courage to explore them. Of such men there are few. But they are worth understanding: none are more worth understanding than they. 'Do you not see,' cried Keats at the moment of emerging from his own wilderness of despair, 'how *necessary* a world of pains and troubles is to school an intelligence and *make it a soul?*' He, at that moment of knowledge, had faced his destiny, and 'died into life.' He ha paid the full price down to the last farthing for that contact here on earth with eternal life which was announced by the founder of Christianity, and is the always forgotten secret of his message. As the priestess of the universe declared to Keats in the sublime allegory of the second *Hyperion*:

> 'That thou had'st power to die
> And live again before thy fated hour
> Is thine own safety. . . .'

It may be that ordinary men cannot themselves attain the wisdom of these heroes. The demand is too great. After all, as Keats himself said many times, 'we never understand really fine things until we have gone the same steps as the author.' To understand a truly great man's wisdom we need to undergo his experience. There is no other way. It sounds impossible and presumptuous; perhaps it is not really so. Any man has at least the capacity to deal honestly with his own undeniable experience, and part of his experience will be the profound response from an unknown self within him to the mysterious words of his great forerunners concerning the soul and its immortality.

A THEOLOGICAL ENCOUNTER

In *The Guardian* of May 8th, 1925, an able theologian criti-
cized, with an unexpected tolerance, the previous remarks
of mine on 'Personality and Immortality.' I was greatly interested in this writer's views, first, because I found them
extremely difficult to grasp in spite of the obvious skill with
which they were presented, and secondly, because his habit
of mind was unfamiliar to me. Though I have read a little in
Thomas Aquinas and a little more in some of the mediæval
Christian mystics, I am a complete stranger to the thoughts
and methods of modern theology.

I have never doubted that the very personal views which
I have from time to time expressed in these essays had points
of contact (though probably of hostile contact) with the conceptions of modern theology. To have ascertained precisely
where these points of contact, or conflict, lay would have
meant my going too far out of my way; for I regard myself
primarily as a literary critic who has been forced by circumstances, both private and professional, to wander for a season
in the debatable land wherein both literature and religion
find their culmination. I have been involved, *invitâ Minervâ*,
in a voyage of discovery, but not in a punitive expedition.
The notion of making a détour in search of enemies is to me
fantastic: I have found quite enough, unsought, on my own
road and in my own profession.

But now that an able modern theologian has planted himself squarely in my path, I have no choice but to deal with
him to the best of my ability, just as I should try to deal with
any literary critic who seriously considered and opposed my
views.

My critic begins his article by admitting the difficulties

and ambiguities which surround the conception of 'immortality.' 'From time to time, therefore, it becomes a duty to face the difficulties and examine with care the nature of the doctrine peculiar to the Church.'

What could be more admirable? I am filled with hope and expectation. It seems to me almost a matter for regret that I should be made to interrupt the exposition. Nevertheless, I am made to interrupt it with my statement that there is no contradiction in 'the simultaneous assertion of a disbelief in personal immortality and a disbelief in annihilation.' To this my critic replies that 'the thought of an immortality less than personal is both ancient and various in form.' There is, for example, the 'attenuated immortality of fame' (excellent phrase!), the immortality of the species, and the immortality which 'consists in reabsorption into the one Eternal Mind.'

At this point I must demur. My statement that I find no contradiction in simultaneously disbelieving both in personal immortality and in annihilation has been quite arbitrarily interpreted. Did I say that I believed in an immortality '*less* than personal'? Might it not be, did not my own essay persistently imply, that I believed in an immortality that is *more* than personal? Did I not maintain that 'personality,' in any current and intelligible use of the word, is a limitation which at various moments of our mortal lives we do in fact transcend, and thereby make contact with a deeper and a truer self? Did I not assert that these momentary and profound experiences of a self beyond, and greater than, 'personality' are indeed our 'intimations of immortality,' and the only ones we have? I tried to make this clear; I believe I did make it clear. Why then am I straightway represented as saying that I believed in an immortality *less* than personal?

I am convinced that this serious and to me crucial misrepresentation of my statements was not deliberate. The internal evidence proves that my critic is an honourable man. Therefore I conclude that this misrepresentation was instinctive: for him an immortality which is other than personal *must* be less than personal. By what necessity, save one of his own temperament?

Henceforward, he is incapacitated from criticizing my belief. He is not controverting me, but some imaginary disputant whom he endows with my name. All that I can conclude from his inability to grasp what I did say is that my conception of immortality is not that of the Church. I never supposed it was. What I know is that some of the greatest sons of the Church have held a belief that is not, in essence, unlike my own. But of the doctrine of the Church itself I know nothing, for the simple reason that I have never been able to understand it when well-meaning people have tried to present it to me.

Fortunately, it is precisely on this point of the Church doctrine of immortality that my critic proposes to instruct me. 'Christianity, it is needless to add,' he goes on, 'can be satisfied with none of these,' that is to say, these doctrines of an immortality less than personal. 'Moreover, we cannot remind ourselves too often that faith in "the resurrection of the body" is radically distinct from the pagan belief in the immortality of the soul.' Here, I fancy, 'should be' is more appropriate than 'is.' Otherwise, what need to remind yourself so often? And, as a matter of history, that 'pagan' doctrine of the immortality of the soul had a very potent influence in softening the asperities of the primitive Christian belief in 'the resurrection of the body.'

Still, my critic is right in insisting that the distinctively Christian belief is in the resurrection, and the immortality, of the body. What I should like to know is whether he believes in it? Whether, indeed, any theologian who is not content with the vain repetition of a dogmatic clause, does believe in it. I understand Saint Paul when he declares: 'We know not yet what we shall be'; I can attach no meaning to a vague and general declaration of faith in 'the resurrection of the body.' I am not saying that those who make that declaration are insincere or perfunctory: I do not know what other men can believe. I merely insist that the mind of a man who can honestly declare that he believes in 'the resurrection of the body' is utterly different from my own. I take it for granted that my critic does believe it, simply, literally, without reservations or symbolic interpretations. He must, for he says, and I agree, that it is the central and distinctive doctrine of the Christian Church. Yet his next paragraph, the substance of which I have met before in Christian apologetic, would make me doubtful.

'We venture to say that "the resurrection of the body" represents, in a philosophical sense, an immense advance upon the older doctrine of the soul's escape from its material prison or tomb. The Christian view is the one effective protest against a dualism which can only end in intellectual disaster. Thus alone does "the body" cease to be a disparate and inimical substance, and thus does the "resurrection of the body" come to signify the survival or restoration of personality in the eternal life.'

On that paragraph one could write volumes. Let me simply ask one or two questions. Was Plato's fate really intellectual disaster? Is 'the resurrection of the body' a philosophical doctrine at all? Does belief in it make the body cease to be a disparate and inimical substance? Did it have that effect on Saint Paul, or on countless Christian ascetics who have followed his noble and vertiginous example? How does 'the resurrection of the body' *come to signify* (dangerous phrase!) anything at all but what it says? If it is become simply a symbol of some ineffable condition, as Jesus' answer to the Sadducees indicates that he held it to be, then why not proclaim it openly?

At this point, however, I re-enter the debate.

'Mr. Murry appears to argue, strangely enough, that because 'this personality' is mortal, it cannot be this same personality which is to pass into the immortal condition. As well almost might one argue that the identity of a human being could not survive the cutting of his wisdom teeth. Outside abstractions like the mathematical unit, there is no identity which does not endure in spite of – nay rather, because of – perpetual development and change. Were human personality – the most complex of all things known to us – exempt from this law, it would indeed be strange.'

Such reasoning, I confess, seems to me disingenuous. The *conception* of 'personality' is difficult, so is the conception of life; but the fact of personality is capable of being apprehended as simply as the fact of life. We know what we mean when we speak of personal possessions or personal charm; we know what men are asking for when they ask for personal immortality, and what they think they are getting when the theologian tells them that Christianity offers it to them. They ask to be reunited with their loved ones, or to be given some share of the earthly felicity that was denied them. The theologian who promises personal immortality promises men that they shall have such things as these. If he were to say to them: 'No, the life everlasting is something infinitely better, an ineffable condition, wherein they are neither married nor given in marriage, and all mundane conceptions, including that of personality itself, are meaningless, a condition which transcends the human existence that we know as far as human existence itself transcends the existence of the brute creation,' they would reply: 'That is not what we want, that is not what you promised.' Nor would they be satisfied if they were told: 'But, my friends, I promised you personality. The conception of personality is fraught with difficulties. But, in general, I may inform you there is no personality which does not endure in spite of — nay, rather because of — perpetual development and change.'

'On any hypothesis, pagan or Christian (my critic proceeds), the philosophy of body and soul is infinitely difficult. . . . It scarcely follows, however, that the whole problem is beyond the range of rational discussion. "If we put resolutely aside the dogmas of theologians," says Mr. Murry, "and refuse to accept anything but the immediate experience of mankind . . . it is to these 'intimations of immortality' that we are reduced for the basis of a faith concerning the spiritual reality of man." On the same principle, we might offer to put aside the dogmas of scientists, and to stick to "the immediate experience of mankind" as the basis of our faith concerning the nature of matter. The two proposals are, in fact, about equally intelligent. Wordsworthian intimations, chorus-endings from Euripides, and so forth, are challenges to the intelligence, not substitutes for thought. The poet's vision, no doubt, is untranslatable into argument, but so is a pain in one's finger. Theologians attempt to explain one kind of experience, physiologists another. The best of their theories or "dogmas" may be no more than shadows; but, as long as men are afflicted with rationality, so long will such theories continue to appear.'

Let me pause at this paragraph: it needs some unravelling. Suddenly we find that the dogmas of theologians concerning immortality are on the same footing as the dogmas of scientists concerning matter. If my critic were a stupid man, I should pass this by as a mere stupidity. Since he is clever, I must suspect him of trying to throw dust in his readers' eyes. For surely this is a travesty of argument. A scientist, quâ scientist, has no dogmas. He has hypotheses which he propounds as an explanation of certain facts; the moment a new fact is discovered that is outside the scope of his hypothesis, the hypothesis is discarded and a new one sought. Science is, by nature, completely undogmatic. Therefore, to declare that my proposal to put aside the dogmas of theologians concerning immortality is equivalent or analogous to putting aside the dogmas of scientists concerning matter is either to be nonsensical, or to imply that the dogmas of theologians are merely hypotheses. That I gather from the concluding sentence, is what my critic means to imply. Or does he merely mean to seem to imply it? He cannot seriously suggest that the theological dogma of 'the resurrection of the body' is a hypothesis? That is a simple fact, for the simple Christian; not a fact at all, for the sceptic. Therefore, I presume that he means that the explanations given by theology of this 'fact' are merely hypothetical. I can well believe it.

But the incidental definition of theology interests me. 'Theology explains one kind of experience; physiology another.' Let us, for clarity's sake, stick to one particular question: 'the resurrection of the body.' Two things are really combined in that phrase. One is a belief in the reality of the resurrection of Jesus in the body; the other is a declaration of belief that all men will be resurrected in the body. One is therefore a belief in the reality of a certain event in history, the other a belief in a certain future event. These are, I presume, the experiences which theology explains. How does it explain them? For the first, I suppose, no explanation is possible or necessary, if you believe that Jesus did indeed rise bodily from the dead. You simply believe that the Gospel narratives of the resurrection, with all their insuperable discrepancies, are true: the event really happened, and happened in several different ways at the same time. I do not see what theology can explain in this; history, psychology, or anthropology might attempt an explanation of the discrepancy of those narratives, on the assumption that the event did not really happen, but was sincerely believed to have happened. But I cannot see what explanation theology can give, or needs to give. The fact was a fact.

And, if this fact was indeed a fact, what necessity is there for theology to seek or give an explanation of the future resurrection of all men bodily from the dead? If the past fact was a fact, there is no difficulty in believing in the future fact. Yet apparently there are difficulties; hypotheses have to be framed and theories propounded, 'so long as mankind is afflicted with rationality.' This is the task and function of theology – to supply rational explanations of matters of faith. It strikes me as a chimerical and fantastic occupation. It was all very well in the Middle Ages, when theological conceptions were the only intellectual conceptions which men possessed, and, for example, substance or matter could be easily and naturally identified with God. Then the theological and the rational activity were one. But now they are separated; and theology (as distinct from the history of theology) presents the pathetic spectacle of trying to find scientific support for beliefs and facts which science cannot recognize.

My critic's next paragraph supplies me with an illuminating example: –

'Annihilation is a doctrine repudiated by natural philosophy in the very hour of its birth. In the lower grades of Nature, where the corruption of one thing is the origin of another, the thread of individuality does indeed appear to be broken at every transition. Yet it has to be remembered that individuality itself, vague and hazy at the lower levels, is for ever advancing towards clearer definition in the long evolutionary process towards human personality. Analogy in such a case, though it must fall far short of proof, is strong enough to authorize the suggestion that the virtual immortality of the germ-plasm may be an anticipation or symbol of the real immortality of the individual soul.'

What on earth has the continuity of the germ-plasm to do with the resurrection of the body or personal immortality? Nothing at all. Moreover, it seems a little – let me speak softly – inconsistent, first to reproach me (falsely) with believing in a 'less than personal' immortality, and then to offer me as 'a symbol' of the true doctrine the least personal kind of immortality my mind can conceive. Is that what theology calls 'explaining an experience'? I should call it whittling away an article of faith, in order that some people who are slightly afflicted with rationality may be able to say, 'I believe in the continuity of the germ-plasm,' but to pronounce it, 'I believe in the resurrection of the body and the life everlasting.' To my non-theological mind there is a difference between these things, and I infinitely prefer the attitude of old Tertullian: *Certum est quia impossibile est.* Then I know where I am; I am bewildered by a science which makes its business to demonstrate (by analogy) that the impossible is possible.

At this point, however, my critic returns, takes his foot off the scientific stool, and plants it, rather circumspectly, on the religious.

'The Christian faith in resurrection rests, however, on no analogies [Why, then, I cannot refrain from asking, make use of them?], but primarily upon belief in the resurrection of Christ as a historical fact. Of those who deny the reality of that alleged event [curious phrase!], something like one hundred per cent. deny it not (as they suppose) for purely historical reasons, but upon some *a priori* ground.'

What is a purely historical reason, I wonder, in the view of my critic? Does the fact that the narratives of that 'alleged event' are hopelessly contradictory constitute a purely historical reason for rejecting them? If it does (and I think of none purer), then the purely historical objection is overwhelming. But it may be said there is the same, or at least a similar, purely historical reason for rejecting all the Gospel narratives of the life of Jesus. If we deny that he rose from the dead on purely historical grounds, then we must be consistent and deny that he ever lived at all. Very few people are foolish enough to deny that. To this extent, therefore, my critic is correct in saying that the great majority of those who deny the fact of the Resurrection do not deny it on purely historical grounds.

But that does not mean that the reasons for which they deny it are *a priori* reasons. They have to deal, in the case of the Gospel narratives of the resurrection of Jesus, with four utterly discrepant narratives of an event which is unparalleled in human experience. Still, it is true that even if those narratives were concordant in every detail, they would reject them. But still not on *a priori* grounds. The *a priorism* is to be imputed to those who maintain that a miracle did, in fact, occur, not to those who deny the possibility of miracle. These reject the Gospel narratives of the resurrection of Jesus in the body, on precisely the same grounds that they reject Livy's prodigies, or the mediæval accounts of men with eyes in their stomachs; and so do I.

But in absolutely rejecting these narratives I am far from denying that Mary of Magdala, or Peter, or Paul, had a real experience of the existence of Jesus after his mortal death. There may well be, and I for my own part am prepared to believe that there are, conditions – 'whether in the body or out of the body' – in which soul may make contact with soul; that men have moments of exaltation when they for an instant possess faculties and acquire knowledge which are quite incommensurable with their ordinary faculties and ordinary knowledge, and cannot be translated into their terms. And I believe that men and women who loved such a man as Jesus was as passionately as his followers loved him certainly did have such moments of exaltation and communion. They described their experiences according to their conceptions and their powers; if they had been educated men of the twentieth century they would have described them differently: that is all.

Here, I think, I touch the root of my dissatisfaction with my critic's attitude, which is, I presume, typical of contemporary theology. It seems to me an attitude that is half of this century and half of rustic Palestine in the first century. It wants to sit on two stools at once, and has acquired the art of transferring itself from one to the other with such rapidity that a momentary illusion is created. Sober reflection tells me that the theologian *cannot* be sitting on both at the same moment: but there is a whirl, a commotion, and a glitter, my eyes are dazzled, and it seems for one incredible second that the two positions have coalesced. It is acrobatics or prestidigitation. Hence comes the general distrust of modern theology and the general disrepute into which it is fallen.

Is it presumptuous to suggest that the only way for modern theology to rehabilitate itself is for it to become truly modern? By that I mean that it should base itself squarely on a critical attitude (which is not a merely sceptical attitude) to the Gospel narratives and the New Testament as a whole. The religious substance that is contained in them, the personality, the teaching, the heroism, the influence of Jesus, the story of the greatest of all human tragedies and the greatest of all human victories, would suffer no diminution. The religious experience exists; it has been and always will be the most universal means of communion with the reality that eludes all intellectual search. There would still be a devoted and heroic Mediator and Saviour, of whom it would still be true that where two or three are gathered together in his name, there is he in the midst of them. The choice in these modern times is not between dogmatic Christianity and no Christianity, as perhaps it was two hundred or a hundred years ago; nor, again, is it a choice between dogmatic Christianity and a kind of ethical humanitarianism. The personality, the teaching, and the heroism of Jesus were not made of benevolence and uplift; he did not preach what Renan called 'la délicieuse théologie de l'amour.' As we see him, and we can see him plainly enough if we look hard enough, he was the man who had the fullest religious experience in human history, and who lived and died completely in accordance with the fullness of his knowledge. For every gentle saying the humanitarians would anthologize there is a hard and terrible one which a truly modern theology would not even desire to extenuate. This harmony in a living man of complete joy in life and complete rejection of it, of extreme love and extreme anger, made Jesus what he believed he was, the Messiah indeed, the prophetic type of perfect man.

There has lived but one man whose life and words and works and death were such that countless generations of men have felt that he who conquered life *must* have conquered also the last enemy, death. The essential Christian faith in the resurrection of the body rests not on the fact of resurrection of Jesus from the dead, which is no fact at all, but on the fact, which is a fact, that no one who knows him (and we can know him as well as the men who saw him) has ever been able to believe that he died. Somehow or other they have created an immortality for him, and always the highest immortality that they could truly conceive. Let modern theology do the same; then it will not need to call 'the virtual immortality of the germ-plasm' to its aid.

CHRIST OR CHRISTIANITY?

I AM now required to define more closely than by scattered remarks my attitude to Christianity and to Christ. Since I have brought the summons upon myself, I will try to respond as quickly and clearly as I can. To attempt this in two brief essays is inevitably to be guilty of injustice, because Christianity is many things: and I believe there are now, as there certainly have been in the past, many Christians whose convictions and lives are of the noblest.

If I seem to be unsympathetic towards the Church, I would ask my readers to bear in mind two things. The first is: that I am fully conscious of the debt that I owe the Church. I regard human history as necessary, inevitable and beautiful. The Church is a part of the scheme of things: without it the memory and the knowledge of Jesus would have been impossible for men. Therefore I acknowledge, and with gratitude, that I am a son of the Church. The second is: that I hold that the finer conscience of mankind has now passed definitely outside the Church. I have tried to explain elsewhere when and why this began to happen.[1] I would ask those to whom this is an intolerable proposition to consider one simple fact: that the reawakening of the sense of the divine in the early nineteenth century, which is sometimes called modern Romanticism, was born outside the Church and imposed upon it from without. The Oxford Movement was merely the belated repercussion of a religious renaissance quite independent of the Church. And the Church has proved itself so incapable of responding to the stimulus that its reaction has been to narrow instead of

[1] See the essay on 'Literature and Religion' in *To the Unknown God*.

broaden its basis. When I think that the spiritual awakening of Keats and Shelley, Coleridge and Wordsworth, in passing through the Church, has degenerated into the sacerdotal movement of to-day, I am confirmed in my conviction that the Church has done its work: it is no longer adequate to the religious consciousness of modern times. Who, during the nineteenth century, have been the prophets of the human soul in England? Assuredly not the priests; but the poets, the playwrights, the novelists, and the men of science.

The essential of genuine religion is that a man should really believe in the God in whom he professes to believe. The religion that consists in pious (or even in desperate) hopes and polite professions is distasteful and meaningless to me. I can accept the religion of no man as a reality if he does not square his acts with his professions. This is a simple test, but the only one. The results it gives are salutary to contemplate. Not one of the professed Christians I have ever met – good men though many of them were – has squared his acts with the very first article of his creed: 'I believe in God the Father, Almighty.'

From this I conclude that, although many people say they believe in God the Father, at least once a week, nobody really does. I am not surprised: it is a very hard thing to believe in. It takes more than a hero to do it. What does surprise me is the willingness of my fellow-men to profess a belief in God the Father on which they will not act. That seems to me less than honest.

The honest thing, it seems to me, is to admit that the conception of God the Father Almighty is belied by all human experience. Men do not believe in Him, because they cannot. If they would acknowledge it, the ground for the future might be cleared.

The question is then: Shall men believe in a God at all?

In answer to that: One thing is certain. It is far better to believe in no God at all than to incur the risk of the lie in the soul, by professing to believe in God the Father Almighty and acting just as though He did not exist.

Man's experience forbids him to believe in God the Father. Then let him stick to experience, in his religion too. The religion that is not built upon experience will fail a man in his need, and, if he is a man with a sensitive conscience, lead him into intolerable equivocations.

But human experience includes experience of God.

In a sense, it does: but not of God the *Father* Almighty. If you have no religious experience of your own to confirm this bare statement, search among the men who have had the deepest religious experience in the past. It is not experience of God the Father. An unutterable experience of an unutterable God, of something – a power – a soul of which all life is the bodily garment. Nothing more? Nothing less.

According to what a man is he will try to formulate that experience of the unutterable. If he is filled with love for humanity, his God will also be filled with love for humanity.

Such was the God of Jesus – the most loving of all Gods, because he was the most loving of all men. Therefore he created God the Father. Created him; and believed in him, steadily, unflinchingly, all his life. He thought that the 'wonderful news' of this God would be received by all men, as glad tidings of great joy. Quite naturally, they did not believe in his message: experience forbade. 'Only believe,' he cried. They could not. A few of them believed in him, which was a different thing, and not what he wanted at all. He wanted them to believe not that he was God's son, but that they were God's sons. They could not believe it. So he, knowing that he was God's son, and finding that men could not believe that they were God's sons, came to that deep and mysterious yet blindingly simple resolution that he must die in order that men should know they were the sons of God. He would trust God the Father to the uttermost, to show men the way to trust Him. He trusted Him; he died in agony; and his last words were: 'My God, my God, why hast thou forsaken me?'

His God, the good God, the loving God, the Father Almighty, did not exist. Jesus died knowing it. No pain in the world of men has ever been like that pain.

That conviction is among the deepest that I have. If I were to leave hold of it for a moment, I should betray the greatest of my heroes and all my experience of life. I have clung to that conviction when it was agony to me. Now it is an agony no more; it gives me a peace beyond my understanding. I do not blame men for refusing to look at the pain of Christ; it is not easy. But it is worth doing, for many things: for one simple thing above all. It makes it easy to die.

The Crucifixion is a mystery. I may be presumptuous; but it seems to me that if men would think out the Crucifixion honestly, to the bitter end, we should be a whole league onward on the road of understanding. But I am afraid the time is not yet come for that. The world is now divided between those who profess Jesus as God, and those who dismiss his story as a fairy-tale; both are precluded from thinking honestly about him.

To those who dismiss his story as a fairy-tale, I have nothing to say. The man who is incapable of sensing the wonderful reality of his life is made of different stuff from mine. To those who read it as the story of a God, I have nothing to say: they also are made of different stuff from mine. Except that I would ask them, Which is better: to contemplate a man who so loved men that he deliberately gave his own life to prove that God was their father, or to contemplate a God who gave his own son to torment, when he could save the world by a thought?

I know that I shall be accused of not understanding the mystery. 'God so loved the world that he gave his only-begotten son. . . .' I can understand a mystery as well as most men and I can understand the thought of the Christian mystic who wrote those words. But things are simpler than that. I refuse utterly the God who would demand such a blood-sacrifice. And when I am told that this proves the unutterable love of God for mankind, my simple reply is: 'Why do you not, then, trust Him?'

Men would *like* to trust God as a Father, no doubt. I know well enough the hunger of the human soul for a Father who cares. But we cannot have all we long for. And which is better: to half-believe in a loving Father who does not exist, or to believe wholly in a loving Son who did? It is this half-belief that is rotting our modern world – belief that does not act. It is this half-belief that has made a mockery of Jesus' words – of all of them. It is this half-belief that drives the intellectually honest man into his aversion from the Church and all its works – this Church of Christ that repudiates the man it worships, repudiates him most utterly *by* worshipping him.

'Therefore take no thought, saying, What shall we eat? or what shall we drink? or, wherewithal shall we be clothed? (for after all these things do the Pagans seek) for your Father knoweth that ye have need of all these things. . . . Take therefore no thought for the morrow; for the morrow shall take thought of the things of itself.'

What does the Church make of that? A word of God? Then it has never dreamed of obeying it. 'Ah, but we *try* to follow it.' Humbug! That is not a word a man can *try* to follow. He can either follow it, or refuse to follow it. There is no middle way.

What is the use, to an honest man, of a Church of Christ which looks upon his very simplest words as so much pious nonsense? There is no middle way of following Christ. Follow him, or leave him alone.

Those words are perfectly simple. They come from a man who really believed that God was his Father and the Father of all men. From that real belief they follow inevitably: they announce the first, the simplest, the most natural act of such a belief – an actual trust in God. Why, a drunken tramp who pads the highways unknowing whence his next meal will come is nearer to following Christ than the whole bench of English bishops. Christ, the friend of publicans and sinners and harlots, would have chosen swiftly between them.

For this modern world does not believe in God the Father; and the modern Church does not either. It puts its faith in pensions, and endowments, and 5 or 15 per cent. And so do I. I have not the faintest intention (if I can help it) of leaving nothing between me and mine and the kindness of God the Father or the mercies of the world. Neither, so far as I can see, have my Christian contemporaries. But I esteem myself by so much a more honest man than they that I refuse to enter a Church and say: 'I believe in the God the Father,' when half my days are spent in taking precautions against his unkindness. I believe in Christ, and I believe in him enough to have tried to find out what it would mean to believe, as he believed, in God the Father. He believed in Him, and he acted on his belief, to the bitter end. If I were to believe in God the Father I should have no choice but to follow him, and to the bitter end.

Here we come once more to the mystery of the Crucifixion. It is hardly a mystery to those who have an inkling of what it would mean to believe in God the Father, the Father of all men, as Jesus believed in Him. If that is true, then there is indeed 'wonderful news' to proclaim; if that is true, then the man who knows it need not, then he *must* not, take thought for the morrow; if that is true, and men will not believe it, as they never have believed it, and never will, then he must die to prove it.

And Jesus died to prove it. He did not prove it. He died, knowing that he had not proved it. But what he had proved was this: that mankind had at last produced a man with such infinite love in his heart that he could not conceive God save as a loving and living Father to all men, and rather than give up this amazing and transcendent faith, he went to a shameful and atrocious death. To have proved that was to have proved a more wonderful thing than even Jesus sought to prove. For what man has been, he may, he will be again. There will, there must come the time when all men will create within themselves the infinite love that he had. Man may, in the long run man must, believe in man. Is that a chilling or a thrilling faith? Is it a *faith* at all? Is it not knowledge, built on a rock, for any man who cares to dig his way to the truth of the Gospel story?

Ah, but Jesus was deceived.

Yes, he was deceived; but he deceived himself. He had created the loving God for whom he died. And the mystery is this: that by dying for him, he did indeed create him, a loving God who was a man, as a *loving* God must be; not that transcendent Father whom men worship with their lips and deny with their acts. Out of that fire of love in himself, which would face the extreme of loneliness and pain simply to lift the pain and loneliness from other men, he kindled the spark of that divine something in man which cares, and will go on caring more and yet more deeply, year by year, century by century, age by age, till the pain and the evil are slowly blotted out of the world.

On that day, which I believe will surely come, in this world in time, his work will be done: that kingdom of God which he believed would come upon men at his death, will be here indeed, and he will be the king.

Wherever is the divine something in men which cares, there is he. For though many great, many lovely, many noble things were in the world before him, that was not in the world. It entered the world when he died for it.

We know more than he did; but when all our knowledge is assayed, perhaps it comes only to this: that we know what was utterly hidden from him in his agony: that what he died for is not a Father that exists but a world that may be; and he has made the coming of that world inevitable.

I may be wrong: perhaps I am blinded by a beam in my own eye that I cannot see, but I must confess my belief that the Church now stands in the way of the onward march. We have grown up to the point where we can look upon Jesus as he was; we do not need, any more, to have the impact of his tragedy mitigated, and our vision of his triumph blurred. We have grown to the point when we can face him. The Church will not face him, and distaste for the Church turns those who would aside from facing him. If we are to have a religion it must be one that honestly accepts life, and squares its beliefs to its acts. When it comes to accepting life, sooner or later you find yourself with the Cross in front of you. Of all tragedies this was the supreme. What do you make of it? An honest man may say: 'Nothing but pain.' But if he is more honest still, he will say: 'No, not pain alone. It is like all great tragedies, only greater than they: there is some unspeakable beauty there.' And then he will go on: with this tragedy and this unspeakable beauty he will wrestle until he sees what was involved therein, and understand what immortal issues were fought in Galilee and won on Golgotha. And, I doubt not, he will end like the centurion, and say: 'Truly this man was a son of God,' and come to comprehend how profoundly mankind may rejoice that there was a son to make the sacrifice, but no Father to demand it.

§

I have said that the life of Jesus enables us to believe in man. Since he veritably was, we can believe in, and we can work for, the creation of a new man. It is the only thing in which we can believe.

'That is impossible. What of the War?

The war proved one thing, and one alone; but proved it finally. The old man, the present man, is doomed to disaster. Somehow man must be changed. We have a breathing space; for ten, for twenty years this blasphemy of humanity which is modern war may be spared us. We have a breathing space. We can use it.

Somehow man must be changed. To change man: that is the problem.

'It cannot be done. Man is not; he is millions of men and women.'

No, we cannot change millions of men: perhaps millions of years are required for that. But to change millions is not required. One man, who was changed nineteen hundred years ago, wrought wonders. Is it not a wonder even to think that if one man in a thousand of those who professed to follow him had taken but one step on his road, the war could not have been? Think therefore not of changing millions, but of changing ones, and those ones – ourselves.

'Oh, but it was not we who were responsible for the war.'

By God, was it not? Who, in very deed, but we? We, the clever ones; we, the thinking ones. Not the politicians, not the priests. We knew them for what they were. Can *we* blame the Church, when we had left her? Can *we* blame the politicians, when we despised them? Were we prepared to do what we knew they would not do – to cry aloud that this thing was a blasphemy, and take the consequences? I pity the man among us, the clever ones, the thinking ones, who has not known, in his hour, that he, and *he alone*, bore the guilt of the war. It is we, who have had that knowledge, or a glimmering of it, who must be changed. We who have wrung our hands over the mud and blood of the muckheap of the world, and have had a sudden sight that it is we, and we alone, who were the muckheap – we who knew and felt, and did not act. There is no one for us to blame, but ourselves. *Nostra culpa, nostra maxima culpa.*

Think therefore of changing ones, and those ones, ourselves.

I have thought of it now, it seems, for years: I have thought of little else. How can one man be changed?

I see one way to do it: to take the life of Jesus as the reality it was.

First of all, then, to *believe* that his life was a reality.

Well, we cannot do that unless we have a sense of its reality. Without that we shall not even be interested. I take the sense of its reality for granted. From that sense we must work, loyally, according to the conditions of a grown mind. We must ruthlessly reject from his story all that makes him incredible to a grown mind. There must be no compromise. Some will say we are thereby rejecting all that makes him 'divine.' Let it be: we do not care. The 'divine' that is incredible to a modern mind is for that mind an inoperative 'divine.' All that we cannot honestly accept as true of a living man must go. Something happened, something of infinite import to humanity, it happened in one way, and one alone. The Jesus we can believe in must be a historical Jesus. It is no use saying, as one sincere correspondent has written to me, that a Jesus without a resurrection is inoperative for men. For heaven's sake let us not be pragmatical! If we are to judge by results, where are we? Has a Jesus with a resurrection been so greatly operative among men? Let us think again of the war, and begin by believeing only what we can believe.

A historical Jesus, then. But what do we mean by that? Only a little of his earthly course can be recovered from the darkness. Let us recover all we can, working like men of science. It is our duty: we desire to recapture a fact. But the fact of Jesus cannot be recreated on a chart. Where he went is little known; what he did, but little more; what he was – let us wait for this.

But of what he did, one thing is certain: he died, and deliberately died, for his belief. We are ruthless with the story, rejecting miracle, pious legend, everything in which we cannot believe. One fact remains. Do what we will to the story as we have it, there is a moment when his face is set to go to Jerusalem – to proclaim the new truth, and to die proclaiming it. He went – no one understood why he was going; he died – no one understood why he died. The historical criticism which would destroy that part of the story is negligible. He deliberately died for his belief, and died for mankind. I have tried to shake that certainty: I have played the devil's advocate against my own exceeding great desire, knowing that I cannot afford to build upon a lie, however dear. Whatever I find to live by, there must be no lie in it. The death, the decision and the purpose of the death of Jesus stand firm. It *was* so.

Here was a *man*. He found it in himself to do what no man, so far as we know, had ever done before; what no man could ever do again. He died lonely, utterly forsaken by his followers, by his God. That could never be again. The Christian martyrs died: they had him with them. The non-Christian martyr has died: he, no less, if he died lonely for humanity, has had Jesus with him. They were not alone. Jesus was.

Here was *the* man. This is no lie. That despairing cry of his was never invented. I know not the mind among all the early Christians from Paul or 'John' to Augustine who could have invented that: who would have dared to invent it – not that extreme of human suffering. If I am told the words come from a Psalm, I shake my head. The words of extreme agony are ever the same. 'And thou, Brutus!' was not spoken once alone in the world's history. Nor was *Eloi, Eloi, lama sabachthani*. But once alone by a man who deliberately died for humanity. Against all my devil doubts, that cry vindicates the reality of Jesus' death. It *was* so.

Here was *the* man. We must look again. Much, infinitely much, depends on this. What was he? Did he die for a dream? If he did die for a dream – may be we also are dreamers, too, and have to die for ours – to make our dreams come true. If he did not die for a dream, what then . . . what then?

Here was *the* man. What was he?

A man who loved all things and all men, who believed that God was the Father of all men, who knew himself the Son of God, who called himself the Son of Man, who deliberately risked, and endured, a death in agony in order to proclaim to men that the God of his belief verily existed, and who was forsaken by his God at the last. Those are the facts, strange facts, simple facts. What can we make of them? Somehow they hang together: mysteriously they fit.

Let us begin therefore at the beginning – his love. Perhaps we shall find the way into the heart of it.

Love – it is a hard thing. Hard to achieve, hard to understand. But his love loved everything. And loved everything naturally. That seems to me, as an adult man, the prime reality of the historical Jesus. To make anything of it we need to know a little about love – to have loved, something or somebody. For then you know it is no use trying to love people or things. You either love them, or you don't. Sometimes a condition of not-loving passes into a condition of loving – miracle of miracles! – but your effort had not much to do with it. It happened. Suddenly you saw that such a person or such a thing was to-be-loved. That he in himself, it in itself, compelled love from you. That is the cardinal fact of love.

That Jesus loved everything means, above all else, that to him everything was to-be-loved. He loved, not by a tense effort of will, nor in a sentimental swoon, but as a man who saw the divine particularity of men and things. 'Behold the lilies of the field: they toil not, neither do they spin; yet Solomon in all his glory was not arrayed like one of these.' There is the secret of the love which is in all great art, so spoken that a child may understand. As with things so with men and women. The man who called James and John the 'Sons of Thunder' was laughing at them, for the naïve children they were. But laughing with love; seeing them as precious and absurd, as they were indeed, clamouring that he should call down fire and brimstone on a village that would not receive them, clamouring that one should sit on his right hand and the other on his left in the kingdom. James and John, 'Sons of Thunder.' That name may convey more to us of the reality of Jesus' love than many volumes. A love that could laugh; a love that must laugh.

Such a love, of all things and all men – a finding of all

things and all men in themselves lovable and lovely. A sense that men could not help being what they were. Could not help it, do I say? Rather, that it was divinely appointed that they should be what they were. Divinely appointed, but only up to the moment when he appeared, seeing them thus divinely appointed – *not an instant longer*.

For when he first wholly saw that lovable creation, he knew in that same moment that it had been created with love. There was the lovable creation; there must be the loving creator. No doubt at all: no possible doubt. He saw the creation: he loved the creator. No illusion here: not the vestige of an illusion. Any man who, for a moment of time, can see the whole creation as Jesus saw it, knows that it is the handiwork of love. Knows it for that moment. All supreme aritsts have known it for that moment. But they cannot remain there: they cannot believe in their vision. Jesus could and did.

Into the presence of that divine and loving Creator he went when he came up out of the waters of Jordan. The Son had found the Father – a God in whom his love could find rest.

No illusion here: I say it again. This was inevitable; this was true. God the Father had been created, because God the Father had been seen; because God the Father had been seen, God the Father had been known. Jesus had not merely loved; he had recognized the lovable. Knowing God's creation, he passed into the presence of its Creator. The Father had found the Son, to know him.

At that moment the divine necessity that men should be what they were was at an end; from that moment it was completely changed. Now men had to be something different: they had to become new men and follow the new man into the knowledge and presence of the new God. They had to see that all things and all men were to-be-loved: the moment they saw that, they would be changed. They would have to change: they could not help it. If they saw, they could not mar the beauty which they saw; they must cease to be discordant, once they had heard the harmony. Once they could see the lovable creation, they must know the loving creator. Then they would know that God was their father and they his sons.

No illusion here: not the vestige of an illusion. Love makes no mistakes, whatever the wise of the world may say. What can be seen as lovable *is* lovable – now and for ever – even though only one man has seen it. A loved creation compels a loving creator.

Is that an illusion? Never. We who cannot love much, but have loved a little, know that in that which we loved the handwork was divine. Though all the rest were the devil's business, so much was divine. Divine that woman whom we loved; that little child divine – that bird, that glint of sky.

Love alone can know love. Love tells us that this man loved all. The whole universe was lovely for him: he loved it and laughed. And it *was* lovely while he was there to see it.

But Pain? The Pain of the world? Was that also lovely? Wait with that question. It cannot be answered now. Remember only this: that the man who saw a divine and manifest necessity that all things and men should be what they were, saw also a divine and manifest necessity that, *from the instant of his seeing*, things and men should be no longer what they were. The moment a man saw the harmony, he must be subdued to it; the moment a man knew the Father, he became a Son.

The Son had found the Father; he could not fail to find him. He had created Him; he was bound to create Him. A God for the new man that he was: a loving God who should have, who could have, not subjects but only sons. He the new man, the man of the new love, had created the new God.

Sublimest of all creations; never-ceasing wonder to the seeing eye; miracle of miracles. You who cannot believe in this man, except as one who changed water into wine, or made one loaf into a hundred, can you not turn for a moment and discern how little is this faith of yours? This man whom you would make a street-corner conjurer wrought a miracle whereat the stars shot from their spheres. This man created God the Father; out of his new human nature he was compelled to create him. Here was he, and he could no other. And because he was, verily and indeed, what he was, the God the Father he created does exist and has existed ever since that moment when Jesus came up out of the waters of Jordan and knew him – but as the God of a new man, known only by a new man. When any man can see the world – the birds, the beasts, the fishes, and mankind – as Jesus saw it, then he too is a new man, and he too is bound to create for himself a new God. He adds existence to the God of Jesus; and that God will wholly be on the great day towards which the whole creation groans and travails, – the day when all men love all things as Jesus loved them. Then every man will know what it is to be the son of God, and be it, and in that company of sons will God the Father have his consummation and his being.

There is the miracle; and there is none beside it. Let a man take this into his soul, and the miracle will begin once more to be in him. Nothing is asked of him, save that he should be a man. Let him deny nothing, surrender nothing of what is truly his; reject no knowledge, accept no faith, only be loyal to the greatest man who ever lived, who spoke the truest words and lived the truest life. Strive to understand him. It is your duty. You believe in knowledge; you believe in history; you believe in fact. What of this fact? Be loyal; be honest. Look at the fact, and look at nothing more. Throw everything away that an honest man of the twentieth century cannot believe; reject it utterly. The fact remains. Stick to the fact. What of the fact?

Was ever love on earth like this man's? Was ever life or death on earth like his? Ever pain? Ever loneliness? Be loyal: be honest. There is but one answer. Never!

What then?

What think you of love? Is it not the highest we know, or dream? Something we touch for a moment and it departs? Something we could give our souls, our lives, to possess?

To love all things, all men. Have not all our greatest striven for this alone? Shakespeare – for what else did he go through his hell and win his victory? What else do his works reveal? What else is revealed by the work of any man whose utterance lives in the human soul, and is not as sounding brass and a tinkling cymbal? What else than love manifest, in the magical creation of love's seeing, distinguishes the true from the false among the words of men? Keats's wasted hand put down his pen with the words: 'I have loved the principle of *beauty in all things*.' What else can a man love? What else is love?

What all our greatest have seen in part and known in part, this man Jesus knew wholly. He lived and died for love of the whole world. For that love, for the God whom that love created, he endured agony of agonies. There is your fact.

Will you now talk of the pale Galilean? Will you condescend to him? Will you say of this man that his God was a dream? Because his God forsook him at the last?

Look closer yet. As surely as that man lived, his God lived; as surely as he died, his God died also. But his God had been. While Jesus lived, he *was*. Whenever Jesus lived again, where alone he can live, in the hearts and souls of men, whenever the love he loved of all things and all men broke into tiny birth again, his God was alive once more. His God is as real as his vision: no more, no less – the most real thing that has ever descended into the soul of man. When he was forsaken at the last by his God, he had paid the last sacrifice of love. It was necessary that the great fact of his life should be completed by that crowning fact. By his cry that God had forsaken him, he made God exist. On the fact of that cry, the fact of his whole life rests secure. This was a man.

Gone are the centuries of faith. Let us be glad. We need no faith any more. We need only to know. This was a man, wholly and for ever a man. Rejoice, again I say rejoice! What could faith give to the faithful that was like this knowledge for them that know? This is how man can love, this is how man can live, this is how man can die, this is what man can believe!

Lift up your heads O ye gates: be ye lift up, ye everlasting doors! for the King of Glory shall come in.

Who is the King of Glory?

The man Jesus, and his brothers in ages yet to be, who will love the wonder of this world in time as he loved it, love the lily of the field and the sparrow and the ass and the harlot and the publican and the sinner. Men who will see, like him, all things new – each single thing, each single man, bright with the bloom of birth.

These are the new men; these are the sons of God, and Jesus was the first-born. Because he was the first-born son he had no Father; his father forsook him in his need. That to all perfect things that were, one wonder at the last might be added – a perfect life of man. The agony that drove God the Father from the Universe, established Him there for ever. Out of the depths of defeat, victory was wrung; out of a discord that jarred the foundations of the world, harmony; out of death, life.

This man who lived and died for love, who lived and died to reveal to men the God of love's creation, wrought at the last one thing beyond his knowing – the beauty of absolute pain. What love could not love, Jesus by his death revealed as to be loved before all things else. Love could love its pain, love could love its death; but not its brother's pain, not its brother's death. But on the day when Jesus died with a loud cry on the Cross, the last great barrier of love was flung down. For the first time love could love his brother's pain, and love the absolute of his pain. The pain of Jesus was Pain: no pain was like that one, nor ever can be – utter, unmitigated Evil. But no man who will face that pain will ever shrink before the mystery of Pain. On that day, Pain was conquered.

Then, for the first time love could love his brother's pain: and then for the last. Once only is it required of him; once only is it necessary. For the one blinding and ineffable moment when he may see that all things and men, all life, in the height and the depth, are to-be-loved. Pain absolute was only once here in this world of men: in that pain is all pain: then it too was lovely, lovely beyond all dream.

Such was the victory of love: it made its own destruction the loveliest thing that love can ever know. Nothing so beautiful as the life and death of Jesus has ever been, or ever will be, revealed to man. Utter love, utter loneliness, utter pain, utter annihilation. Look on it well, look till your eyes cannot see for tears.

'I cannot look!'

Look, look! Have you no love? This was a Man. Do not turn your eyes away. Hold on, I conjure you, though your heart be ashes and your mind a frozen thing. It is nothing to what he suffered for you. Suffer this for him. Not for him – for your own soul's sake. What do you see?

'I see Beauty, Beauty Absolute; I see Perfection of all Perfections – the love of a loving *God*.'

§

It is as I feared: that once embarked upon this ocean, the voyage would never be done. Whatever I write upon this subject, so soon as the words are in cold print, appears to me altogether insufficient; and I dare not leave it there.

In the two previous papers I have tried to convey two attitudes of mine towards Christ and Christianity. I hold these attitudes simultaneously, knowing well that they are contradictory. I make no apology for that, because I believe that a religious *truth* is, by nature, incapable of being formulated save by means of contradictions. As Keyserling says, 'Remote truths in particular can only be represented in powerful contrapuntal opposition.' And as though immediately to prove the truth of that statement, I must qualify it by saying that the remotest truths are always the nearest of all. We reach them by long and tortuous journeyings; but at the last we see them face to face: closer than that – for the final realization is that the truth is ourselves and in ourselves. To know what we are is the end of all the search for religion and for wisdom – the end; not merely the beginning, as the old Greek said.

I have tried in these papers to follow the spontaneous movement of my mind in its effort to extract a real meaning for itself out of the contemplation of Christ and Christianity I have found my mind working – in a manner now familiar to me – by means of contradictions, such as that the completeness of Jesus' triumph is apprehensible only through a realization of the completeness of his defeat. The choice is between contradictions and silence. Perhaps if I were older and wiser than I am, I should have chosen silence.

The contradiction in my last two papers may be summed up, in personal terms, thus. On the one hand, a contemplation of the life and death of Jesus makes absolutely impossible a belief in the existence of God the Father Almighty; on the other hand, the life and death of Jesus are the supreme revelation of a loving God. To those two assertions in their fullness, and in the fullness of their opposition, I adhere.

The life and death of Jesus reveal the love of a loving *God*. There is the emphasis. The love of God is not as the love of man. We have a blinding glimpse of its nature in the perfection of the Crucifixion, which is the archetype of the perfection of all true tragedy. In the Christian conception of God as the Almighty Father, a human love is ascribed to God. That conception is to me utterly impossible. I do not even desire it. The extreme of human love was manifested once for all, as it must be manifested, in a man. Him I worship. A man can worship a man.

The worship of Jesus, as the perfect exemplar of human love, and the knowledge of God as revealed by his life and death are two utterly different things; they belong to different orders. What is inacceptable in the Christianity of the Church is that these two distinct things have been somehow fused into one, to produce an amalgam – a divine Christ, a loving God the Father Almighty – in which few if any professing Christians really believe, if their lives be regarded (as they must) as the test of the reality of their faith.

I think the time is past for these half-beliefs: they stick in my throat, and they stand in the way. We have, as modern Europeans, to accept ourselves for what we are. We can think, and we can think more clearly than our forefathers. Let us think, therefore. But, precisely because we can think,

119

let us not be cockahoop about our thinking. Simply because the old statements of the Christian verity are empty, were in fact emptied four hundred years ago, let us not imagine that Christ or Christianity is out of date. The old statements are useless to us. The 'intellectual' *convert* to Catholicism to-day is a renegade to humanity. By his works ye shall know him: and there is always something rotten in his works. The man who is born and bred a Catholic, on the contrary, may well achieve within his religion, as final a knowledge as any man outside it. The Protestant is in a different case. His business is to follow the Protestant spirit to the bitter end, and on his journey thither to restate frankly, in a manner that admits of no equivocation, the Christian verity for to-day.

What I believe to be that verity I have tried to show. But I will state it again. The cardinal revelation of reality, or of God, for a Western European is in the life and death of Jesus, considered and pondered as credible historical fact. It was so in the past; it remains so to-day. What has changed is the method of conceiving historical fact. We do not need, for instance, to complete Jesus' life by a bodily resurrection: simply because we can resurrect him in our own way by striving to understand him. To the early Christian the mighty fact about Jesus was not what he said or did, not that he died, but that he rose bodily from the tomb. To us the mighty fact is that he said what he said, and did what he did and died with a loud cry on the Cross. But, so far as the religious verity is concerned, the early Christian belief in his bodily resurrection, and ours in his bodily extinction, have the same potency and value. They are both means to a knowledge of that which is beyond both life and death – of God. The difference is really on the side of the subject, not of the object: we no longer need to distort facts to make them symbols of the divine. To us facts themselves, if we have eyes to see them, are divine – 'the garment we see Him by.'

The further question is whether and to what extent we shall follow the man Jesus along the road which he declared – the road of universal love. This again is a question to be pondered by men as men. There are clear-sighted and deep-thinking men who do not at all believe in the gospel of love. They envisage the history of mankind very much in the same way as I do, as necessary, inevitable, and beautiful; but, they say, as wars have been, so they must be: the pattern changes, but the elements are the same. Evil and pain are necessary.

Here, it may be, I confess my limitation, and prove myself no philosopher. But I cannot and will not accept this. Though I fully and freely accept the fact that 'truth on one side of the Alps is falsehood on the other,' that Christianity is the professed religion of but a portion of the world, that to men of other climates a different revelation of the nature of God and man from our own is and probably will always be necessary, – still I know that I am, in my own sense, a Christian. Christian culture is in my blood, and, I hope, a spark not to be quenched of Christian love in my soul. I cannot see the universe as the Moslem sees it, I cannot know God or myself as the Hindu knows them. I belong to my race: no more than the Ethiopian can I change my skin. For this race to which I belong, the very constituents of whose blood have been altered by two thousand years of Christianity, Jesus remains the prophetic man. Its problems are not the problems of the Moslem and the Hindu. It is travelling along a different path into the unknown future: the woods, the trees, the rivers, the sky, the joys, the dangers – all are different.

In other words I am a European, and I believe that the conceptions, the habit of feeling, the spiritual atmosphere of Christianity is, and will for ever remain, an essential part of the European consciousness. I am not merely a European, but an Englishman; therefore the Christianity which is native to me is a Protestant Christianity. That is to say, I am not vitally concerned any more with the great Catholic tradition. I am the heir of a long succession of rebels against spiritual *authority*. Christianity is for me simply what I can find in it that is of use to me in my effort to live my own practical and spiritual life. I am, by nature and by consideration, opposed to the Catholic ideal. It has served its turn; I recognize that it was a great ideal – once. But my forbears abandoned it centuries ago: I am glad they did, and I am convinced that any movement of return is a movement backwards.

Whether or not Protestantism will move forward to a religion of personal loyalty to the man Jesus, is of course beyond my power to prophesy. I hope it will. For that is the least incomprehensible way I can find to describe the only path I see of escape from the abyss that suddenly yawned under our feet in the war. The morality of Jesus is the morality we can follow with some faint hope of achievement. I do not mean that we should follow the Sermon on the Mount literally: a great deal of it depends upon a belief in God as a loving father which, in spite of all professions, not one man in a million truly holds. Not one man in a million *can* hold it.

Not Jesus as son of God but Jesus as son of Man – in the non-eschatological meaning of the phrase – is our ideal perfection. And we have the right and the duty to distinguish between his own native morality, that which made him what he was, and the morality that sprang from the combination of his native morality with his God-consciousness. When we have learned to love as Jesus loved, then it will be time for us to talk of our loving God, or of God's loving us. By that time he very likely will.

For, though it may sound a queer proposition, I hold that we humans have it in us to make God what we desire. If we truly desire a loving God, we can have him – at the price. What we do, God does. If we could get that primary truth into our souls, perhaps a new illumination would come to us. Then we should see quite simply why and how God the Father was Jesus' own creation. If we also want God to be our Father, then we must follow Jesus, the living man, implicitly, not as a pattern, but by our own spontaneous impulse, though the impulse may have been kindled by him. The existence of God the Father depends absolutely upon the number of his veritable sons.

For my own part I do not desire God to be a father. I am too conscious of the price; and I am by no means a hero. But I love my fellow-men sufficiently to desire that God should be a good deal more like a father than he actually is. So I am prepared to do something towards making God what I want him to be. The method of God-creation is simple: you have only to remember the simple fact that what you do, God does; what you are, God is. Even to the uttermost: if you disbelieve in God, then God *pro tanto* disbelieves in himself. Every man has the responsibility for God upon his shoulders.

That is, essentially, my creed. Until this moment, strangely enough, it never entered my head to express it to myself in this simple fashion. It is a red-letter day to me that I have said something so clearly to myself as this: What I do, God does: what I am, God is. Perhaps it may give others something of the simple satisfaction it gives me.

I am afraid it will not sound very logical. What I am to-day differs greatly from what I was three years ago: there-fore God is greatly different from what he was three years ago. Well, why not? My part of him, his whole of me, is greatly different from what it was. I am content. I am not

123

offering a faith for everybody, though it is one that everybody can hold. This creed of mine is meant only for those whom it suffices: I aim at no proselytes.

Yet it might be a good thing if this simple creed were to gain adherents? It is pleasant to imagine that the landlord of a slum-tenement who has kept the place in a foul and filthy condition should suddenly realize, when praying with the rest of his respectable fellows in church on Sunday, that what he is, God is: and that he should have a sudden sight of the heavenly mansion reserved for him, without a sink or a privy.

But, above all, it is a practical creed. It adjusts itself to every issue in a man's life. If he wants to find God, then God wants to find himself also. The unfortunate thing is that the simple truth of the matter will not have dawned upon him in that condition; nor will it greatly pain a man who disbelieves in God to be told that God disbelieves in himself. I do not think it would have greatly pained me ten years ago. Which serves me as a reminder how great is the distance I have gone – hopping, skipping, jumping, wriggling – ever since I began my *confessio fidei*; how innumerable have been my attempts to formulate to myself the one reality of whose existence I have long been convinced, how desperate my efforts to avoid being committed to a formulation I could not accept, how close I have seemed, even to myself, to come to Christianity, how certain nevertheless I have been that that haven was not mine. Perhaps I have found my resting-place.

A resting-place in my own creed: a fit end for an individualist. A resting-place which has no rest in it: which is what I have always desired. *What I am, God is; what I do, God does.* Yes, I think that will last me my time. And now that I have it, and read it, and stare at it, I wonder whether it can mean to any other soul, what it means to me, whether indeed for another it can have aught of meaning at all. For I think I can see some of the ways in which it can be misunderstood: I can imagine the lifted eyebrow of disdain for the complete romantic, who believes that the divine endorsement descends upon all he is and does.

That is not what my creed means; it is, indeed, the very opposite of what it means. Yet I look at the words: *What I am, God is; what I do, God does.* What other meaning can they bear?

I do not know that I can explain, or even that I care to try to explain. But I may put the difference as simply as I can in this way.

The obvious meanings of my creed are two. One is, that I put the responsibility for myself upon God; the other is, that I take the responsibility for God upon myself. The second is the meaning which my creed has for me. But what inclines me to believe that there is more in this creed than I can ever explain is that both these interpretations are true. Only the first belongs to one phase of growth, the second to another; or, again, the first belongs to one kind of perception, the second to another. Any man can say, and say truly, God is responsible for all he is and all he does God *is* responsible. If he be a liar, or a coward, or a lecher, or a doer of cruel deeds, God is what he is, by the same necessity whereby, if he be the servant of the truth, or a hero, or a man who will die for his friend, God is what *he* is. But there is this – and the mystery and the simplicity of the mystery lies here – that if a man can truly say to himself: 'What I am, God is' – then from that moment he will cease to be a liar, or a coward, or a lecher, or a doer of cruel deeds.

But, by going on in this strain, I may only add confusion to a simple thing. I do not want to defend my creed; though I should be happy to think that anyone had derived from it a fraction of the peace it has brought to me. I am prepared, I shall be delighted, to be told that it is obvious – after all, a creed that is obvious would be a welcome change – or that many men have thought of it before me. In this matter I have no desire to be original; nor have I any overwhelming anxiety even to be understood.

RENAN'S DREAM

THE other day I began to read for the first time Renan's *L'Avenir de la Science*. It is an astonishing book for a young man to have written, even though he happened to be young Renan – the most exquisite intelligence produced by France in the nineteenth century. *L'Avenir de la Science* is a moving book; it moves first by its passion and then by its pathos, and in recollection by its pathos most of all.

For how few of those who have followed in the seventy years since Renan wrote his book have understood 'science' so widely, so nobly, and so subtly as he? Let the average man of to-day read on a book the title: 'The Future of Science,' and what will he expect from it? A dissertation upon chemical warfare, or a plea in favour of eugenics, or at best some hair-raising speculation on what may happen if the energy of the atom is liberated. He would throw aside with disappointed impatience what Renan had to say under that head – for it contains no sensations, no thrills, no time-machines. The future of science was for Renan simply the future of human knowledge. How dull it sounds! How exciting it was to him! How exciting it still is for those who care to read it!

If science itself has not grown narrow since Renan wrote, the general conception of science has. The very word 'rationalism,' which was so teeming with hidden promise for him, has become as chilly and *mesquin* as a corrugated-iron tabernacle. What has happened in these seventy years? A big thing and a simple thing, I believe: of the two distinct yet complementary processes which for Renan together composed the magnificent whole of science, one has been neglected and forgotten. The exploration of the universe without – that has indeed marched forward; but the exploration of the universe within – of the metaphysical and moral reality – that has retired discomfited. It has occurred perhaps to none save Renan himself that in this realm the qualification of the man of science was delicacy, that here, above all, he had to be assured of the quality of the object.[1] The kingdom has been invaded by men who could not, in things spiritual, distinguish a rose from a cabbage. Psychologists have demonstrated to their own exceeding satisfaction that the vision of the supreme artist or the supreme saint is just the same as that of the brass-voiced Salvationist at the street corner: it is all epilepsy, or it is all sex, or it is all a vague something or other called Libido or Hocus Pocus.

Naturally, this science, of which Renan hoped so much, has got nowhere. And people who are weary of the fruitlessness of a science which seeks to unlock the spiritual world with a mechanical key turn desperately to the old superstitions, or to new ones without their element of truth. The Catholic Church at least did once contain the whole wisdom of mankind. There were wise men in the Middle Ages – their wisdom has not wholly perished out of the Church that first contained it. It can be found: but one needs not to be, one had better not be, a Catholic to find it. But better that than to turn to the slick and second-rate consolations of newfangled religions, or the abracadabra of occultism. Yet in these last few weeks I have read in a serious review of novels in the *New Statesman* unmitigated praise of the spiritual truth of a story written by some poor victim of demons and black magic. Those who have no sense of quality had better by far stick to the great Church: without that sense they can only delude others as well as themselves.

The basis of Renan's science of the future was the axiom:

[1] It occurred, of course, to Nietzsche also.

'There is no such thing as the supernatural.' How different an axiom from that of those who have stumped their way with hobnailed boots into the holy places: 'There is no such thing as the non-mechanical!' Yet, apparently, most people can see no difference between them. In the one ear cries the priest: 'Deny the supernatural, and you abolish religion'; in the other the rationalist: 'Accept religion, and you accept the supernatural.' Children! All the religions that have ever been are but more or less clumsy symbols of an eternal verity of man's nature – that there is a hierarchy and a progress in the human consciousness towards another and a fuller mode of comprehension than our quotidian faculties allow. It is not easy to reach, and few men have reached it; but when they have, their fellow-men have paid homage to what they have achieved. Paid homage, but not recognized it for what it was, a mode of consciousness that any man might attain. No, here was something which veritably was, and was beyond their comprehension: so they called its possessor god or saint or genius. They had to invoke the category of the 'supernatural' to explain something which was beyond their understanding.

Nevertheless, it was and is eminently natural. That there is such a progress and hierarchy in the human mind is clear from our commonest judgments. When I say that this poem is better than that one, what on earth am I saying but that the mind which produced it is finer and truer than the mind which produced the other? And how is it possible for one mind to be finer and truer than another if there is not some mysterious capacity for development in the human mind? When it has reached its pinnacle we say 'saint' or 'genius.' We do not say 'god.' We have grown out of that; the category is not necessary any more. There have been no new gods for a thousand years or so, or if there have been they have not made good. Not because the Christian revelation was the final revelation; but because men had to some extent grown up.

But they have not grown up very much. It is not much advance to call a man 'saint' or 'genius' or 'great man' instead of 'god,' if you pay no attention to his words or his beliefs. The simpler minds which did say 'god' at least paid some attention to 'god's' words. But now that we are quite certain that the great man is not god – that he has no power to blast us with lightning if we pay no heed to him – we have the best of excuses for not listening; if we are tinged with the rationalistic tar-brush, we have a still better excuse for turning away, for we know what he is without listening to him: he is abnormal.

Which, of course, he is: abnormal and natural. For, luckily, the normal is not natural. If it were, life would be a nightmare indeed, save that it would have perished æons ago. Every man is abnormal in some degree: when he begins to be considerably abnormal he is worth attending to. I myself am moderately abnormal, or I should never be writing these lines, or hoping that other moderately abnormal persons will read and understand them. But I am interested in much bigger abnormalities than my own – in men who could write and speak and act with infinitely more power than I can, who because of their great abnormality have impressed themselves on the memory of mankind. It seems to me strange that so few people should be interested in trying to discover how these men came to speak their words of wisdom and authority. It is not enough for me to say simply that they were 'inspired.' Inspiration is a meaningless metaphor to me, unless I know how they achieved it. And when the rationalist tells me that they were afflicted by an abnormal state of consciousness, I feel like George II when they told him Wolfe was mad: 'I wish he would bite my other generals.' Superstition whispers 'inspired'; rationalism sniggers 'afflicted.' I don't care which; I care only for the fact, not the name, and the fact is that these inspired and afflicted have spoken words which have seemed to generations of men fraught with a secret wisdom and illumined by a strange vision.

Where did they get it from? That is what I want to know; and, as I say, I am surprised that so few are eager in the search. I am astonished that in this age of complacent rationalism the arch-rationalists should be content to wave these facts aside with 'A miracle!' Of course, the facts *are* miracles to them. Half the facts of the universe – and all the important ones – are direct interventions of the supernatural on the rationalist hypothesis. If I were a rationalist, I should hide my head in shame at my own silly superstition. But I am not; I am a mere naturalist.

As a mere naturalist, I observe that there is an order of spiritual creations, and that some of these creations are greater than others. I see in them a hierarchy gradually descending to what is palpably within my own compass; and I conclude that it is possible to make the upward ascent to the height of genius. I do not mean that it is possible for me to be a genius; but it is impossible for me in precisely the same way as it is impossible for me to be Prime Minister. I cannot make the effort, in either case. The difference is only that in the latter case the effort is not so well worth making in the opinion of such a one as I. Therefore in the former case I do try to make the effort, and though I do not succeed, I do not wholly fail. I succeed to some degree in finding out the way the great men went; I succeed to some degree in going along their path; I succeed to some degree in attaining glimpses of the knowledge which they possessed; and above all I succeed to some degree in seeing the possibility and the necessity of holding to the reality of their experience, without degrading it by supernaturalism, for I begin to discover a law of spiritual progress which has been obeyed in all times and all places.

It may seem strange that seeing so much, and believing that the highest spiritual progress towards a mode of consciousness deeper and truer than the ordinary is natural to man, I am not indignant with the destiny that has meted me out one talent instead of ten. The strange thing, and the thing which most persuades me that what I have discovered for myself is no illusion, is that I have gained in the course of my pursuit a profound sense that it is just and equitable and right that I should have but one talent instead of ten: provided I do not hide it in a napkin it is enough.

Finally, I am bold enough to imagine that it was of some such science as that of which I begin dimly to discern the elements that Renan dreamed when he wrote in his book these words:

'It is not without intention that I call by the name "science" what is ordinarily called "philosophy." I should like my life to be summed up as a life of "philosophy"; nevertheless, since this word in the common usage expresses only a partial form of the inward life and implies only the subjective fact of the solitary thinker, when one adopts the point of view of humanity it is necessary to use the more objective word – *to know*. Yes, the day will come when humanity will no longer believe, but will know; a day when it will know the metaphysical and moral universe, as it already knows the physical universe; a day when the government of humanity will no longer be left to hazard and intrigue, but to the reasonable discussion of what is better and of the most efficacious means of attaining it. If such is the aim of science, if its object is to teach man his end and his law, to make him grasp the true meaning of life, to compose together with art, poetry and virtue, the divine ideal which alone gives value to human life, – can it have serious enemies?

'But, it will be said, will science fulfil these marvellous destinies? All I know is that if science does not, nothing will, and that humanity will be for ever ignorant of the secret of things; for science is the only legitimate method of knowing, and if the religions have been able to exert a salutary influence on the progress of humanity, it is solely because of the element of science – of the regular exercise of the human spirit – which was obviously mingled with them.'

Yes, science *is* the only legitimate method of knowing: but there is a science of quality which has been neglected, while the science of quantity has been cherished. Until they can learn to work together, each respecting the other's realm as inviolable, humanity will not have begun to make the next great step in its progress.

SCIENCE AND KNOWLEDGE

A VALUABLE book has lately been published on the relations between science and religion.[1] It consists of essays, well planned and ably edited, by various eminent men of science – an anthropologist, a physicist, a psychologist, a biologist – indicating the position that may be occupied by the religious perception as a valid apprehension of reality without challenge from the sciences they practise. Not one of them is engaged in apologetics: what they have in common is a more or less definite surmise that there is another method of cognition, another kind of knowing, than the scientific.

It may be said that there is nothing new in this; and indeed there is not. But there is something new in the feeling which these men of science evidently share that it is their duty to forward a new synthesis of science and religion. Some people will hasten to call it a *rapprochement*. Reunion is in the air. Well-meaning people are pathetically anxious nowadays to reconcile irreconcilables; they press forward to sing, with the unconvincing voice of a curate at a beanfeast: 'We all go the same way home.'

There is no such taint of *union sacrée* in this excellent book. And it was a stroke of inspiration to obtain a substantial epilogue from Dean Inge. I am not sure that I like Dean Inge: but he *is* something. He has a first-rate mind and an admirable gift of expression; he is not the man to humbug himself or to suffer others to humbug themselves, if he can help it. I am sometimes doubtful whether he possesses his full share of 'the one thing needful' to a Christian apostle. He is occasionally metallic where he should be

[1] *Science, Religion and Reality.* Edited by Joseph Needham. (Sheldon Press. 12s. 6d. net.)

gracious. But I am sure of this: that if Dean Inge is a little lacking in Christian *caritas*, he is not likely to mistake for it (as his opponents do) unction and woolliness. If Dean Inge could have his way the Church of England would become at least intellectually honest.

Instead of uttering a pious benediction, in the familiar archiepiscopal style, over the laudable efforts of the scientists to show that there is room for everything in a modern mind, Dean Inge keeps the debate on a slightly higher level of intellectual rigour than some of the men of science themselves. And in his brilliant epilogue he drives home the real moral of the book. There will be no facile reunion: science and the Christian religion *are* in conflict: they have been in conflict ever since the Renaissance. If there is to be a new union it must be a real union, between a science and a religion both adult, both truly conscious of their limitations, and both genuinely secure in their complementary validities. At the present moment it is 'religion' which has to make the sacrifices, and make them not grudgingly, bargaining in the hope of an arrangement with its creditors, but honestly and with conviction.

What Dean Inge asks for, in short, is a gesture from the Church comparable in candour and clarity with the gesture of the scientific contributors to this volume. As Dean Inge puts it, 'we must take religion seriously.' To take religion seriously, at any rate for a grown man, is to face the fact that science and the religion of the Church have been in ever-increasing conflict for four hundred years. Ideally, one might have supposed that the effect of the exploration of the physical universe which began with the Renaissance would have been a purification of religion. Actually, it was the reverse. Instead of the Church being prepared to hand over the physical realm to free inquiry, and consolidating her own possession of *meta*physical truth, she fought the new spirit at every turn. And the reason for her ugly and vindictive resistance was the secular reason for such conduct: she was insecure on her own ground. Where she should have been infallible, there the Church was weak: where she had scarcely the right even to an opinion, there she claimed infallibility.

It is easy to condemn the mistake of the Church; but it is unfair: for it is asking that the Church should have been conscious of the distinction between physical and metaphysical which could only be established as the result of that very process of inquiry which she resisted. After all, the claim of the Church to be competent *de omni re scibili*, concerning all things knowable, was freely and universally admitted for many centuries. There were no martyrs of science in the Middle Ages: for the great mediæval theology was elastic enough to include all contemporary scientific inquiry. The God of religious apprehension could be intellectually apprehended as matter. The scientist (if such he could be called) did but investigate the material modality of God.

One cannot help regretting that this pregnant synthesis could not maintain itself: for it is one to which humanity will be compelled to return. But it was inevitable that, when it came to details, scientific inquiry should come into conflict with religious dogma on two main points. Science was forced to deny the physical reality of the Christian cosmogony. That difference might have been accommodated had it not been for the Reformation. Intellectually, the Reformed was far less liberal than the unreformed Church. Rome made Galileo recant: Geneva would have burned him. And it is at least probable that but for the fanaticism of the Continental Reformation the Church would have been more liberal still. But it could not afford to be outbid in the rigour of its orthodoxy by the heretics. The Reformation was in fact a curiously paradoxical movement. It was supremely unconscious of its own true significance. Its conception of the sacrosanctity of the word of Scripture was in itself far more stifling to the spirit of man than the Papal authority which it was used to undermine. Therefore it was impossible for a man of true enlightenment like Erasmus to be with the Reformers; he had to sit on the fence. But behind the appeal to the infallibility of Scripture lay concealed the veritable principle of free inquiry. That ugly and uncouth husk contained the seed of a freedom which has still to be fully achieved.

Only an uncomely soul can *revere* the Reformation. Its spirit was almost as unpleasant as Mr. Kensit's; a caricature of the spirit of Renaissance, with which it is so often confused. How could Shakespeare not have disliked the Puritans? He was bound to take the same attitude as Erasmus; he, like so many others, would have desired to remain a Catholic, if – but the if never has been, and never will be realized. The Church may let the old Christian cosmogony fade away; but on the question of miracle it cannot yield. The future (if it belongs to a Church at all) belongs to the Church which will yield ungrudgingly on the question of miracle. Yet how much has to be yielded with it! The resurrection of the body;[1] the very conception of God incarnate, held as a physical reality. Yield these, and Christianity

[1] Since so many priests of the Church of England forget what they have *bound* themselves to believe, I will quote the fourth article. They have bound themselves, moreover, 'not to put their own sense or comment to be the meaning of the article, but shall take it in the literal and grammatical sense.'
'IV. *Of the Resurrection of Christ*. Christ did truly rise again from death, and took again his body, with flesh, bones, and all things appertaining to the perfection of Man's nature: wherewith he ascended into heaven, and there sitteth, until he return to judge all Men at the last day.'

yields everything. Refuse to yield these, and there can never be a real synthesis of science and religion.

And yet of course by yielding these the Church would yield nothing – absolutely nothing – of what is eternal in herself. After all, her eternality lies wholly within the person and the teaching of Christ. It is this, and this alone, which has and will always have the power to *change* men and to make them new. But that is not what men ask from religion: in so far as they ask anything, they ask to be made comfortable, which is another matter. And there is something which makes for comfort of a certain kind in the very idea that science and religion are in conflict. The notion that the truth lies nowhere in particular gives a potent excuse for not looking for it: and unless they have looked for the truth pretty hard, with the conviction that their lives depended on their finding it, men never attain the capacity for belief in any truth at all. What passes for belief nowadays is chiefly the desire to be relieved of the trouble of finding one. As Dean Inge puts it, 'The real sceptic does not write books on agnosticism; he never thinks at all, which is the only way to be perfectly orthodox.'

Dean Inge himself is an intellectual mystic; he has more than a touch of Spinoza's *amor intellectualis dei*. Therefore on the positive side his epilogue is a harmonious completion of the attitude generally taken by the scientific contributors to this book. Dr. Charles Singer concludes his essay with the words:

'There remain two religious points of view that can never be affected by any extension of the scientific realm. The one would completely separate internal experience from external experience. The man who does that is safe; he has fled, as have many before him, to a haven of peace down the mystic way. The second would regard man's soul not altogether as his own possession, but as part of a great world-soul. This combination of determinism and pantheism is a refuge, not infrequently sought in antiquity, to which many a student of science has turned in modern times, from the days of Spinoza onwards.'

Dr. Singer is by no means at home in this region of thought and experience. He betrays his own unfamiliarity by his naïve conception of the 'mystic' as 'fleeing' and taking 'refuge.' One has a pretty clear vision of Dr. Singer forlornly holding a large bag of salt for a bird which has flown away. He would fain have caught the bird, and rather resents his airy-fairy vanishings. He grudgingly confesses that there is no getting at him. The attitude rather reminds one of Mr. Bertrand's famous chapter on 'Mysticism and Logic.' Mr. Russell also has a logical apprehension of what may be called the mystical possibility.

But, unfortunately, this logical apprehension is of little use, save to those who, having knowledge of the fact behind 'mysticism,' desire to make their position intellectually impregnable. The two points of view between which Dr. Singer professes to distinguish are in reality one and the same; and his description of the second as 'a combination of determinism and pantheism' must cause a smile in anyone who has some experience of the reality he is trying to describe from the outside. One may describe a rainbow as a combination of rain and light: but it is hardly a *valuable* description.[1]

For my own part I shrink from the word 'mysticism.' I have not the least objection to being described as a mystic, if I am one; just as I should have no objection to being called a Plymouth Brother, if I were one. But the word 'mysti-

[1] Perhaps in this simple example will be apparent the absolute distinction between two kinds of truth to which we return below.

cism' seems to me, every day, more misleading. It has a tinge of secrecy and occultism. The whole thing is very much simpler, far more open to the light of day. The real difficulty about the important truths of 'mysticism' is not that they are mystical, but that they are obvious. They have their root in a matter of everyday experience – the absolute distinction between the qualitative and quantitative judgments. The former are not, the latter are, capable of immediate verification. If you say to some one: 'There is a pound of apples,' and he disputes it, you don't argue: you go to the nearest scale. But if some one says to you: 'Agnes is an angel, I am going to marry her,' you can only say, 'Don't be a fool: angels neither marry nor are given in marriage.' You may be right, you may be wrong. There's no settling it for a year or two.

But the qualitative judgments are more important to a man's life than the quantitative ones. It is far better for the real business of living to develop one's sensitiveness to quality than to be a perfect whale with the micrometer. There is, of course, not the least reason why you should not be both. But the naked fact is that you do not *live* in the world of quantity, which is the world of science: nobody does. If you must make a choice it is better to become expert in the world of quality, which is the world of life.

'Mysticism,' or the valuable part of it, is simply expertize in the world of quality. Ineffable communion with the One is too rare to be important in men's lives. The important part is to train yourself not to make mistakes in your judgments of quality. For though the logicians call these judgments subjective, they happen, as any man may quickly find, to correspond to a reality. It is not in the least a matter of indifference that you should call some one an angel while your friend calls her a devil. Disagreement of such a kind you must take most seriously of all. If your friend holds the moon is made of green cheese it doesn't really matter; but that he should say X is good, while you know him bad – your whole life may turn on this.

All living life moves in the world of quality. It behoves you therefore to sharpen your awareness of it. You devote yourself to it. What happens? You find yourself pursuing a truth that is utterly unlike what most men hold for truth. Truth is for them ultimately a matter of the scales, or of pointer-readings, as Professor Eddington says. The truth you find yourself pursuing is quite different. It is a quality shared by human beings, and by yourself in loving them; by lines of poetry, and yourself in understanding them; by Beethoven sonatas and paintings by old Crome, and yourself in responding to them; by words of wise men and the beasts and flowers they are fond of talking about – shared in short by an extraordinary number of things which seem at first sight to have nothing in common. The intellect makes nothing of the apparent jumble. But an obstinate voice, which you unfortunately recognize for true, persists that this strange heterogeneous truth is one.

So off you go again: and it slowly begins to dawn upon you that all these things are perfect expressions of Something-or-Other. Something-or-Other shines through them, and yet is them. You cannot know this Something-or-Other save in them, and yet it is not them. And as you come to know them more fully, you find strangely enough, that a Something-or-Other is being created in you in order to know them. And this Something-or-Other, as it gathers strength in you, begins gradually to take possession. You have to obey it; and in this obedience you find an utterly unfamiliar freedom. It goes on: you know more, and more knows you. Only by more knowing you, do you know more. It is all very odd. The more you find yourself becoming simply a vehicle, the more you find yourself a self. Till one day you wake to the amazing conjecture that you are coming *alive*.

That is indeed what is happening. Life is breaking through the barrier of consciousness. That Something-or-Other which you discerned in all those heterogeneous things and felt in yourself in responding to them was simply Life – organic, spontaneous, ineffable. Strictly ineffable: for it is not uttered, it utters itself. And at long last it is uttering itself through you. Now at last you can say you believe in Life: because you are Life.

Though the process thus vaguely indicated may appear highly mysterious, it is in reality very simple; but it is, by nature, incapable of description in terms of the scientific consciousness. The qualitative can have no quantitative equivalent. In the attempt to describe it, one is compelled to use words in senses which they do not usually bear. This Truth is not the truth of the intellect; nor is this Life what the intellect understands (if it understands anything) by life. In this world of quality Truth and Life are identical. Perhaps it can be explained, or a hint of explanation given, thus:

There is a plain and immediately known sense in which an animal is *true*. Nothing it does is wrong; it is a perfect and complete expression of life.[1] Not so with human beings, save in infancy. They are corrupted: they no longer act from a living centre, out of wholeness: they become in a thousand different ways *untrue*: they are at best extremely imperfect expressions of life. The cause of this discord and dissension is the domination of the intellectual conscious-

[1] I have no choice but to refer my readers to my own book *Keats and Shakespeare* for an attempted demonstration in the life of what I am saying here. See the chapter: 'Dying into Life.'

ness, or the intellectual will. Because a man has the *idea* of justice, he believes he is just. The possession of the idea of a state or quality is held to be the same as the possession of the state or quality itself. Pious (and sincere) professions are taken as real declarations of faith. People who talk Socialism are supposed to *be* Socialists. Religions and philosophies are wholly divorced from the living life: men's conscious motives are quite different from their real motives. Under one aspect or another the condition is familiar to every one, and it is accepted as part of the inevitable human heritage. We do not look deeply into it, because it appears to us an ultimate. But the true diagnosis of this universal sickness is that knowing is divorced from being.

In the animal knowing and being are one. Therefore, the intellectualists say the animal does not know, and they talk of instinct as something sub-human. This is simply nonsense. The animal does know. Its very life is a knowing that is never divorced from being. The problem of human life is to reachieve the organic unity of knowing and being which exists in the animal and is lost in us. Some men who have seen this (Rousseau and Tolstoy, for example) have demanded that we should virtually return to the animal condition. That is impossible, retrograde and wrong. What we have to do is to regain the spontaneity of the animal or the child, and sacrifice nothing of our human faculties. *This can be done.* This is the eternal rebirth which is the secret of true mysticism, and of the teaching of Jesus himself. It and nothing else is 'the mystery of the Kingdom of God.'

I have attempted to describe the process in one of its many forms: but the form in which I have described it is the one which is, I believe, the most natural to a modern man. It can be, rather baldly, described as the loyal and unremitting cultivation of that knowing which is an immediate function of being. In the qualitative world knowledge is always immediately dependent upon being: yet, no matter what the logicians say, it is always a true knowledge.[1] That is to say, it is not subjective illusion. Though nine hundred and ninety-nine out of a thousand may be utterly unaware of the truth-beauty (or Life) of *Antony and Cleopatra*, that truth-beauty (or Life) *objectively* exists. And its objective existence is not diminished, but only defined by the fact that a certain fullness of Being must be achieved in order to know it. From this whole realm of objective but non-measurable reality, science is absolutely excluded by its own nature, and for the simple reason that in this realm the progress of knowing is always an organic function of the process of being. In this realm the wise man is the perfect man; in the world of science the genius *may* be a villain.

The facts are simple. All that part of 'religion' which is conflict with true science is not religion at all. Essential religion *cannot* conflict with science. For essential religion is one valid, coherent, harmonious way of knowing reality; and science is another. Where they appear to be in conflict, there is error and misunderstanding; for conflict is only possible *in pari materia*.

But we have reached a point in human evolution where the name 'religion' is itself misleading. To speak of religion nowadays is immediately to be misunderstood, or exploited in a sectarian sense. The religion of which we have need, the religion which is slowly evolving, can be most fitly described as *the knowledge of life*. Apprehend it thus, and the reason why a conflict with science is impossible is immediately apparent. Apprehend it thus, and you are not appre-

[1] A true knowledge in the sense that it is a knowledge of a reality: not, of course, in the sense that no mistakes are possible.

hending a *new* religion. All true religion has always had the science of life at its centre. But this has been disguised and overlaid. It is time that it appeared in its own supreme autonomy.

'TRUTH TO LIFE'

FROM the beginning in these essays has been expounded (perhaps more truly, explored), with varying degrees of clarity, the conviction that literature and life are one. Since the propagation of this conviction, in all its implications, is the chief reason for my literary activities, it may be well to restate it, if possible, in such a way that the apparent digressions of the past may appear with something of the inward coherence which, I believe, they really possess.

With the obvious sense of the bare statement, that literature and life are one, many would be found to agree who by no means agree with (or even understand) its implications. There are quite a respectable number of people, themselves respectable, who hold that the value of literature depends upon its 'truth to life.'

'Truth to life' is, however, a highly ambiguous conception. It can be shown to possess a whole hierarchy of different meanings. At the lowest and most tangible the demand for 'truth to life' corresponds with the demand made by Aristotle that the writer should represent 'things that would probably happen.' That seems plausible enough, until it comes to mind that singularly few great works of English literature, from *Lear* to *Tess*, represent things that would *probably* happen. At the most, so far as the external events are concerned, they represent things which might possibly happen.

In fact, violation of mere probability is the commonest of all happenings in the work of a great writer. I do not know why this plain and palpable characteristic of great literature, that it triumphantly disregards mere probability, should itself be so triumphantly disregarded by criticism, unless it is for the very reason that it blunts the edge of the handy little conception of 'truth to life,' and forces anyone who looks at the facts into the admission that if 'truth to life' be indeed the requisite of literature – which we do not deny – then 'truth to life' is obviously of more than one kind.

What we demand of the literature of representation[1] is not that the events should be probable, but that the actions of the characters should be inevitable. The mere outward events can be highly improbable, but the reactions of the characters to those events must be inevitable; and in so far as any of the events are wholly determined (in the moral sense) by the actions of the characters themselves, those events must be wholly inevitable. The finding of the hand-kerchief in *Othello* is improbable; but the improbability does not matter in the least. It is an external event; it might happen – and that is enough. Not so the murder of Desdemona by Othello, and Othello's suicide. These, being internal events, are not merely probable: they are inevitable.

So that 'truth to life,' in so far as it is a valuable criterion of literature, immediately resolves into truth to human character. Not what is done to men, but what men do; not what they suffer, but what they are – this is the life to which literature must be true. It must reveal men as men are.

But that is not all. Not only must literature reveal men as men are; but it must reveal them as intrinsically noble. That really is rather astonishing; yet it is the fact. Think of all the great literature you know. In high tragedy, whether in drama or the novel, it is obvious. What we require and what we receive from it is the sense so magnificently expressed by Milton:

[1] Merely for convenience' sake I omit 'subjective' literature – lyrical poetry and the like – where the problem of 'truth to life' is much simpler.

'Come, come: no time for lamentation now,
   Nor much more cause. Samson hath quit himself
   Like Samson.'

Where a work of literature awakens that consciousness within us, there we pronounce, without hesitation, that it is great. But this sense of human nobility is aroused in us not merely by high tragedy, but by comedy and satire. The very substance of the greatest of all pure comedies, Molière's *Misanthrope*, is Alceste's nobility; that nobility is rigid, therefore Molière laughs at it. But he is careful not to laugh too much. He sees to it that Alceste inspires affection in his friends and sympathy in us. The satirist, however, does not deal with noble characters – if he did, he would not be a satirist – but he nevertheless reveals human nobility. He condemns humanity by an ideal: precisely because it is not noble, he castigates it. We admit the justice of such a castigation for a double reason: because we are not noble, and because we know we ought to be. He recalls us to our duty.

Here, then, is a paradox. Men are not noble, and they know it; yet they demand of literature that it should either represent men as noble, or be angry with them for not being noble – anything rather than simply accept them as ignoble. If a writer does that, it is all up with him. Not merely because men will not stand it, but because they have an ineradicable conviction that a writer who can see without anger or dismay only the ignobility of man is himself hopelessly ignoble.

The truth is, of course, that man is at once noble and ignoble. Pascal gave splendid expression to this truth in his *Pensées* on 'the misery and grandeur of human life.' Nevertheless, men feel that the nobler part of man is the truer: therefore, they demand that the emphasis of literature should be on the nobler part.

None the less the writer must not tell lies: he has to *reveal* man as noble, not to make him out to be noble. We have to feel that the writer is revealing the absolute truth about men, but that – wonder of wonders – this truth is a hidden nobility. Not in all men, of course: we have no objection to a villain or two, or, in the extreme case of satire, to a whole world of them. But somehow and somewhere, whether directly or by implication, nobility must be revealed.

But this word 'nobility' is awkward. It is rather statuesque, in its immediate suggestion inflexible. We must soften it a little, by taking note that Sir John Falstaff is a member of this nobility, not by virtue of his knighthood, but by virtue of his capacity to rise superior to circumstance (as in the case of the buckram men) and to inspire a deep affection. This last is perhaps the most suggestive. Bardolph's longing to be with his dead master wherever he was, in heaven or hell, stamps Sir John (and Bardolph himself) with the nobility of which we are in search. So, also, when Enobarbus kills himself for having deserted Antony, though every voice of prudence and of justice urged him to dereliction of a master whose reason stood captive to his will, Antony and Enobarbus are by a single stroke both enrolled in the golden book of this nobility. If Falstaff and Antony, Enobarbus and Bardolph, alike share this nobility, as they do, we may grip it a little harder and from it squeeze an essence – noble indeed, for it is generosity of soul.

Generosity of soul in men and women – that is 'the truth to life' which men demand from literature. Of no use to say that this is not 'the truth to life.' Men do not go to literature for a lie or a dream. They do verily go to it for 'truth to life'; and they find it in this thing – generosity of soul, either in the created character, or in the creator. Without this thing, in embryo or in plenitude, somewhere or somehow, literature is ashes in the human mouth. If this is absent, you may pound on the door till Doomsday with your asseverations of perfect art and truth to life: men will not listen to you. If they do listen they will reply: 'This is *not* perfect art; this is *not* true to life.'

That, on the face of it, is a very strange phenomenon. For, after all, generosity of soul is not the most obvious quality of the human race: nor is it the one which it most obviously respects. In actual life an Enobarb who had made himself comfortable at Cæsar's side would have the general approbation; and a Bardolph who insisted on being with Falstaff after death would be dismissed with a caution as a reprobate old fool. But the truth is that actual life is the last thing we want from literature – we get too much of it; we want truth to the life wherein men are generous of soul.

The cynic says that this life does not exist: poor humanity clamours that it does, and that, although in fact it spends most of its time overreaching its neighbour, this life is the only one it really cares about. This inclines one to suspect that it may be the life of the Kingdom of Heaven.

'Truth to life' – 'generosity of soul' – 'the Kingdom of Heaven.' There is something about that concatenation that excites me with the childish feeling that I am 'getting warm.' Generosity of soul – surely it is the one thing needful to a man who would enter the Kingdom. That was the thing the Master loved, wherever he found it. Of course, he at first demanded more than that: that man should be born again. That is still the only way of being sure of getting into the Kingdom, simply because only then do you *know* you are in it. But that was not, and is not, easy; the Master found it was in fact altogether too hard for men. And he loved men far too much to resign himself to the idea of their being left out. So he conceived the extraordinary plan of making himself men's Judge: it was not, he felt, safe enough to leave it

to God. God was all very well; but the surprising thing was
that nobody knew about him except the Master, and the
certain thing was that everybody would be terrified out of
their wits by him unless they saw the Master was about.
After all, even to the Master himself there remained something inscrutable and incalculable about God. It was much
the safest that he himself should be men's Judge. So, in
order to become this, he died, and alas! in dying he found
that God was far more inscrutable and incalculable than he
had feared. But before he died he had announced the terms
on which he was going to judge mankind when the day came.
The Churches, of course, have forgotten all about those
terms long, long ago, because they say absolutely nothing
about the necessity of belonging to a Church or even of
going to one. It was a reprehensible omission on Jesus' part.
(Most of his sayings and doings were, I fear, very reprehensible indeed from the point of view of the Churches. Indeed,
I often wonder why they put up with him at all. They could
easily get somebody else much better for their purposes.)
However – for the ordinary simple person the terms are
there to be read in the twenty-fifth chapter of Matthew:
they are very simple, very clear. One little, nameless, un-
remembered act of love – nothing more: only *one*: and the
Kingdom of Heaven was yours.

Well, the tragedy of mankind is that Jesus will not judge
it. Or is it the hope? The hope, I suppose: for only when
men learn that they must judge themselves will they make
the effort to get into the Kingdom by the way Jesus first
meant them to. That is a digression, and what went before
it is, if you like, a fairy-tale. But the point is this: that men
in what they demand of literature show that they want to be
judged *precisely* as Jesus would have judged them. They
want to be represented to themselves as capable (whether in
great ways like Othello, or little ones, like Bardolph) of enter-

ing the Kingdom of Heaven. I am not talking in metaphors: I mean exactly what I say. This, and nothing else, is the truth to life on which men insist in literature.

And literature is important, supremely important, because it gives this thing to men – the certainty that man is capable of the Kingdom, just in the same sense as the Master saw that he was. He wants to have it proved to him that the world is wonderful, though he cannot see it for himself; that he has an immortal soul, though he does not know how to get at it; that life triumphs over death, though he knows not how; that – in a word – generosity of soul is utterly immune from defeat and disaster; and that even a touch of it will save a man at the last.

In a thousand ways this is what true literature does give him. Its function is to demonstrate over and over again, in the heighth and in the depth, those fundamental truths of life which Jesus proclaimed. 'He that would save his life shall lose it, he that would lose his life shall save it' – so with Enobarb, so with Antony. And in the very creation of literature itself what is that but the spiritual law behind the simple fact that the most truly impersonal work is the most indelibly personal?

To this we may return at another time. What we have so far tried to establish is the complete congruity, nay, the perfect identity, between the morality of great literature and of the essential teaching of Jesus. At first sight that, because it is extraordinary and unexpected, may seem far-fetched. One may be inclined to grant, in the general case, that 'ethics and æsthetics are one,' as indeed they are; but still, in the particular instance, inclined to suspect legerdemain. There is none. The reason why Shakespeare's practice as an artist is completely congruous with Jesus' precept as a teacher is simple enough: both were wise with spiritual truth, and spiritual truth is one. Both saw men as capable of the Kingdom of Heaven; both knew that generosity of soul was the one thing needful; both judged men with the generosity of soul that was their own.

But, it may be asked, why did Western humanity have to wait till Shakespeare for this complete rediscovery of the verity of the Master's teaching? There are very good reasons for that, and I have expounded them elsewhere.[1] Here one can say, simply, that it was because Shakespeare was the first man of truly commanding genius since Jesus himself who had fought himself free of orthodox religion. It is very odd, but people never can remember that Jesus himself was absolutely free of the Christian religion: he knew nothing about it, and if he had, he would have given up the ghost with a more bitter cry than that he uttered. Jesus at one end, Shakespeare at the other, of the Christian epoch – and both free of it. Imagine them thus, as they were, and it is not so hard to understand why they should say the same, and be the same. I know of no two spirits more profoundly alike than theirs.

Now, perhaps, it becomes easier to understand why the religion of Christianity, as such, is dead, and its place long since taken by literature. That does not mean that there are not many and many good people who go to church, but they go less and less. But even though forty million inhabitants of these islands recited the Apostles' creed every Sunday, still Christianity would be dead. It was killed nearly 400 years ago: Anglo-Catholicism is a sort of belated death-rattle. But the rest of the dying may take another 400 years, for aught I know. Time is of little account in these cosmic affairs. Does it matter in the least that only a few dozen people to-day understand the meaning of Einstein's theory? It is absolutely true, none the less. Similarly, it makes no difference that possibly a quarter of the inhabitants of these

[1] *To the Unknown God*: essay: 'Literature and Religion.'

islands still believe that Christianity is alive. It is absolutely dead, none the less. What is alive, and will become more and more alive as the years go on – is the wisdom of Jesus. We are only just beginning to be able to understand it, and we have got to that point through the labours of the great writers, the great thinkers, and the great men of science since the Renaissance. Very slowly the English Church will evolve, if the Anglo-Catholics do not kill it meanwhile, into a sort of sacred school for teaching the Master's wisdom. But that wisdom will have been taught outside the Church for many years before it finds a way inside it.

Great literature came into existence in this country to satisfy the profound need of the human soul which had been once satisfied by the Christian religion, and was no longer satisfied by it. It still satisfies that need, and it satisfies it more largely, more generously, more humanely, than any religion can, or will. To put it bluntly: no man who truly understands Shakespeare can honestly profess any form of Christianity in existence to-day. He can understand any form, he can sympathize with it; but he knows more, and more truly, than can be expressed through that form. In so far then as humanity has moved on and come to look for the spiritual truth it must have, or starve, in literature rather than religion, it is actually moving nearer towards a comprehension of the real teaching of Jesus. A modern man will more quickly and more truly find what the Kingdom of Heaven means from Shakespeare than he will from the New Testament itself.

Therefore, it follows that the writer who slips back into the bosom of the Church to-day is, quite simply, an insignificant writer. It is a summary test, but quite infallible. He may perfectly well have a touch of genius – Francis Thompson had – or a quiverful of talents – G. K. Chesterton has; but there is inevitably something childish in him, as there is

in these two men. The Kingdom of Heaven was not promised to the childish, but to the child-*like*. It belongs to children when they are born, and to men when they are reborn.
But men have to grow up first.

Above all, writers have to grow up: that means, among
other things, that if they are born outside Churches, they
have to stay outside, and if they are born inside them, they
have to get outside. To be a writer is itself a veritable priesthood, a sacred calling with obligations of its own: it can
admit no others. If a writer does not know this – he need
not shout about it, still less be solemn about it – then he is
not grown up, and he will remain, for all his streaks of
genius and touches of talent, essentially a nursery-rhymer –
charming enough, perhaps, but totally without the power to
engage the depths within us. That is – I say it unashamedly
– the true business of literature. The rest is lollipops.

For to write truly is to be truly alive, and to understand
true literature is to understand life, in the very deepest
meaning you can attach to those words. Literature when it
is real, and life when it is real, are alike spontaneous. Hardly
a man, hardly ever a writer, has been spontaneous all the
time. Most of us, in our lives, have to be content with
flashes; so have most writers. But of both it is true that
only in our spontaneity are we real and significant. Those
moments of generosity of soul which bring a man into the
Kingdom, are the moments which take a writer into immortality. Our business here on earth is to prolong those
moments into minutes, minutes into hours, hours into days:
from the writer we learn, in secret and mysterious ways, how
to do it. We go to the writer for truth to life; if we perse-
vere with the quest, we find that we get from him – what,
though we did not know it, we were really asking for – truth
to eternal life, which is, after all, just ordinary life, only made
completely significant.

P.S. – For simplicity's sake, I have put aside the interesting question of the constant development of literature towards an ever closer approximation of the inwardly inevitable to the externally probable – what is called realism. That is, in the main, a technical question: for the demand made upon realistic literature is precisely the same as the demand made upon any other kind – for generosity of soul. Nevertheless the evolution towards realism means that a more exacting demand is made of a modern writer than of his predecessors. He is required, like Jehovah, to look upon all creation and see that it is good – to include everything within his own generosity, and to find a vestige or a potentiality of that generosity in everyone. No wonder that modern literature is so extraordinarily chaotic. The act of acceptance required is prodigious, and the few who are capable of making it, like Tchehov, are incapable of expressing it on a grand scale. Significant literature nowadays can be divided into two – the work of those who express the struggle towards this acceptance (Mr. Lawrence's 'thought-adventurers'), and the work of those who attain it.

THE PARABLES OF JESUS

WHEN I have read, with a vain expense of labour, the arguments of those who would prove that Jesus never existed, I have often wondered whether there is some absolute chemical difference between their brain-stuff and my own. For I cannot understand why they cannot understand that their painful efforts to show that there is no proof of the historical existence of Jesus are wholly beside the mark. After all, the recorded events of Jesus' life are few indeed; and about half of them are so saturated in the miraculous that they have little or no meaning for a modern mind. It is easy enough, if your taste lies that way, to throw doubt on the remainder. But the attempt can have value on one condition alone: namely, if there were, apart from this meagre handful of events, no reason to believe in the real existence of Jesus – if the significance of his life lay in events alone.

One must suppose, therefore, that this is, in fact, the conviction of those who prove to their own satisfaction that Jesus is a myth, or imagine that they have disposed of him by some casual remark to the effect that he was a Vegetation-God. Such a conviction astonishes me. I do not say – very far from it – that the events of the life of Jesus have no significance; nor do I say that these events, compared to his recorded *words*, are even of minor significance. But I do say that, apart from those words, the events of Jesus' life would be meaningless. It is the words that are primary.

To suppose for one moment that these words were not uttered by a living man is altogether beyond my capacity. On the contrary, it is to me self-evident not only that the most remarkable of those words (and these, at a guess, amount to at least one half of the words recorded in the

157

Synoptic Gospels) are the utterance of a single man, but that they are, on the face of it, the utterance of one of the greatest men that ever lived. The case is simple; for surely no one who is capable of responding to these words at all could imagine that they were a collection of pregnant sayings from many sources. A unique personality is stamped indelibly upon them. Critical nihilists talk glibly of the many parallels and analogies to the sayings of Jesus. But when they produce their parallels, one can hardly believe one's eyes. Can they really suppose that those are like these? Is there for them no difference between gold and brass? It seems incredible.

Sometimes, when I have been vexed by this insensibility, I have conceived the notion of making a complete separation between the events of Jesus' life and Jesus' words. I have desired to imagine that nothing had come down to us but the teaching and the parables of Jesus; and I have fancied that, with these alone before us and, beyond, a complete ignorance as to whom he was, or how and when he lived, he would still, as the speaker of those words alone, come to hold as deep a place in men's hearts and be as intimate a figure to their imaginations as he now holds and is.

This is, no doubt, a vain speculation: no man can so completely empty his mind of the Christian tradition that he could approach the words of Jesus as though they had been discovered for the first time to-day. But it still seems to me that some sort of approximation to this attitude would be possible, and valuable. Anyhow, I propose to make the attempt in a deliberately restricted field; I propose to imagine that I have been given a small – a terribly small – pamphlet containing some thirty parables newly copied from a papyrus roll, by someone who invites my considered judgment upon them.

Accordingly, I read them carefully. Some, most of them,

I do not understand at all; some are simple and wonderful as the sunlight on a flower. The one that makes the deepest immediate impression upon me is the Prodigal Son. It floods my heart with the revelation, "Here is love indeed," and I know that I have been in the presence of a rare soul. When I recover from my wonder at what seems to me at first a miraculous simplicity, I notice the print of the finger of genius. The son says to himself:

'I will arise and go to my Father, and will say to him: Father, I have sinned against heaven and in thy sight, and I am no more worthy to be called thy son. Make me as one of thy hired servants.'

But when he comes, his father sees him far away – he had been constantly on the watch – and runs toward him, and falls on his neck, and kisses him. The son speaks the words:

'Father, I have sinned against heaven and in thy sight, and I am no more worthy to be called thy son –'

That is all. No syllable of 'Make me as one of thy hired servants,' as he had planned and intended. Why? We scarcely need to ask. The father has interrupted him, calling to the slaves, 'Quick! Bring me out the finest robe, and put it on him.' The love of this father is too impatient to stay to hear.

And how strange is the love of this story! Something in us sympathizes with the grievance of the elder son. It *is* unfair. Never has such a banquet been made for him; and in making this one, they have not even waited for him to return from his work in the fields. They have begun without him. It is worse than unfair; it is cruel.

No, we protest, this love is extravagant, unjust; and yet, we listen to the old man's pleading:

'My son! thou art ever with me and all that is mine is thine. But it was meet that we should make merry and be glad: for this thy brother was dead, and is alive again; and was lost and is found.'

In spite of ourselves, we are conquered. This is love, indeed. Unjust? Yes, truly; for now we know that there is no justice in love.

Our minds turn back to another parable, which we have read without understanding, The Labourers in the Vineyard. Here is the same plenitude and supererogation: the same final touch of what our sober judgment calls the sheer extravagance of love. Not only do the labourers of the eleventh hour receive the same payment as those of the first, who have truly borne the heat and burden of the day: but they are paid first. Like the elder son, who had toiled his life long in his father's fields, the day-long labourers must wait till the late-comers are satisfied. It is the same utter annihilation of justice; the same complete abrogation of desert and reward. But, with the memory of the Prodigal Son present to our minds, something that eluded us in the almost forbidding words of the Master of the Vineyard eludes us no longer.

'Friend, I do thee no wrong. Didst thou not agree with me for a penny? Take that which is thine and go thy way. I will give unto this last even as unto thee. Is it not lawful for me to do what I will with mine own? Is thine eye evil because I am good?'

The seeming hardness is dissolved away when we remember:

'My son! thou art ever with me, and all that is mine is thine . . . but this thy brother was dead and is alive again; and was lost, and is found.'

Then we understand that those fellow-labourers are fellow sons; and that the lord of the vineyard is not a master only, but a father. The sons, if they are true sons, will rejoice with their father's joy that the prodigal is preferred to themselves, and the latest labourers the soonest paid; for they will love with their father's love. It is no less than a deliberate holocaust of all our human values in the consuming flame of love.

These stories stand apart in all the literature of the world, not for their beauty, though it is surpassing, but for the conception of love which they enshrine. But this conception of love is, of course, not a conception: it cannot be. Such love was never conceived. It was felt, it was experienced. The man who spoke those parables had experienced that love: it cannot be otherwise.

We look to the stories again. The Prodigal Son follows two others – two little ones. One tells of the man who lost one sheep of a hundred, and left the ninety and nine to seek the lost one. He found it and carried it home on his shoulders rejoicing; and he called his friends and his neighbours together. 'Rejoice with me, for I have found my sheep which was lost.' Then come the words of explanation. 'I say unto you that likewise joy shall be in heaven over one sinner whose heart is changed more than over ninety and nine just men that need no change.' The other tells of the poor woman who swept her floor until she found the lost shilling. 'I tell you, such is the joy among the angels of heaven over one sinner whose heart is changed.' And at the beginning of the Labourers in the Vineyard are the words, 'The Kingdom of Heaven is like the master of a vineyard. . . .'

Heaven – angels – the Kingdom of Heaven. What is this Heaven, what are these angels, what is this Kingdom? There is much in these parables about that Kingdom; little about those angels. Let the Kingdom wait; angels are stranger. But there is a word concerning them. It speaks of children also. Children have much to do with the Kingdom: 'The Kingdom is made of such as they.' The word is, 'See that you despise not one of these little ones, for I tell you their angels do always behold the face of the Father.' Thus, small and living children have their angels who live with their Father and do not leave him, while they are children. We may guess that, when their angels do leave him, the children have become prodigal sons, and that, when they return, their angels also return: they were dead, and are alive again. It may not be crystal clear, this matter of angels; but there is a gleam. We catch a glimpse of the reason why they rejoice over the sinner whose heart is changed: he is a brother-angel, come back again. When he was tiny, his angel was there, basking in the love of God: then his angel disappeared, but his place was kept, and his dear face remembered; suddenly, he came back again, and his brothers cried for joy. There he was, in his old place, full in the light of God's eyes.

A queer business – this of angels: well worth the trouble of looking into, a parable, no less than the others. The angels turn out to be so lovely, and so loving, and so near. We have them, and we lose them, and we find them: we are them, and we are not them, and we are them again. All that is required of us to regain the angelic birthright we have lost is that our hearts be changed ('metanoein'), our minds turned upside down. Oddly enough, we find, as we read these stories of the Prodigal Son and inquire into the nature of the angels who are so intimately related to him, that our minds *are* turned upside down, and that something suspiciously like a change of heart is threatening. There is a queer sensation as of a seed, sown in our hearts and bursting swiftly into flower, choking us almost, with the urge of a new creation.

THE PARABLES OF JESUS

Let us leave the angels, and back to the Kingdom. There is a brief sequence of words and parables about it; they are the only parables in the earliest of the gospels, and they are knit into a context which speaks, quite definitely, of the 'mystery' of the Kingdom of God. And strangely, that same metaphor of the seed which compelled itself from the pen of one man in his mere effort to describe the effect of two other parables, is the sole theme of the parables of the 'mystery' of the Kingdom of God.

'The Kingdom of God is as when a man casts seed into the earth, and sleeps by night and wakes by day, and the seed sprouts and grows up, he knows not how.'

Can this be mere coincidence? Mere coincidence, the parable of the swift springing of the infinitesimal grain of mustard seed into a tree? Mere coincidence, the growth of the seed the sower scattered on the good ground, 'that brought forth, some thirty, some sixty, and some an hundred fold'; with the explanation that these 'are such as hear the word, and receive it, and bring forth fruit.'

It is inconceivable to me that this is mere coincidence. Jesus is describing precisely what does happen, even to men like ourselves, when they hear the word of the Kingdom as he uttered it. There is this swelling of the seed in the heart, we know not how; this choking with the urge of a soul in travail to be born into some new condition where 'all things are forgiven and it would be strange not to forgive.' These parables of seed are not, what they are often said to be, allegories of the growth of the Church; they are quite simple descriptions of what happens to men's hearts when the word of the Kingdom is dropped into them. That is what Jesus said they were; and that is what they are. And again, 'The Kingdom of Heaven is like unto leaven which a woman took and hid in three measures of meal till the whole was leav-

163

ened.' It is the same secret, swift and mysterious growth, not of an institution in the world, but of a new vision and a new truth in the hearts and minds of men.

'Again, the Kingdom of Heaven is like unto treasure hid in a field, the which, when a man hath found, he hideth, and for joy thereof, goeth and selleth all that he hath to buy that field.' There it is, once more, the gleam of a new vision, to which, when a man sees it, his impulse is to sacrifice his all. 'Again, the Kingdom of Heaven is like unto a merchant man seeking goodly pearls, who, when he had found one pearl of great price, went and sold all that he had and bought it.' To the man who bought the field the vision came, as it were, by chance; there is nothing to say that he knew the treasure might be there: but to the merchant of pearls it came as the sudden, incredible reward of long searching.

Nevertheless, sudden, miraculous, incredible though it is, it does not come by chance. The soil is ready, even though the seed be despaired of: and that despair may be the perfect preparation. The vision does not come by chance, as Jesus made clear in the words that are knit up with the parables of seed.

'Look hard at what you hear. For by the measure wherewith you measure, it shall be measured to you again, and more added. For to him that hath it shall be given, and from him that hath not it shall be taken away, even that which he hath.'

There is, to speak baldly, a potentiality of response in men's hearts, which is co-extensive with the degree of understanding which they possess; and this response and this understanding are aspects of one indivisible motion. We may say that the understanding is of the mind, the response of the heart; but the secret is that these are no longer separate: the intellectual and the emotional parts of man become one, because the word of the Kingdom is dynamic, and creative. It actually *creates* in the man who can receive it, a new condition and a new faculty; he sees something new and he *is* something new.

It is almost a kind of sacrilege to venture on this clumsy explanation, which is like turning a perfect poetry into pedestrian prose; yet the risk is worth taking, if there should be a thousandth chance that a glimpse of the real meaning of Jesus' words should come, by this means, to a single person who had it not before. In these fundamental parables of the Kingdom, Jesus is describing the effect of the dynamic word of the Kingdom. That a word should be dynamic, creative by its inherent virtue, is hard to conceive. But this is, in the case of the words of Jesus, no recondite or mystical fancy. We have only to remember the story of the Prodigal Son. That is dynamic enough. It seems almost impossible that any man could read it – 'looking hard at what he hears' – without feeling some indescribable and mysterious change within him, a sweet convulsion of which he knows himself in no way the cause, the pain and joy of the travail of some new birth, of new understanding and a new world to be understood. Thus actually, as a matter of simple experienced fact, the word of the Kingdom does create the Kingdom; it does directly work the change of heart which brings men into the Kingdom. In virtue of that change they are members of the Kingdom.

And, of course, the change happens, and the Kingdom is entered and established here and now. It is hardly necessary to say it: the fact is obvious. All these fundamental parables of the Kingdom refer to a process that happens here and now. There is really not even the faint possibility of mistake. The Prodigal returns in life, not after death; the joy among the angels is not in some remote, transcendent heaven – the angels are the little children who have never left, and the grown men who have returned to, the presence and the love of God: homely and familiar angels it may be, yet, perhaps, incomparable in beauty if we could but keep the eyes to see them. 'Heaven lies about us in our infancy,' said Wordsworth, and it is good; but not so good, by far, as 'Truly I tell you, their angels do always behold the face of my Father.' And as for Wordsworth's further lament over the fading of the vision splendid:

'Where is now, the glory and the gleam?' –

Jesus knew better. The glory and the gleam are always there, waiting to be discerned. Wordsworth himself, when a grown man, had had his glimpse of them, and if he could find them no more himself, he should have looked hard at the words of Jesus and discovered in them what any man may discover, experienced from them what any man may experience – that there is a virtue in them that *can*

'bring back the hour
Of splendour in the grass, and glory in the flower.'

Those words of Wordsworth's, with their resignation and their despairing appeal to 'the philosophic mind,' a greater poet than Wordsworth once, in a moment of extreme suffering, declared were true. John Keats, who had endured in a year more than Wordsworth had to endure in a life-time, wrote at the nadir of his fortunes:

'I must choose between despair and energy – I choose the latter – though the world has taken on a quakerish look with me, which I once thought was impossible –
Nothing can bring back the hour
Of splendour in the grass and glory in the flower.
I once thought this a Melancholist's dream.'

But he chose energy; and a Melancholist's dream it proved

indeed to be. Not that his fortunes improved: they grew more desperate and terrible: he tasted the very dregs of misery. Yet, from the last onslaught of Destiny, he emerged one autumn morning, with these words:

'How beautiful the season is now. – How fine the air – a temperate sharpness about it. Really, without joking, chaste weather. – Dian skies – I never liked stubble-field so much as now. – Aye, better than the chilly green of the spring. Somehow, a stubble-field looks warm – in the same way that some pictures look warm. This struck me so much in my Sunday's walk that I composed upon it.'

What he had composed upon it was the most perfect poem, of its length and kind, in our language of perfect poetry – 'The Ode to Autumn':

'Season of mists and mellow fruitfulness,·
Close bosom-friend of the maturing sun . . .'

The splendour was indeed in the grass again – it was in a stubble field.

§

I have followed my thoughts, and they have led me, it may seem, far from my subject. I do not think so; I believe I am winding my way to the heart's core of it. The splendour in the grass has, if I am not mistaken, much to do with Jesus:

'Consider the lilies of the field, how they grow: they toil not neither do they spin; and yet I say unto you Solomon in all his glory was not arrayed like one of these. Wherefore, if God so clothe the grass of the field . . .'

This conjuncture, though it was not premeditated, is not fortuitous; neither, I incline to believe, is the strange coincidence by which in a passage from Keats's letter which I quoted, the word 'quakerish' occurs. I had forgotten it was there: it came to me with a shock. I held my pen. Should I substitute another word? Should I forgo the quotation? I decided for the word, and for the quotation. For in them is implicit the real point of what I have to say, and the real purpose I had in accepting an invitation of a kind which, though I esteem an honour, I do not covet.[1] Let me say, once more, that this is, indeed, a coincidence, unpremeditated by me. I had not the faintest idea that I should be using that quotation from Keats, and when I looked to find it, I had forgotten that the word was there.

But there it is, unmitigated. 'Lately the world has taken on a QUAKERISH look with me, which I once thought was impossible –

> Nothing can bring back the hour
> Of splendour in the grass or glory in the flower.'

Those are the words, and I will try not to shirk them. It is, I believe, an article, perhaps *the* article, of your belief that a man's words may be and should be guided by the spirit. Perhaps something of the kind, as like and as different, as are my belief and yours, has guided mine. At any rate, I felt that to conceal the word, or forgo the quotation, would be an act of treachery.

Keats was writing more than a hundred years ago, when the attitude of your noble society was different from what it is now. Nevertheless, granting to the full that the attitude of Friends has changed – that plays are no longer to them an abomination, nor the simple passionate sensuousness of

[1] This address was delivered to the Summer School of the Society of Friends at Jordans Meeting House in June, 1927.

literature a snare; granting also that Keats used his adjective with the vehemence of youth: it is still worth while to consider the implications of his casual judgment. Even if the word slipped from his pen, it may be not the less significant for that.

Let us examine the position. The world looked Quakerish, to Keats, when 'the splendour was no longer in the grass nor the glory in the flower,' and he felt that nothing could bring it back again. And I was trying to show, or to hint, that precisely this vision of the splendour in the grass is inseparable from the vision of the Kingdom in the teaching of Jesus. It would follow, if logic were everything, that Keats identified the moment when the vision faded, and seemed irrecoverably lost, with what he thought to be the attitude of Friends. That forthright conclusion would be preposterous. You have your vision, and it has been proved by the glorious history of your Society, more steadfast and abiding than the more opulent revelation claimed by others. It is assuredly no mere negation which has upheld, and been upheld by, the Society of Friends. But, if I may express the distinction in the subtler terms of poetry, which have entered inevitably into this exposition, I think it possibly *is* true that the Society of Friends, by tradition, perceptibly inclines towards the attitude of Wordsworth rather than the attitude of Keats.

Even the most sensitive words are clumsy tools for this discrimination. I know well enough that there lives in the heart of the Society of Friends a flame of spiritual joy that is of the very essence of true Christianity. But unless I am as gravely mistaken as was Keats himself, it is not integral in the fabric of your tradition that this joy should be received from the whole of the created universe: in other words, there is a certain ascetic and life-renouncing element in your tradition. The emphasis falls perceptibly on the inward-going movement of the religious life: there is a constant sense of what the Catechism calls 'the pomps and vanities of this wicked world': the movement is rather towards withdrawal than participation. Now this movement is, certainly, an essential part of the religious, or, as I prefer to regard it, of the spiritual life; it is, most certainly, an essential part of the spiritual life as Jesus experienced and taught it. But it is only one part of that experience and that teaching. Just as essential to it is an outward-going movement of spontaneous delight in the glory of the created universe, as the manifest work of God; a deep and joyous awareness that the world *is*, and that no part of it may be refused.

This is the most difficult and mysterious element in the teaching of Jesus, though it seems simple to me. The difficulties, I know, seem simpler still. To find a manifest glory in a world where there is cruelty and pain? This is evasion, self-deception; good is good, and bad is bad, and the harmony that transcends them a dream. True enough; judge the world with cool intelligence, look at it with the eyes of what is called falsely reason, and it is for ever discordant; the heart of the universe is gnawed by an eternal pain. But the secret of the teaching is that the eyes must be changed, and that they can be changed; and that with this change of vision the old distinction between good and bad is indeed transcended. The teaching is that there is a power and faculty attainable by man by which he can feel and know that there is something beyond good and evil both in the world outside him and in himself: in other words, that it is truer to see than to judge, better to be whole than to be good.

If it can be put into a word, this is the fundamental distinction between the teaching of Jesus and all other religious wisdom that I know: that he taught not goodness, but *wholeness:* and this both in the inward man, and in the outward world. Wholeness in the man himself means that the soul is not a partial faculty of man; it is not something that can be opposed to and distinguished from mind and heart: it is a creation which includes both these within itself. The soul is simply the condition of the complete man. And to this completeness in the man, which is his soul, there corresponds a completeness and harmony of the world of his experience; it also, without abstraction or denial of any of its elements, suffers a like transformation, and becomes organic, harmonious – it becomes God.

I know well enough that a statement such as this provokes many objections, and I do not pretend that it is of a kind to carry conviction. These imperfections and disabilities I accept, because I know that they are, in the nature of things, inevitable. The mystery of the Kingdom of God is, what Jesus declared it to be, veritably a mystery; and he further declared that it could not be revealed by the direct and intelligible word, but only by means of parable. That, and no other, is the meaning of the words that occur in the midst of his primary parables of the mystery of the Kingdom:

'Is a lamp brought to be put under a basket, or under the bed, and not to be put on the stand? For there is nothing hidden save in order that it should be manifested; neither is anything made secret, save that it should come to light.'

What parable essentially is, I have tried to convey: it is the dynamic and creative word. It is the imaged speech which veritably does create within us a new vision, a new faculty, and a new soul. It sounds fantastic – believe me, I am just as aware of the seeming extravagance of the idea as the most rational and contemptuous of my critics – nevertheless, it is true. This dynamic utterance, with its apparently miraculous virtues, does exist; and those who submit themselves to its power gain a glimpse of the mystery of the Kingdom of God.

It stands in the nature of such a process of soul-creation that it should be able to occur in all times and all places. The process can take place in any man; it is, if it is not merely an illusion, an eternal truth of man's inward nature. Not only this: but the dynamic utterance which is the agent of such a change cannot be confined to the words of a single man. Unless we realize that the mystery of the Kingdom of God is 'concealed and revealed' in the words of other men than Jesus himself, we have not a real understanding of the mystery as he taught it. That does not mean that the revelation made by Jesus is not final; it is. The discovery of a true and a new potentiality of the human soul is final, just as the discovery of articulate speech by some incredibly remote and forgotten ancestor is final. But other men, travelling different paths, have reached the same finality.

One such man was Keats. To regain his vision of the splendour in the grass he paid just such a price as Jesus said was necessary to be paid – he lost his life to save it. Through great and terrible suffering, he became whole, and regained more completely than he possessed before, the power of dynamic utterance. 'The Ode to Autumn' is as authentic a revelation of the mystery of the Kingdom as the story of The Prodigal Son. I say that with complete conviction; but if I am asked to make my statement good, I do not know even how to attempt it. And any attempt is bound to fail, unless it is addressed to those who realize that the mystery of the Kingdom is essentially the mysterious birth within us of a new condition, a new awareness of ourselves and the universe and of our relation to the universe.

The love that is uttered in The Prodigal Son involves the universe; it brings to birth in him who can receive it a condition wherein 'all things are forgiven and it would be strange not to forgive.' Because the word is dynamic, it does not so much describe as create love; and the love thus

172

created flows out to its own sole and proper object. We shall not say that it flows out to God, unless we are speaking to those who understand that the nature and reality of God is comprehended only by this love. The man who loves with this love knows God; and God is apprehended in his verity whenever the love which burns in The Prodigal Son is kindled in our hearts and minds towards the universe which is His and Him. For this love is not an emotion. It is kindled in the heart, but it is not an emotion of the heart; it is endorsed by the mind, but it is not a judgment of the mind. This love is of the soul; and it is not a feeling, but a seeing and a knowing. It is a union of the soul of man with the only object of the soul's knowledge, which is God.

That does not mean, at least in the ordinary sense of the words, that the soul loves God and nothing besides; it means that whatever the soul loves *is* God. The soul is as it were the divining rod, discovering God in the universe: and the soul discovers that there is nothing that is not God. It is this essential activity of knowing that lies at the heart of the soul's loving that is hardest of all to convey. Regard it, if you can, in this way. Remember, first of all, that the soul is created within us: we achieve it, we bring it to birth, or, more truly, we bring ourselves to a condition wherein the soul cannot remain unborn. The soul is simple and mysterious; it is ourselves in a new wholeness, without division. The loving of the heart, the knowing of the mind, have fought together, and no matter which may triumph, each has failed. Each has failed, because each must fail. We are all seekers after God. What we mean by God will be only known when we have found him. The heart seeks for God; the mind seeks for God – in all men, without distinction – for God is simply that which brings repose to our seeking. The wealth of the man of business, the good works of the social reformer, the truth of the scientist, the beauty or the truth of the artist (whichever it be) – these things that all men seek are, by virtue of their seeking, God; and in so far as there is no rest in them, they are not God. We seek the rest of our hearts, in love for another, and death tramples it to fragments; we seek the repose of our minds in facing all the truth that we discern, and it is ashes and bitterness in our mouths. Our hearts cry out and will not be comforted. There is no God, and we cannot live without him. For truly to live is to be at peace; not to rest, but to rest in a surety; to be no longer at the mercy of destiny, no longer to find our childish hearts dismayed by the barren judgments of the mind, no longer to find the resolution of our minds discomfited by the cry of our hearts in pain.

Surely it cannot be that this is the end – division, and dismay, and no repose. Something there must be, to bring divided man into oneness with the universe, with the lily that toils not, and the ocean that has no regret. Can life not come to him as it comes to a child, and death as it comes to a flower? Can he not, too, be whole?

And the answer is, Yes, he can. His wholeness is his soul. In it, mind and heart are at one, and are no longer what they were. Now, what the mind knows, the heart loves; because the mind is no longer the mind, nor the heart any more the heart. The loving of the soul is not as the loving of the heart, or the mind would deny it; and the knowing of the soul is not as the knowing of the mind, or the heart would refuse it. The knowing and the loving of the soul are one – and the object of this knowing and this loving is all things, which are God. And since in this knowing and loving there is a peace which cannot be shaken (for the mind thenceforward can know, and the heart can feel, nothing that is not transmuted by the soul's alchemy) we may say that in it we know and love God indeed. We have found what we sought – the peace of wholeness; we are whole, and we are one with the whole: and the outcome of this peace is a perfect activity, for only when we are whole are we sure what we must do. We long no more to do what our hearts desire, or what our minds determine; we act simply as we must, and as we are.

It is sometimes said of a truly beautiful woman, whose act was as expressive of her soul as the leaves and the flower of a plant are expressive of the life that informs it, that 'to know her was to love her.' Extend the meaning of those words till the whole universe is embraced by them, and you have the knowledge and the love of God that is the soul's activity and purpose. Just as the woman was known and loved by reason of her complete expressiveness; so the universe is known and loved for its complete expressiveness. That each thing (the soul itself not least among them) must be what it is, is the triumphant knowledge of the soul, which knows and loves it for its perfect expressiveness of God. Wherever knowing and loving are one, there perfectly expressed in the object is God. Where knowing and loving are one, that is the point. Not where we love and do not know, not where we know and do not love. In the first, the love, in the second, the knowledge, is not of the soul; and the object neither of the love, nor of the knowledge, can be God.

Now at last I am come by devious ways to my goal. The highest literature, the truest literature, can be known by this, and only by this, that it enables us to know and to love some fraction of the universe with a knowing and a loving that are one. This is what the great writer feels towards the creatures and things that he depicts, and this is what we feel towards them through the magic of his words. The writer who makes us know without loving, may be a powerful, may be in the common sense of the word even a great writer; but he does not belong to the elect. His words are not, in the final judgment, dynamic. And the writer who would make us love without knowing – though this miracle is hard to work upon an honest mind – may be an attractive and a popular writer; but there is no virtue in him. The great writer is he alone who makes us know absolutely, and love absolutely: for he brings to birth the soul that is within us, he effects the union of our mind and heart, he, like Jesus himself, drops the seed of the Word into the earth of our being, where it grows we know not how; and he, like Jesus, is the prophet and the priest of God.

But, alas, it is not so simple, or the Kingdom would have been established ages ago. It is not easy for men to receive a parable of Jesus, or the words of a great writer, into their hearts. The ground is shallow, or stony, or a well-trod pathway where there is much traffic and no repose. The earth has to be tilled, wrought over and over by suffering and circumstance, by struggle and despair. It is out of this travail that the dynamic utterance of great literature is born; and out of this travail is born the power to receive it. 'We only understand really fine things when we have gone the same steps as the author.' For literature, in the highest, is a communication from soul to soul, a creation of soul by soul; it is always a parable, and a parable of the same virtue and the same meaning as Jesus' own.

POETRY AND REALITY

TOWARDS the end of his stimulating book, *Principles of Literary Criticism*, Mr. I. A. Richards discusses what he calls the 'revelation' theory of poetry; that is to say the theory that poetry, in its highest forms, does actually reveal somewhat of the else hidden nature of reality. The theory was first maintained in this country by the 'romantic' poets of the early nineteenth century. It is to be found also in Goethe. Centuries before that we find palpable hints of it in Plotinus; and the enthusiastic sometimes discover it adumbrated in Aristotle's famous dictum that 'Poetry is more highly serious and more philosophic than history.'

Mr. Richards is distinctly scornful of the suggestion.

'The joy (he writes) which is so strangely the heart of the experience [of high tragedy] is not an indication that "all's right with the world," or that "somewhere, somehow there is justice"; it is an indication that all is right here and now with the nervous system.'

He is ruthless, you see, with our little illusions. When we respond to *King Lear* or *The Cherry Orchard*, and leave them with the sweet solemnity of a *Nunc dimittis* sounding within our souls, a conviction that our eyes have seen our salvation, we are the victims of romantic delusion, pardonable perhaps in such foolish children of earth as we, but to be regarded by the cool-headed expert in knowledge with a blend of amusement and pity.

And yet, I wonder . . . 'All is right here and now with the nervous system.' It is downright enough. Mr. Richards is obviously quite certain that he knows. Yet Goethe, Coleridge, Keats . . . were no fools either. We had better take another look at the new theory before we bid a long farewell to the old one.

'All is right with the nervous system.' Queer that we should read *King Lear* only to find out that. The last thing that entered Keats's head, when he sat down once more to read the play:

> 'O golden-tongued romance with serene lute!
>   Fair-plumèd Syren! Queen of far away!
>   Leave melodizing on this wintry day,
> Shut up thine olden volume, and be mute.
> Adieu! for once again the fierce dispute
>   Betwixt damnation and impassion'd clay
>   Must I burn through . . .'

He misunderstood himself. What he was really after was to determine whether he could stick it. He ought to have known that Monk Lewis was a better test of nerves.

Probably we misunderstand Mr. Richards. The 'nervous system' sounds a very businesslike affair. No humbug about that, so to speak. And yet, I fancy, it is as vague and nebulous a conception as the 'soul.' In spite of his appearance of scientific rigour, Mr. Richards is saying no more than that the strange and profound satisfaction that comes to us through great tragedy is purely emotional and subjective. We feel it, and that is all. If that is what he means, he might have chosen a less ambiguous way of saying it. Simple things are best said simply.

But, in actual fact, he says more than this. He says that the profound satisfaction we derive from tragedy is an indication that *all is right* with the nervous system. Whether he meant this, we cannot tell. Perhaps his audacious pen ran away with him. For we must ask why the tragic satisfaction indicates that *all is right* with the nervous system? Is it because that strange satisfaction is the correct response to tragedy? But who is to determine what is the correct response? From the fact, on which Mr. Richards is so anxious to insist, that all we can say of great tragedy is that it calls forth a certain emotional condition in certain people, it is quite impossible to conclude that the presence of that condition is evidence that nothing is wrong with their nervous systems, or their souls, or their bank-accounts, or their drains.

Mr. Richards cannot have it both ways. He has chosen a complete subjectivism; then he must stick to it. He declares that the fact in question is that certain people, after reading or seeing *King Lear*, experience a strange satisfaction. Very good. But if we are to accept it as a statement of the fact, he must not go beyond it. The moment he attempts to make deductions from the fact, new and unwarrantable assumptions enter in. Mr. Richards' assumption is that to the people to whom this strange satisfaction comes it comes because their nervous systems are in order. First, it is an unwarrantable assumption; and it is a very doubtful one. It would be laughed at by nine neurologists out of ten, for the chances are that the soundest nervous systems belong to eupeptic Philistines, who would be bored to extinction if they were compelled to read, or even to see, *King Lear*.

Mr. Richards may reply that in his view the nervous systems of our friends the Philistines are not in order. But in that case he means by the nervous system something quite peculiar – never before described by that name. He means the very delicately refined sensibility which, he believes, is required in order to respond fully to *King Lear*. I do not doubt that it is required. But the only reason for believing that a refined sensibility is necessary to respond to *King Lear*, is that *King Lear* is a very delicate and subtle object. Our response to *King Lear* can prove that we have a refined sensibility on one condition only, that it is, *in itself*, something which requires a refined sensibility to respond to it. Except we know the nature of the object, nothing can be deduced as to the nature of the subject.

Mr. Richards has attempted an illegitimate simplification of the problem of poetry. Two things are given in the poetic experience – the poem, and the reader. It is only possible to say a clever thing, such as that the joy of the tragic experience is an indication that all is right with the nervous system, by unconsciously doing a stupid one – namely, to leave the tragedy out of the reckoning. The truth is that the strange joy that comes to the reader of high tragedy is the outcome of the meeting of two elements: some quality in the tragedy itself, and a delicate sensibility in the reader. If the experiencing of that joy indicates that the reader possesses a delicate sensibility, it indicates equally, and by precisely the same logical compulsion, that there is in the tragedy itself as object some quality which causes the delicate sensibility to function in a way so strange.

It is tedious, no doubt, to be compelled thus painfully to indicate that an egg is an egg and not a taste; but subtle logicians like Mr. Richards have to be tediously countered. At any rate, we are now in a position to rewrite his bold sentence to accord more closely with the facts:

'The joy which is so strangely the heart of the experience [of tragedy] is an indication that our sensibilities are delicate and responsive: whether it is an indication that 'all's right with the world' can only be decided by an inquiry into the nature of those qualities possessed by the tragedy, and responded to by our sensibilities – an inquiry into which I have not the patience to enter.'

So far from having demolished the 'revelation' theory of poetry, Mr. Richards has touched it not at all. Like most writers on literature who are æsthetic philosophers rather than literary critics, he has bemused himself with a phrase. Mr. Richards' talisman – 'the nervous system' – has failed him.

I am not anxious to embark upon the inquiry which Mr. Richards has thus avoided. To attempt it in the few pages of this brief essay would be fantastic. For it would involve a long and minute investigation into the creative process of the poet, which has never yet been attempted by any critic. Coleridge intended to undertake it, and left behind him valuable hints for the work – but they are hints, and no more. I confess that I have only glimpses of the way the work should be done; it is something which I hope, not indeed to do, but to have helped in the doing, before I die.

But the present point is that the 'revelation' theory of poetry and art emerges completely unscathed from Mr. Richards's demolition. He has delivered his blow on the empty air. That is not to say that the 'revelation' theory is right, but that we may with a good conscience retain the theory held by Goethe, Coleridge, and Keats, and still believe that the chances are that they, being at once great poets and subtle thinkers, were not wholly deluded.

Nevertheless, though it would be idle to undertake a systematic defence of the 'revelation' theory without a careful and minute investigation of the creative process, it may be worth while to point out that the real objection to the theory springs generally not from a consideration of the facts, but from an *a priori* repugnance to the implications of the theory. The philosopher cannot admit the poet's implicit claim to 'know' reality, or the reader's claim to attain through the poet's work a 'knowledge' of reality. 'Knowledge' is the privilege of the philosopher, and he very strongly resents the attempt of the poet to claim it. Therefore, he feels himself compelled, by hook or by crook, to prove that the poet's conviction of knowledge is merely subjective: it is an emotional condition. By some mysterious means (into which the philosopher never really inquires) the poet with this sense of 'knowledge' creates something which arouses in the sensitive reader the same sense of 'knowledge.' This also must be merely subjective: an emotional condition. The decision is *a priori*. For if the strange condition of soul, experienced by the poet, and called by him 'knowledge,' which is communicated to us, and called by us 'knowledge,' be not relegated to pure subjectivity, then the philosopher's monopoly of 'knowledge' is threatened. But, unfortunately for the philosopher, his effort to relegate this queer poetic experience to the realm of subjectivity fails, as we have seen it fail in the case of Mr. Richards.

Of course, those who uphold or incline to the 'revelation' theory of poetry do not claim that the poet's 'knowledge' is of the same kind as the philosopher's or the scientist's – it may be remarked in passing that the scientist is just as scornful of the philosopher's claim to knowledge as the philosopher is scornful of the poet's. Roughly, the 'revelation' theory holds that there is a reality outside the perceiving mind and that man has evolved several ways of seeking to know it. Of these several ways the poetic, or æsthetic alone is concerned with the real in its particularity: it does not seek to subsume particulars under universal concepts, nor does it confine itself to the measurable aspects of the world. It is primarily concerned with the world of ordinary human experience; and the materials with which the poet sets about his work are unusually vivid perceptions of real and particular objects. Like Antony in the streets of Alexandria he 'notes the qualities of people,' and of things not for any practical purposes, as an employer may note the qualities of men for a particular job, or a mason the qualities of stones for a particular building, but simply and solely for his own delight in observation. Towards the world o particulars he is passive and receptive, that not one of its qualities may be lost. It is perhaps peculiar that he should take delight in this: it is because the pursuit gives him delight. He has 'more than ordinary organic sensibility.' In fact he alone is able to *see* the world of particulars, where ordinary men, as it were, see only the headlines, and take note only of those salient features of the world which are useful for their practical ends.

This rare faculty of vividly perceiving particulars is the primary poetic gift: no one can ever be a great creative writer without it, though not all who have it become great creative writers. What further gifts are necessary, what further operations are carried on the mind of the great poet beside this incessant intuition of particulars, cannot be discussed now: it is a fascinating and difficult inquiry. But even this brief consideration of the primary poetic perception is sufficient to show that when the poet claims to reveal reality he is not talking idle nonsense. By his most elementary act of perception and description, he does reveal, and he reveals the real.

We may surmise that the poet's activity, when he is a Shakespeare and writing *King Lear*, though infinitely more complex, is of the same kind. Just as a life-time of observation of particular things has given him the power of making us see them when he describes them, so a life-time of observation of the behaviour of men and women (above all, perhaps, of himself) has given him the power of making us understand them when he represents them. We see that they *must* act as he makes them act, speak as he makes them speak. True, they use a language which in real life they would not use. The characters of a high Shakespearean tragedy speak as poets. It is necessary that they should so speak. The poet alone can utter himself; and the characters of a great tragedy must utter themselves. And that strange peculiarity of high tragedy that its heroes speak rhythmical

and recondite poems has its simple explanation in the fact
that poetic utterance alone is completely expressive of the
living man.

Thus the characters of high tragedy are the more real,
because they are not realistic. They are presented complete,
as it were in the round, to our consciousness; and as they
move to their destinies we have an immediacy of contact
with them which is unattainable through any other literary
form. When Cleopatra cries:

> 'O, see, my women,
> The crown o' the earth doth melt. My lord!
> O wither'd is the garland of the war,
> The soldier's pole is fall'n: young boys and girls
> Are level now with men; the odds is gone
> And there is nothing left remarkable
> Beneath the visiting moon.'

she is uttering an emotion which in real life is never expressed – not because it is not felt, but simply because men
and women have not the power to express it. High tragedy
brings us into contact with creatures who experience the
most grievous human vicissitude, feel the deepest human
emotions, and express themselves. Therefore, in one sense
they are not human. Not Shakespeare himself could have
expressed his emotion at the moment that he felt it. When
his dark lady betrayed him, he laughed wanly and said,
'That's a blow!' just as feebly as the rest of us. But the
shudder of loathing of himself and her remained with him:
he could recall it. One day he did recall it, and wrote:

> 'The expense of spirit in a waste of shame
> Is lust in action . . .'

This added faculty of utterance, that can be given to the
creatures of a poet's imagination alone, makes them more

real than men actually are, precisely as the poet's description of an object makes it more real than it actually is to the ordinary perceptions of men.

But, it may be said, when the poet describes a primrose, there *is* (or there was) a primrose which he sees and describes; when Shakespeare gives utterance to Cleopatra, there is no Cleopatra. How can he then be revealing the reality, when there is no reality to reveal? The answer is simple. He is revealing his own experience of the real, of which his Cleopatra is but one of a thousand incarnations. Thereby you admit (comes the reply) that the only reality with which we make contact in a Shakespearean tragedy is Shakespeare's experience. True, so far as it goes. But Shakespeare's experience – his emotions, his thoughts, his habits of emotion and thought – is experience of the real. His 'more than ordinary organic sensibility' was exposed, day in day out, to contact with the real world; by it he was shaped to what he was. When he utters himself through the immense complexity of a tragedy it is his experience of the real world that he utters. One man's experience of it, if you insist. But such another man you will not find in the world's history. What he brought to the equal marriage with reality was what the high gods gave him, 'an experiencing nature' the like of which they gave to no other man.

Through that experiencing nature we little men are privileged to make our nearest contact with the real, one far closer, far more comprehensive than the most sensitive among us could make – a contact that seemed prodigious and miraculous to poets of genius – to Goethe, to Coleridge, to Keats. This real is not the real of science, nor of philosophy; it is not the reality of the specialist of any sort, but it is the reality with which we ordinary humans are all our lives concerned, the world in which we suffer and delight, are defeated and conquer. To know that reality as it is may not be 'knowledge' for the philosopher, or for the scientist; it is 'knowledge' to us, and it is the only knowledge we greatly care about. We go to Shakespeare to learn it, and to learn how to learn more, to have our own small experiencing natures enlarged. We do not go to him in order to learn whether our nervous systems are in order; nor do we get any answer to that doubtless important question through him. The joy that comes to us after a tragedy of his is not indeed a sign that we know the secret of the universe, however much we may feel that we do; but it is a sign that the truer and more complete experience of reality we gain through Shakespeare does bring us, what we sometimes dream all true experience of reality would bring us were we but capable of it, joy and serenity. Once break this contact with the real, once persuade men that high tragedy has not its roots in outward life, there would be no joy and acceptance in the tragic experience any more. But in attempting to break that contact with the real, you are attempting the impossible. Every man capable of experiencing a Shakespearean tragedy at all knows, with the same certainty he has of his own existence, that he is making contact with the real. He is making contact with art also. That he sometimes forgets. But by forgetting it, he gets to the root of the matter, which far cleverer men miss by remembering it, namely, that art is but a means – the most potent of all means – of bringing reality nearer to us than we have power to bring it to ourselves.

THE PHILOSOPHY OF POETRY

In a recent essay Sir Henry Newbolt discussed the conceptions of Time and Eternity that have found expression in poetry, and in conclusion, with the aid of some rather difficult speculations by the late Dr. McTaggart, tried to indicate a path of thought which (he thought) might lead some future poet to a more comfortable creed concerning these high subjects, and so to a more comforting achievement. The light of a new dawn glimmers, for Sir Henry Newbolt, in Dr. McTaggart's contention that 'events in Time take place in an order – a fixed and irrevocable order. But there is in the mere form of Time itself nothing to determine what this order shall be.'

'What then does determine the order of events in Time, on the supposition that Time is only an illusory way of regarding a timeless reality? The philosopher believes tnat there is good reason to hold that the order is determined by the adequacy with which the states represent the eternal reality, so that those states come next together which only vary infinitesimally in the degree of their adequacy.'

Dr. McTaggart (according to Sir Henry Newbolt) held that he was justified in believing that the representations of reality presented to us in the time series are becoming more and more adequate, and will continue inevitably to do so until 'we reach the last stage in the series, and enter upon the perfect vision which lies beyond time.' An inspiring philosophic faith, which if a future poet were to embrace, 'surely his poetry would have the power to give, as only poetry can give, consolation and encouragement in the evils of the present.'

I doubt it – for many reasons. The simplest of them is that I cannot understand the theory. Perhaps, in the long practice of literary criticism, what little metaphysic wit I once possessed has worn away; but I can make nothing even of the primary notion that though events in Time take place in fixed and irrevocable order, 'there is in the mere form of Time itself nothing to determine what this order shall be.' What is this 'mere form of Time' that can be thus abstracted from events? The events in their order are our datum; the category or form of Time is derived from our contemplation of them. Time without events, events without Time, both are inconceivable. And, since my earth-bound wings refuse this first flight into the empyrean, the subsequent speculations upon the growing 'adequacy' of events in the time series to the eternal reality remain as remote from me, and as impotent to console me (did I need consolation) as the farthest of the fixed stars; nor can I imagine that any poetry which accepted and proclaimed such a theory would have more potency over men.

Not, at all events, in virtue of its theory. In virtue of the passion of mind with which the imaginary poet embraced it, perhaps. I am totally unmoved by the cosmology of Epicurus, deeply thrilled by the response it awakened in the mind of Lucretius; for there I find a secular passion of the human soul – to be freed from blind ancestral fears – uttered with a constrained intensity of emotion. And, no doubt, if the imaginary poet were to find in Dr. McTaggart's theory a deliverance from a spiritual bondage comparable to that once experienced by Lucretius, his pent-up soul might leap to a like magnificence of contemplative rapture. But it is improbable that he would bring much more comfort to his readers than Lucretius has brought to his. Yet Lucretius was passionately convinced that he was bringing a message of hope to his fellow-mortals. His message leaves us cold; it is his ardour alone which kindles us.

In other words, Sir Henry Newbolt appears to have involved himself in the old mistake that it is the philosophy of philosophical poetry that moves us. What moves us is the poetry; and, though it is difficult to separate the poetry of a philosophical poet from the intellectual argument which gives it form, the fact that we can and do continually refuse the philosophy and accept the poetry points to the likelihood that the philosophy merely serves the same office in philosophical poetry as the plot or myth in other kinds. We give to the one as to the other 'that willing suspension of disbelief which constitutes poetic faith'; if the poet is great enough to create, by means of his philosophy or his story, a significant order in the chaos of human experience, we ask no more from the philosophy.

So much at least seems true of the philosophic poetry of the past. Whether philosophic poetry is likely to be written in the future depends, therefore, upon the possibility of a metaphysical theory giving to the intellectual and emotional nature of a great poet a satisfaction comparable with that given to Lucretius by the theory of Epicurus, or Dante by Thomism. And that, I think, is improbable.

In considering the question we have to take into serious reckoning the fact that we have no real philosophic poetry in English. Sometimes, it is true, Shelley is called a philosophical poet, sometimes Wordsworth; but in both cases by a manifest indulgence. Of the process of intellectual argument they contain nothing; each, indeed, possessed a certain metaphysical faith, but, from the point of view of the logician, it was irrationally held. Shelley's Platonism was certainly not the outcome of Plato's dialectic, and Wordsworth's Pantheism was the product of immediate experience. They are philosophical only in the vaguest sense of the word, and it would be much nearer the mark to call them simply religious, as probably they would have been called had not orthodoxy in their day possessed a monopoly of the epithet.

Of Coleridge, on the other hand, it might fairly be said that he did possess the capacity to write a true philosophic poem; he could think severely and sustainedly, and, what is of no less consequence, the processes of his own abstract thought were attended by real emotional responses. To his intellectual dialectic there was, so to speak, a constant emotional corollary. Yet, strikingly enough, he made no attempt at the philosophic poem which he so much desired to be written, and seemed so abundantly qualified to write; he contented himself with urging the much less appropriately gifted Wordsworth to the task. Why did he thus draw back? It is not enough to whisper the word 'laudanum': very few of the problems of Coleridge are explained by that easy word. It is more relevant to make clear to ourselves what Coleridge meant by 'a philosophical poem.' In a remarkable letter to Wordsworth he expounded his idea of what such a poem should be.

'I supposed you first to have meditated the faculties of man in the abstract, in their correspondence with his sphere of action, and first in feeling, touch, and taste, then in the eye, and last in the ear, – to have laid a solid and immovable foundation for the edifice by removing the sandy sophisms of Locke, and the mechanic dogmatists, and demonstrating that the senses were living growths and developments of the mind and spirit, in a much juster as well as higher sense, than the mind can be said to be formed by the senses. Next I understood that you would take the human race in the concrete, have exploded the absurd notion of Pope's *Essay on Man*, Darwin and all the countless believers even (strange to say) among Christians of man's having progressed from an ourang-outang state – so contrary to all history, to all religion, nay to all possibility – to have affirmed a Fall in some sense, as a fact, the possibility of which cannot be understood from the nature of the will, but the reality of which is attested by experience and conscience. Fallen men contemplated in the different ages of the world, and in the different states – savage, barbarous, civilized, the lonely cot or borderer's wigwam, the village, the manufacturing town, seaport, city, universities, and, not disguising the sore evils under which the whole creation groans, to point out, however, a manifest scheme of redemption, of reconciliation with this enmity with Nature – what are the obstacles, the *Antichrist* that must be and already is – and to conclude by a grand didactic swell on the necessary identity of a true philosophy with a true religion, agreeing in the results and differing only as the analytic and synthetic process, as discursive from intuitive, the former chiefly useful in perfecting the latter; in short the necessity for a general evolution in the modes of developing and disciplining the human mind by the substitution of life and intelligence (considered in its different powers from the plant up to that state in which the difference of degree becomes a new kind [man, self-consciousness], but yet not by essential opposition) for the philosophy of mechanism which, in everything that is most worthy of the human intellect, strikes *Death*, and cheats itself by mistaking clear images for distinct conceptions, and which idly demands conceptions where intuitions alone are possible or adequate to the majesty of Truth. In short, facts elevated into theory – theory into laws – and laws into living and intelligent powers – true idealism necessarily perfecting itself in realism, realism refining itself into idealism.'

If we set aside the initial 'demonstration' of the absurdity of the sensationalist psychology which Coleridge demands, we see that the rest of the contemplated poem deals with man 'in the concrete.' The philosophical phases are simple. First, a Fall 'in some sense' would be affirmed on the evidence of experience and conscience; second, the way would be pointed to 'a manifest scheme of redemption,' which, significantly, is equivalent to 'a reconciliation of this enmity with Nature'; and third, nothing less than a revolution in philosophy itself is to be proclaimed – 'intuitions alone are adequate to the majesty of Truth."

In order fully to grasp Coleridge's intention we need to call in aid other passages in his writings. His conception of the 'Fall in some sense' is illuminated by his words in an appendix to *Lay Sermons*. 'The soul, regarding Nature, seems to say to herself: "From this state hast *thou* fallen! Such shouldst thou still become, thyself all permeable to a higher power." ' And again, 'What the plant is – by an act not its own and unconsciously, that thou must make thyself to become.' The 'manifest scheme of redemption' thus consists in the conscious achievement of a condition of pure spontaneity, in which state man should be so completely obedient to and expressive of Life as the rest of organic Nature appears to be. We may suppose that this belief, which recalls certain of the sayings of Jesus, was reached by experience and intuition; and that it is itself an example of that superiority of intuition to conception which the whole poem was to establish. This process of intuition applied to living nature is what Coleridge calls 'Reason,' and, like Goethe, resolutely distinguishes from understanding. Indeed, Goethe's words to Eckermann provide the aptest commentary on Coleridge's thought:

'The Godhead is effective in the living and not in the dead, in the becoming and changing, not in the become and set-fast; and, therefore, similarly, the Reason is concerned only to strive towards the divine through the becoming and the living, and the Understanding only to make use of the become and the set-fast.'

Finally, with the identification of realism and idealism at the end of Coleridge's letter, we may compare his conviction that Nature is 'a symbol of the ideas of reason established in the truth of things'; and that 'a symbol is consubstantial with the truth of which it is the conductor.' So, 'the language of Nature is a subordinate Logos, that was in the beginning, and was with the thing it represented, and was the thing it represented.'

Thus we may describe the theme of Coleridge's philosophic poem as the supersession of intelligence, by intuition; of understanding, by reason. This process, achieved in the individual man, was redemption; by it man became one with Nature, for the spark of intuitive Reason is kindled in him by a contemplation of Nature. The conflict of emotion and thought within himself is resolved, and his consciousness becomes as it were organically whole. This reintegrated consciousness has an immediate apprehension of Truth which is not abstract or ideal, but concrete and real. Nature *is* the Truth; and as man, by the attainment of Reason in himself, is reconciled with Nature, so he himself becomes part of the Truth – 'all permeable to a higher power.'

The doctrine may seem difficult, or at least difficult to distinguish from a sort of Rousseauism. With Rousseauism it has little in common, though it has affinities to Rousseau. But it is, certain nuances of terminology apart, almost exactly identical with Goethe's philosophy; it is, again, very intimately connected with Keats's quite independent thinking, as will be apparent to anyone who studies, with the care which it demands, Keats's famous letter on 'the Vale of

Soul-making.' But the point for immediate emphasis is that this philosophy of Coleridge's is, like the related philosophies of Goethe and Keats, the philosophy of a poet. That is not to say it is inferior to the philosophy of a philosopher – I myself am convinced of the contrary – but it is profoundly different. For the true poet, the man 'gifted with more than ordinary organic sensibility,' ſtarts with an ineradicable faith in intuition. The faith may be unconscious, and very often it is never brought into the full light of consciousness; but the faith is there. The poet cannot help believing in intuition: he has it; and he is a poet because he has it. But all these three men – Coleridge, Goethe and Keats – possessed besides their native poetic gift very great intellectual power, by which they were enabled to make the workings of their own mind diſtinct to themselves and to contemplate the nature of that intuitive faculty which was their birthright. Essentially, their philosophies are a reasoned juſtification of their own poetic processes of mind. Abſtract conceptual thinking seemed to them always a mere clumsy subſtitute for a finer method of attaining truth of which they had actual experience.

Inevitably there muſt, to the philosopher, appear to be something paradoxical, if not wholly intangible, in this philosophy of poets; and that is the reason why the thinking of these three great men (even of Goethe) has never received any serious attention from professional philosophers. To follow their arguments a certain capacity for the sideways glance is required. For here are men who, though certainly not inferior to the average philosopher in the faculty of discursive thinking, possessed another gift besides, to which they attached infinitely more importance, and which had and was bound to have, a very potent influence on their abſtract thinking. Though capable of abſtract thinking they were unable to *believe* in it as an inſtrument for attaining truth; for the simple reason that the divorce between the abstract and the concrete from which discourse takes its rise was overcome by their own peculiar faculty of intuition. The distinction between universal and particular could never be to them a distinction of the real, but only a distinction – and to them in their highest moments an unnecessary one – imposed upon the real. For them the particular *was* the universal, the real *was* the ideal. The identification may be disconcerting to the philosopher, but he ought to reckon with the fact that there is a kind of mind, and a very powerful kind of mind, to which that identification is necessary and inevitable – the unconscious beginning and the conscious end of thinking.

One may get a pretty clear glimpse of the process of poetic thinking by reading Goethe's account of his reconciliation with Schiller, who had been infected with Kantian idealism. The dispute between the two men – did Goethe's drawing of a typical plant represent an 'idea' or an 'experience'? – touched the centre of the problem. The dispute, it is true, was a dispute between two poets; but, in reality, it was a dispute between the purest type of poetic mind, with a reasoned and justified awareness of its own peculiar powers, and one less pure. Schiller combined – and in this he was very like Shelley – an impulsive, undisciplined poetic fluency, with an acquired philosophy. There was a *liaison* of discordant elements. Goethe, on the contrary, was *totus, teres atque rotundus*. And probably it was Schiller he had in mind when he wrote:

'There is a great difference between a poet who seeks the particular for the sake of the universal, and one who seeks the universal in the particular. The former method breeds Allegory, where the particular is used only as an example, an instance, of the universal: but the latter is the true method of poetry. It expresses a particular without a thought of or a reference to the universal. But whoever has a living grasp of this particular grasps the universal with it, knowing it either not at all, or only long afterwards.'

It reminds one, very distinctly, of the letter Keats wrote to Shelley in August, 1820, in acknowledgment of a copy of *The Cenci*.

'There is only one part of it I can judge of – the poetry and dramatic effect, which by many spirits now-a-days is considered the Mammon. A modern work, it is said, must have a purpose, which may be the God. An artist must serve Mammon; he must have "self-concentration" – selfishness, perhaps. You, I am sure, will forgive me for sincerely remarking that you might curb your magnanimity and be more of an artist, and load every rift of your subject with ore.'

One further sentence from Goethe's letters to Schiller will make clear the relation of thought between the two statements. 'The non-poet, just as much as the poet, can be moved by a poetical idea, but he cannot transfer it *into an object*, he cannot express it with a claim to inevitability.' The power, the universality, of poetry lies in its concreteness. The true poet's unremitting insistence upon particularity which seems to the uncomprehending eye the service of Mammon, is to the discerning vision his own peculiar and inimitable service to God, to 'that subordinate Logos' of Nature – to repeat Coleridge's characteristic phrase – 'which was with the thing it represented and was the thing it represented.'

Of course, it is evident that the most abstract and apparently logical of these statements is largely metaphorical. When Goethe insists that the true poet expresses a particular, and that whoever grasps this particular grasps the universal also with it, he is not speaking of the same universals and particulars as the logician. The man who grasps the particular person delineated by a dramatic poet, or the particular emotion expressed by a lyrical poet, cannot be said in either case to comprehend a logical universal.[1] Something other than a concept is grasped, and another faculty than conceptual thinking is at work. The universals of poetry are not concepts, nor have they conceptual equivalents; Goethe was perfectly clear about that. What he was really saying is that in the true poetic activity of mind the logical distinction between particulars and universals is ignored because it is invalid for that activity of mind. In poetry, *quâ* poetry, there are neither particulars nor universals, abstracts nor concretes.

That is to say that, in the very method of poetry, a metaphysic is implicit. This was the metaphysic which Coleridge wished Wordsworth to make explicit in his 'great philosophical poem,' the scheme of which he outlined in his letter. Yet Wordsworth did not write it, and Coleridge himself made no attempt. What was the reason for the failure?

We must remember that Wordsworth did make a beginning and that Coleridge was once enthusiastic over it. It was 'The Prelude.' We may suppose that Coleridge believed this was the right way to begin, namely, with an account of 'the growth of the poet's mind.' The poet would then show how the faculty of poetic thought came to be what

[1] What he grasps might well be called an 'essence.' By so calling it we should adopt the terminology independently employed in recent times, by the two subtlest and most satisfying of modern esthetic thinkers – George Santayana and Marcel Proust. There is a real and important distinction between an 'essence' and a 'universal,' which was well and truly made by Aristotle and the Schoolmen, but has been ignored by modern logic.

it was, and how intuition, unconsciously active from child-hood, came consciously to claim for itself the supreme posi-tion in the poet's mind. This was possible; this to a considerable extent Wordsworth actually did. But what then? Was not something very like a paradox imminent?

For if the poet was indeed the person he claimed to be, who by his intuition apprehended the truth, manifest where alone it could be manifest, in the infinite particularity of the universe, why trouble to explain what must in the nature of the case be either self-evident or not evident at all? Why not simply pursue his own natural task of making poetry in which the universality of the particular, the ideality of the real, should be made plain to those capable of seeing? What indeed was the purpose of a specifically philosophic poem, seeing that all true poetry – all poetry written according to Goethe's 'true poetic method' – contained, implicit in itself, a philosophy superior to all others? And, finally, how could such a philosophical poem be written, seeing that this true philosophy, proceeding from particular to particular, to in-tuition from intuition, was, by hypothesis, incapable of being fully embodied in anything but non-philosophical poetry? Whether or not Coleridge ever presented this diffi-culty to himself in direct connection with his demand for a philosophical poem, that he recognized it clearly enough in other contexts is evident from the nature of his praise of Shakespeare, whom he holds up constantly and with un-varying conviction, and not in a figurative sense, as the supreme philosopher.

In fact, Coleridge's position, stated in the simplest terms, was that the purest poetry was the purest philosophy. He had infinite difficulty in stating this in an intelligible form, because by definition a philosophy which proceeds from in-tuition to intuition is incapable of being apprehended save by intuition; and he was, moreover, involved in the impos-

sible task of trying to find a conceptual language for processes of mind which were not conceptual at all. For this
reason he has been, naturally but quite unwarrantably,
accused of confusing poetic with conceptual thought in his
criticism. He knew perfectly well – no man better – the difference between intuitive and discursive thinking; but he
was compelled by the nature of his attempt continually to
have recourse to clumsy intellectual equivalents for his intuitive processes. Thus when he describes Shakespeare's
method as 'the observation of a mind, which having formed
a theory and a system upon its own nature, remarks all
things that are examples of its truth, and, above all, enabling
it to convey the truths of philosophy as mere effects derived
from what we may call the outward watchings of life,' the
'theory,' the 'system,' the 'philosophy' of which he speaks
are not at all what the ordinary metaphysician would understand by such words. Coleridge is trying to find utterance
for a thought which haunted him. We might gather together
from his writings a dozen other efforts to declare it. One
shall suffice. 'It was Shakespeare's prerogative to have the
universal which is potentially in each particular, opened out
to him, the *homo generalis*, not as an abstraction from observation of a variety of men, but as the substance capable
of endless modifications.' The power which Coleridge is
attributing to Shakespeare is precisely the same as that
which Goethe also made frequent efforts to distinguish; the
anschauliche Urteilskraft, the *exakte sinnliche Phantasie* –
the power precisely of seeing the universal in the particular,
of penetrating by intuition and self-knowledge into the
creative force which is, and is recognized in, its differentiations.

The same inherent difficulty of language which has led to
Coleridge's thinking being dismissed as transcendental and
mystical must inevitably have recurred in an avowedly

philosophic poem. It would have been well enough if Coleridge's mind had been inflamed by an alien system of philosophy; but that was impossible. He was a poet, with the poetic experience; the only philosophy that could satisfy him was the philosophy which set poetry in the supreme position which, he was intellectually convinced, it rightly occupied. The only way to express that philosophy was to practise it, and the only way to practise it was to be simply a creative poet.

It may be said that Coleridge's failure was the failure of a particular man, and that we must not draw a general conclusion from it. The objection is only plausible if we are prepared to challenge the truth of Coleridge's thought upon the nature of poetry. This, I think, is possible only to those who do not understand it. Therefore Coleridge's failure, and Wordsworth's, is really prophetic of the failure of all serious philosophical poetry in future. The attempt will be possible only to a poet who is less of a poet and less of a philosopher than he ought to be; it is condemned beforehand to second-rateness. Philosophical poetry can never again be great with the greatness of Lucretius or Dante because, whenever a poet appears with a comparable poetic gift and a comparable 'depth and energy of thought,' his intellectual power will be applied, as the intellectual power of Coleridge and Goethe and Keats was applied, to the justification of his own specifically poetic processes of mind.

The essential condition of philosophical poetry is that the poet should believe that there is a faculty of mind superior to the poetic; that was possible for Dante, tremendous poet though he was; but since Shakespeare lived and wrote it is not possible. Shakespeare created a new order of values, independent of the great mediæval Christian tradition, yet spiritual through and through; a system of values, so far as we can see, completely divorced from any faith in immor-

tality or after-justice, compatible, indeed, with a real agnosticism, yet in the height and breadth of word profoundly
religious. This system of values – which seems to us to have
been produced like a creation of nature – makes a deep and
undiminished appeal to us; generation after generation of
men have meditated upon it, only to discover that this system
of values is not a system at all. It satisfies, yet it cannot
be analysed. The order is there, but it is the inscrutable
order of organic life. And this extraordinary thing was produced by the poetic spirit, working free and autonomous,
by a poet who trusted, as no poet had done before or has
done since, his own poetic genius.

The poets who, since Shakespeare, have been capable of
philosophic poetry have had Shakespeare before them to
show them what philosophic poetry can be. Perhaps, without his works before them, Goethe and Coleridge and Keats
might not have reached the conclusions and certainties they
did reach. Certainly no poets have ever been deeper and
more understanding students of Shakespeare than these;
and it is impossible that any poet of real stature who comes
after them should not see Shakespeare largely through their
eyes, and approach him by the road which their genius
opened. The poet who follows them has no choice; he must
realize that there is a profounder truth in Shakespeare than
is contained in any system of philosophy, and that the poet
becomes a truly philosophical poet, not by taking a philosophy for his subject-matter or his inspiration, but by becoming wholly that which he potentially is – a revealer of
the real. To the degree to which he follows the true method
of poetry the problems of philosophy cease to exist for
him.

What, then – to return to the first cause of these reflections – can the prospect of an intellectual reconciliation of
the conceptions of Time and Eternity from which Sir Henry

Newbolt expects so much, offer to a poet for whom the particular is, in fact, the universal? The reconciliation will be meaningless to him, because the divorce has never taken place. The things of time, the real world, truly seen, are to the poet completely significant. There is nothing higher than complete significance. The conception of an eternity, or of an eternal reality, different from the temporal, springs only from a sense of a partial or mutilated significance in the actual.

It is precisely this sense, which may be natural to man – *l'ennui commun à toute creature bien née*, as Marguerite of Navarre described it – which the great poet overcomes within himself. He does not judge experience; he submits himself to it: and he finds that the reality which presented itself to his intellectual consciousness as imperfect is received in a quite different way by the totality of his being. By the impact of that seemingly imperfect reality upon him, something is created in himself which declares that it is perfect. He recognizes the inevitability and beauty of his own painful experience, and with the same act of recognition bows himself to the inevitability and beauty of the things that are. Time is not to him a discordant and corrupting element; it is but a word for an aspect of the secret force of life itself, for the effective Godhead which, as Goethe said, is 'effective in the living and not in the dead.' Time is but the intellectual abstraction of that reality which he knows immediately in himself as life – the pulse of his being. To shrink from Time is to shrink from Life itself.

That is not to say that poets have not given voice to the anguish of the temporal – many have – nor that the poets who have done so are not poets. The contention is that, in so far as they remain in that predicament, they are incomplete and partial poets, who, through some defect of power, cannot make their rightful inheritance their own. The sense of exile is not the mark of major, but of minor, poetry; its persistence betokens a failure in poetic energy, an impotence to realize, or to be loyal to, the poetic nature. It is true that the note is recurrent in much of the poetry that is most generally admired; but that is because this emotion of exile is itself the most widespread in human hearts. The poetry of dream, in ages such as ours at least, finds a more ready response than the poetry of reality. But a growing nature quickly tires of it; it has no substance, it cannot satisfy. And to suppose it will gain substance by embracing a recondite philosophical notion of the ultimate convergence of Time and Eternity is an illusion. The anguish of the temporal will not be assuaged either in the poet who feels and communicates it, or the readers who respond to it, by any shadowy promise that in the dim and distant future men will feel it no more. The demand which the human soul makes is for satisfaction here and now; men's eyes must *see* their salvation.

It is this visible salvation, if the phrase may be forgiven, that great poetry does offer. It faces the real, it extenuates nothing, shrinks from nothing; it gives us life as it is. And we discover that we can desire nothing more perfect, for we can conceive nothing more perfect to desire. That seems miracle enough, yet that alone will not suffice. For when the influence of the great poet's alchemy has passed from us, a question remains. If that which is possesses this perfection, then why struggle to achieve a better condition? This doubt often eats at the hearts of those religious souls who are in some degree responsive to the achievements of great poetry. It is the cause of that frequent revulsion in those who ponder the idea rather than experience the attitude of mind which often is called Pantheism. The great poet, no doubt, is a Pantheist, but he is primarily a poet. The Pantheism which, held as an intellectual creed, might engender a Stoic resignation is, as a poetic reality, a thing of potency – a *sursum corda*. For the poet's revelation of the perfection of what is kindles in our souls the desire to be able, with unaided vision, to see the perfection for ourselves.

POETRY AND RELIGION

THERE are many reasons why I find Mr. Santayana the most stimulating of living philosophers. The chief of them is that his philosophy is the expression of a real attitude to life; it is capable of being lived – the *life* of reason. It is therefore also capable of being expressed in terms congruous with itself. The exquisite care which Mr. Santayana gives to the writing of a paragraph is an act of loyalty to his own metaphysic: there is a necessity of his own fastidiousness in his vision of the sum of things. One cannot take seriously a philosophy of the beautiful that is written with a barge-pole.

It is true, I do not find Mr. Santayana's philosophy wholly congenial. But what of that? I seek in it not a creed, but a contemplation: and completeness of achievement is always satisfying. To disagree with Mr. Santayana is an incessant challenge to one's own convictions and one's own powers: for he is a thinker whom it is quite impossible to *dismiss*. Yet how many clever thinkers may be simply ignored! Indeed, it is almost a law that a philosopher's propensity to beg the main question is in direct proportion to his intellectual subtlety – a law to which Mr. Santayana is, in these days, one conspicuous and proving exception. It is because he is aware of more data, because he has a more comprehensive view of what is to be accounted for, because his powers of *reason* are by a whole degree more acute than those of his fellow-philosophers that he is neglected by them. Read any compendium of modern philosophy; it is ten to one you will look in vain for an account of Santayana – even for his name. Philosophers in blinkers find him invisible.

He has been recognized by the literary critics: first, because they sometimes know a writer when they see one;

secondly, because he has shown himself deeper in the theory and more expert in the practice of literary criticism than any contemporary. He *comprehends* his subject; he knows where it belongs; and he places it there with the swift and easy gesture of a woman arranging a lovely vase in a lovely room of a lovely house. But the room is the world of literature and the house the universe of reason. With such a certainty you disagree, at your peril, knowing that if you insist on moving the vase the responsibility of creating another room and another house is upon you.

To be perpetually alive to implication and perspective is the main reward of reading Santayana – an almost inestimable reward in these curious days. Consider the following on 'Poetry and Religion.'

'Poetry is metrical and euphuistic discourse, expressing thought which is both sensuous and ideal. Such is poetry as a literary form; but if we drop the limitation as to verbal expression, and think of poetry as that subtle fire and inward light which seems to shine through the world and to touch the images in our minds with an ineffable beauty, then poetry is a momentary harmony in the soul amid stagnation or conflict – a glimpse of the divine and an incitation to a religious life. Religion is poetry become the guide of life, poetry substituted for science, or supervening upon it as an approach to the highest reality. Poetry is religion allowed to drift, left without points of application in conduct and without expression in worship and dogma; it is religion without practical efficacy and without metaphysical illusion.'

I do not believe it is possible to carry the rational analysis of poetry deeper than that. To pass beyond that point you must take a mortal leap which will land you beyond philosophy, perhaps into another life than the life of reason. Moreover, Santayana's statement, considered as applying to poetry as a whole, is true. Poetry exists chiefly in a state of imperfection: for the most part the harmony in the soul of the poet out of which it is created, and the harmony in the soul of the reader which it creates, are alike momentary and evanescent. There seems, indeed, no link between this glimpse of the divine and men's actions in the world: nor is there generally more than a precarious connection between what a poet is and what he utters.

For this reason the most obviously impressive of great poetry is that which is, so to say, ancillary to religion; poetry wherein the poet accepts the religious formulation of the divine reality he apprehends, and identifies the unity of which he is conscious with the God of the religion in which he believes. Then the connection between poetry, religion and conduct is indeed organic. But that identification is possible only at periods when religious belief is vivid and unquestioned. In those periods it is spontaneous. It was not by the compulsion of a theocracy that in the Middle Ages art and religion were identical: the mediæval artist, the mediæval thinker, was not conscious of constraint: he could not surmise that the ultimate reality of which he was conscious might be other than the God in whom he believed: because he did believe in God.

It is no use looking back with envy to the Middle Ages. The thing is gone: we are different. Slowly at first, now ever more swiftly, the unity of the European consciousness has disintegrated. It will disintegrate still more, and still more swiftly, because men do not believe in God, in the churches or out of them. The extraordinary thing is that so many excellent people believe they believe in God, when they have not the faintest idea of what belief means. I should say there are not, in the whole European world to-day, more than a few hundred thousand men who *believe* in a God of any kind. And, by the same token, there are not more than a few hundred thousand men who *disbelieve* in God. The whole Western world is become Laodicean.

Hence the increasing importance of the great solitary souls who belong to the period of disintegration: of whom the chief are poets. In most of them there was the same lack of organic connection between their poetry and their lives as there is in their readers. But one or two were different. Consciously or unconsciously, they understood that their mission was to achieve, in themselves and alone, that unity of being which had been lost through the disintegration of the European consciousness. And they saw that the combination of ideal and sensuous in which the most perfect poetry consists could only be achieved through the attainment of a new condition of knowledge for which the ideal and sensuous were one. In Christian language they had to reach a point from which they could see the universe as the handiwork of God. Of course, they did not express it in those terms: it was the same immediate knowledge, but the frame of reference was no longer Christian.

This complete interpenetration of the ideal and the sensuous – that is, the knowledge and the power to reveal that everything is significant – which is the perfection of poetry, is of a supreme practical efficacy. In order that the poet should realize it, he needs to be changed, to be reborn; in order that we should understand what the poet is saying, we also need to be changed, to be reborn. And poetry in this its highest form has *direct* power: its spiritual significance is so concentrated that it acts upon the receptive soul as that leaven which 'a woman took and hid in three measures of meal.' Poetry at its highest does not *mean* anything, it *is*; it cannot be understood, it can only be received; it is a pure conduit of mysterious and ineffable life into man's being. He, too, becomes touched with significance.

The intimacy of the connection between pure poetry and

religion may appear if we realize the relation – one almost of identity – between the interpenetration of the ideal and the sensuous, which is poetry, and the fundamental Christian conception of the Word made flesh. Accretions apart, the eternal verity of Christianity is that a man was once wholly filled with divine significance: the eternal verity of Jesus's own teaching is that any man may be so filled. And this complete significance the poet attains, often only for a moment of incandescence, but sometimes it becomes his steady and assured possession.

Great poetry is of two kinds, therefore. The one accepts, not passively but actively, a religion that is vitally believed; the reality which the poet apprehends as poet is the God which he apprehends as believer. The poetic and the religious noêsis[1] in Æschylus or Plato or Dante are one and the same. The other kind arises in a period when religious belief is lost. There is no specifically religious noêsis; but there is the poetic faculty. Then the complete interpenetration of the ideal and the sensuous after which the poet unconsciously strives as the highest poetic excellence, intuitively perceived, serves, in the man of supreme genius, as an earnest of a condition to be achieved within himself. The interpenetration of the sensuous and ideal, which he pursues as art, inevitably becomes an ideal of conduct and of life. So through a loyal obedience to the poetic noêsis the full perfection of religious noêsis – the Word made flesh – is re-achieved.

[1] Noesis may be an unknown term to some of my readers: it is Plato's name for the highest kind of knowledge; supra-intellectual and immediate. The word has no equivalent in the English language.

POETRY AND PRAYER

IN France for eighteen months there has been raging an acute literary controversy such as, I fear, would be scarcely possible in this country. It is hard to imagine the Press, in London and the provinces, given over to a heated discussion of the question: What is pure poetry? It is hard to imagine that a summary of such a debate in volume form would run through ten editions in a week in our English book-shops.[1] The idea that poetry is a thing of extreme importance, concerning which it is at least as necessary to make up one's mind as it is concerning the merits of Free Trade and Tariff Reform, will take a few years yet to become acclimatized in these islands. We have the poets: Why think about them?

Not that I dream that captains and corporals of industry, newspaper proprietors and eminent journalists will ever wake up to find themselves passionately interested in poetry. 'There's nothing in it'; and there's an end. But what I should like to be able to impress upon the attention of bishops, priests, deacons, ministers and other apostles of religion in this country is that this significant controversy in France has been inspired and guided by an Abbé of the Roman Catholic Church. No ordinary Abbé, of course; but then there are many Abbés of the Catholic Church in France who are not ordinary – men whose intellectual sympathies, power of thought and faculty of expression make them the equals (sometimes the superiors) of the finest literary intelligences of their own country.

It is strange to me that no famous champion of religion in

[1] *La Poésie Pure; Prière et Poésie*. Par Henri Bremond. 15 francs and 12 francs each. (Paris: Grasset.) The second volume has been translated by Mr. Algar Thorold.

this country has ever had a glimpse of the opportunity offered by the poetic experience as a corroboration of the religious experience. A dangerous corroboration, perhaps, but surely one worth attempting to secure if only as a means of interesting the more cultivated minds in religion once more. For the divorce between religion and culture in this country is painful. In part, I suppose, it is due to the Puritan and Protestant tradition; but more certainly in these latter days to the intellectual quality of many of the men who enter the priesthood or the ministry.

The Abbé Henri Bremond is a member of the French Academy. In October, 1925, at the annual séance publique of the five Academies, he read a lecture entitled 'La Poésie Pure,' wherein, with the purpose of contributing towards a *rapprochment* between literature and religion, he maintained that the specific poetic experience, that is, the experience of the true reader of true poetry, is non-rational: it is, essentially, a mystical experience; and the Abbé concluded by restating the famous sentence of Pater that all the arts aspire to the condition of music. 'No, they all aspire, each by its own proper magical medium – words, notes, colours, lines – they all aspire to the condition of prayer."

With another than M. Bremond I might demur (even violently) to the phrase; but I have read his remarkable *History of Religious Feeling in French Literature*, and I know that to prayer he gives the profoundest meaning: it is nothing less than the means to a perfect communion with that which is mightier than ourselves and beyond our knowledge. In such a sense I do agree that poetry and prayer are allied. Nevertheless, I cannot accept the statement that poetry aspires to the condition of prayer.' It would be truer, in my opinion, and as I shall try to show, to say that prayer aspires to the condition of poetry.

But let us leave the further question aside for the moment,

and suppose that prayer and poetry are parallel and analogous. Then we must make a necessary distinction. Prayer has two meanings. It is the words which are prayed; it is also the condition attained by the soul by their means. 'Our Father' – those two words are a prayer; the condition of soul of the man who can truly say them, while he says them, the condition of simple certainty that there is One, unutterably close, to hear – this is *prayer*. To say that poetry aspires to the condition of prayer may mean either that the perfect poem is a prayer (which is not true) or that the condition of soul created within the man who truly reads a great poem is either identical with, or analogous to, the condition of soul created within the man who truly prays a great prayer.

That these conditions are allied, I do indeed believe; but they are not identical. If we say over to ourselves the two lines –

'Thou still unravished bride of quietness,
        Thou foster-child of silence and slow Time . . .'

a quietness begins straightway to descend upon our souls. The fever and the fret which agitate our waking lives are stilled. By the magic of fourteen words we are become listeners, true listeners, listeners who listen to the silence, and can hear the creative word stirring within its womb, then rising to the lovely gravity of life and death, as that perfect poem moves with labyrinthine simplicity to its triumphant close. At the end, it seems we know, even as we are known.

I believe that every great poem, every great work of literature, whether it be short or long, leaves behind it a sense that can be truly described only by some such words as these. This sense has precisely the same quality of feeling that used to come to me as a boy when I listened to the *Nunc dimittis*. It is not the same feeling, of course: the *Nunc dimittis* aroused in me a feeling, deep and memorable indeed, but only a feeling. A great piece of writing leaves me with knowledge, but the quality of feeling with which this knowledge is pervaded is the same as of old. It is strange, I sometimes think, that it should have been the *Nunc dimittis* that moved me thus, more than twenty years ago, seeing that the words of the chant express more nearly than any others the content of the knowledge which great literature brings. 'Lord, now lettest thou thy servant depart in peace: for mine eyes have seen thy salvation.'

If you care to say that such a condition *is* a condition of prayer, I will not rebel; if you are willing to acknowledge that such an experience is fully the equivalent of the experience of the Christian soul in prayer, I should accept the acknowledgment and rest content. But of course, not even the Abbé Bremond can do that. The poetical experience is always inferior to the religious experience. It must be, of course, for Christian orthodoxy. As M. Bremond writes in a note to his book *Prière et Poésie*:

' "Poetry is not prayer; poetry does not, by its nature, end in prayer," lately wrote Dom G. Aubourg. That is so self-evident that I did not even imagine I could be suspected of doubting it. By its nature, that is so long as it remains poetry, it cannot end in prayer. . . . Dom Aubourg continues excellently: "Poetry is a sign: it is the index of a high faculty within us capable of receiving God, but impotent in itself to apprehend Him." Why is poetry impotent to apprehend God as prayer apprehends Him? Because the smallest prayer worthy of the name, not only the prayer of contemplation, is a supernatural gift of God.'

Whereat I become intransigent. The simple thing would be for me to confess that I am ignorant of the experience of prayer; untouched by the necessary divine grace. That would be simplest, and best. But, unfortunately, it would not be quite honest. I may not know very much about prayer, but I do know a little about mystical experience, in which prayer should culminate.

However, not to lose ourselves in abstractions yet, let us have a poetic fact sharp before our eyes, and vivid in our memory.

> 'Unarm, Eros: the long day's task is done,
> And we must sleep . . . Off, pluck off:
> The seven-fold shield of Ajax cannot keep
> The battery from my heart. O cleave, my sides!
> Heart, once be stronger than thy continent,
> Crack thy frail case! Apace, Eros, apace.
> No more a soldier: bruised pieces, go;
> You have been nobly borne. From me awhile. . . .
> I will o'ertake thee, Cleopatra, and
> Weep for my pardon. So it must be, for now
> All length is torture: since the torch is out,
> Lie down, and stray no farther: now all labour
> Mars what it does; yea, very force entangles
> Itself with strength: seal then, and all is done.
> Eros! – I come, my queen – Eros! – stay for me:
> Where souls do couch on flowers, we'll hand in hand,
> And with our sprightly port make the ghosts gaze:
> Dido and her Æneas shall want troops,
> And all the haunt be ours. Come, Eros, Eros!'

What shall we say of that? Does it aspire to the condition of prayer? Surely not, if that condition is something other than it has attained already. I read it, and am content. Here, I know not how, is truth; here, inseparable from it, is beauty. The beating brain is once more at rest.

No, though I am willing – none more willing – to grant an affinity between the poetic and the religious experience,

I cannot for one moment allow that the poetic experience is a subaltern form of the religious experience. On the contrary, the poetic experience is the perfection of the religious experience. To turn M. Bremond's phrase: it is prayer that aspires to the condition of poetry.

I hesitate, very naturally, to criticize M. Bremond's conception of the mystical experience; nevertheless, I believe that it is imperfect. I am too ignorant of the history of mysticism in the Catholic Church to be able to say whether that aspect or moment of the mystical experience which I think M. Bremond neglects was deliberately banished out of the Church: but it is certainly true that the greatest of all Christian mystics, and the one who most nobly insisted on the neglected element – Meister Eckhart – was condemned (though after his death) for heresy.

In the complete mystical experience there are two phases or moments. There is the ascent into complete communion with the One, or with God, which is commonly supposed to be the end of the mystical path. It is not; the true and perfect mystic only ascends to the One in order to descend once more to the Many with the knowledge of its Oneness to sustain him. This is the doctrine of Plotinus and Dionysius the Areopagite and Meister Eckhart; but far more important even than these great masters of the mystical way, it is the doctrine of Jesus himself. Jesus was the most *perfect* mystic of whom we know, and his doctrine is as crystal-clear as his practice: he went apart to commune with his Father, he returned to live and work in the world of men – and not to live and work among them like a missionary, but to be really of them, brother among brothers, the friend of publicans and harlots, a man who came eating and drinking. His practice is plain as day; so is his doctrine. It was a doctrine of the perfect beauty and divine particularity of the universe, seen and known as the creation of a loving Father's hand.

'Behold the lilies of the field: they toil not, neither do they spin: but Solomon in all his glory was not arrayed like one of these.'

That is the true end of the mystical path. The true mystic, as Meister Eckhart nobly said, is as one who, having looked upon the sun, thenceforward sees the sun in everything. What falls short of this consummation is an imperfect mysticism, and, I believe, a still more imperfect Christianity: a cloistered as opposed to a living virtue, a withdrawal as opposed to an acceptance.

Now the mysticism of descent can find its full expression in two ways alone: in life and in poetry. The poet cannot be truly conceived as a man who, instead of surrendering himself like a real mystic absolutely to the One and being silent, struggles to give voice to his ecstatic experience. The mystical poets of this sort are few, and certainly not very important. The poet, *quâ* poet, is not concerned with the One at all: he is, by nature, concerned with the Many. He actually does see the beauty and significance of real things – at first quite naïvely, and perhaps he may never get beyond the stage of naïvely recording his delights.

> 'And shall I ever bid these joys farewell?
> Yes, I must pass them for a nobler life,
> Where I may find the agony, the strife
> Of human hearts.'

I will not attempt to outline, with a misleading brevity, the evolution of the poet to poetic greatness which I have tried to present in 'Keats and Shakespeare'; but I must insist upon the fundamental difference between the poet and the mystic as he is commonly understood. The mystic is but half-way to the perfect poet (as he is but half-way to the perfect Christian). On the other hand, a complete mysticism and a complete poetry are all but identical. Keats's principle of 'beauty in all things' and Eckhart's vision of 'God in all things' are practically indistinguishable. And, in fact, the complete mystic is, invariably, a great poet.

Jesus was a great poet. It was necessary that he should be. There is no means of uttering the truth he had to utter save through poetry – the living, creative and significant word. For the secret of true religion, or at least of his religion, than which none truer will ever be found, lies simply in the rediscovery of the actual – a rediscovery which can be fully accomplished only through a process of rebirth and reintegration.

This rediscovery of the actual is the poet's final mission. To achieve it completely the same process of inward reintegration is necessary. Only harmony within can respond to the harmony without: organic wholeness to organic wholeness. Many poets – and great ones – fail in the attempt. They lack courage, they lack humility, they lack honesty; and the plenitude of youth ends in the desiccation of age. They have shrunk from the lonely and painful task of being loyal to their experience. Who are we to accuse them for failing? But we know that there are others who have not failed, and because they have not failed, the revelation of the actual that their words contain will never fail. The others will amuse and delight; they may throw gleams of illumination upon the chaos of experience, but the gleams will be fitful: the light of the great ones is steady, it spreads into the dark places, and suffuses pain and disaster.

It is not poetry that aspires to the condition of prayer, therefore, but prayer to the condition of poetry. There will be, I am sure, no reconciliation between literature and religion unless this be accepted. We are not going back to religion; we are going forward to it. This is a time when our creativeness is critical; when many minds in many realms are at work to discover the implications of their own real

217

experience. They know that they are religious; they know that the religion of to-day has no *meaning* for them; they know that the words that have meaning for them are the words of the poets.[1] In them alone they find that rediscovery of the actual which, I believe, will be the religion of the future – the knowledge that we are and the world is. There is no answer to the riddle of the world, save to be able to see the world.

It may be long before this religion of simple experience will take hold of many minds. Those who can understand it, it will satisfy. But to those who feel that it gives them nothing to hold on to, we can only reply that it is the having nothing to hold on to, nothing that can be held on to, that will be the strength of the future. It is their very being that men will live by, and living by that, they will live by the being of that which is not themselves.

For these dark sayings I am sorry. I would not hazard them but that I dread compromise. I am for ever being embarrassed by those who say to me, But how near you are to this religion, or to that! And, indeed, I am very near. But also very far away. It is as though I were near every religion, before it *is* a religion, before formula and creed and worship: but so soon as it is a religion I am by the whole breadth of a spiritual universe removed from it. The religion that can become *a* religion is, by that very fact, quite alien to my way of thought.

P.S. – In the foregoing, for the clearer statement of the essential point, I have excluded from consideration the repetitive-rhythmical, incantatory element in poetry, which distinguishes the genus verse from the genus prose in the large species of true *poiēsis*. By insisting upon this incan-

[1] I use the word, of course, in the largest sense. Tchehov is our greatest modern poet.

tatory element a more specious case for the identity of poetry and prayer can be produced; but it is based on a confusion of accidents with essentials. What is essential to poetry – its quiddity – is an apprehension of the real in its concreteness, the real of direct, unabstracted, pure experience. The poet is distinguished from other men in that he is capable of uttering this experience without the intermediary of the falsifying though necessary concept.

THOUGHTS ON PANTHEISM

In his comment upon Goethe's rhapsody on Nature which he translated, Thomas Henry Huxley spoke of those who 'dislike Pantheism almost as much as I do.'[1] The sentiment is unexpected; it seems discordant with Huxley's enthusiasm for Goethe's poem, which both Goethe and Huxley agreed in finding more than a little Pantheistic. The fact of the matter is, I suppose, that Huxley liked Goethe's Pantheism – the Rhapsody in Nature had been, he said, 'an inspiration to him from his youth up' – and disliked other brands.

I cannot say for certain; but I fancy that at the time when Huxley was writing (1869) the Wordsworthian Pantheism counted many adherents in this country. *The Prelude* had been published only nineteen years before, and in *The Prelude* Wordsworth had not only given a first-hand account of romantic Pantheism, but, with a little careful manipulation, had made smooth the path from romantic Pantheism to Orthodoxy. Probably Huxley disliked the reconciliation extremely. *The Prelude*, as Professor de Selincourt has just revealed by printing the original side by side with the published version, is a dishonest poem. Wordsworth had no right, and must have known he had no right, to modify his statements of belief to suit his subsequent orthodoxy, and yet present them to an unsuspecting public as the beliefs held by him in his young maturity. An unpleasant savour of hypocrisy emanates from the poem.

I may be quite wrong in ascribing Huxley's avowed dislike of Pantheism to a dislike of Wordsworthianism. But it gives a probable explanation of something that needs ex-

[1] I have reprinted at the end of this volume Huxley's translation of the poem.

plaining; for it is plain that Huxley did not dislike Pantheism as such. On the contrary, he had adopted Goethe's Pantheistic rhapsody as his own credo. Not only had it been an inspiration to him all his life, but it would, he thought, prove to be a final, because poetic, statement of the truth.

Part of the trouble lies in the fact that Pantheism is a vague word; moreover, it is generally a term of abuse. I cannot recall an instance of a man of mark saying boldly and gladly, 'I am a Pantheist.' The epithet will be flung at him surely enough, without his running to meet it. And yet most men of mark, since the Renaissance, have been Pantheists of some sort or other. They could not help it; for there is no other refuge for the mind which refuses both Christian orthodoxy and mere rationalistic mechanism. *Quartum non datur.*

That seems to me clear; and it seems clear also that the normal movement of the modern mind which troubles at all over these things is, first, rebellion against orthodoxy, then a recoil from mechanism, and finally an advance into 'some sort of Pantheism.' Champions of orthodoxy would add a fourth and final phase – return to orthodoxy. In that I do not believe. It has happened – it happened to Wordsworth – it will happen again; but it happens, I believe, only to tired and broken men.

Of such tired and broken men there will always be a few; for Pantheism, if truly held, must make exacting demands upon the holder. To say to oneself, and mean it, that whatever is, is best, requires an incessant effort of self-discipline. To those who know nothing of it Pantheism seems an easy creed, a flowery path that leads to the everlasting bonfire. But, in fact, it could be said of it more truly than of most orthodoxies that 'Narrow is the gate and strait is the way: and few there be that find it.' For Pantheism, like charity, begins at home; it means, first of all, an acceptance of one's own experience. That is easy enough, if your experience has been pleasant; but in that case you do not need and generally do not seek any religion. And, after all, it is astonishing to find how pleasant is the experience of many men. They have a mysterious faculty of shutting out unpleasant experience: nothing short of a piece of shrapnel in their own belly will convince them that there is such a thing as pain in the world. They shut their eyes to it, and lo! it is not. Pantheism is not for these happy ones, but for the less fortunate, who are compelled to try their religion by their experience. They rebel against orthodoxy because their minds cannot reconcile the pain of the world with the omnipotence of a personal and loving God. They have 'proved upon their pulses that the world is full of heartbreak, misery, pain and oppression'; upon their pulses also must be proved the reality of a personal and loving God.

I do not say it cannot be done; I believe, on the contrary, that it has been done: but I do not believe it will be done again, save by minds more simple than the rest. The personality and the love of God are, for the grown mind, only metaphors. In the history of religion one metaphor succeeds another, because it is truer than the one which went before. But we have reached a point when we know that our metaphors are only metaphors: we can no longer mistake them for the reality.

The reality: but what is the reality? It is the religious experience. But here is the root of the trouble, the source of unending confusions. For the religious experience, with its manifold differences in degree, is in all its degrees a thing *sui generis*, unique and incommensurable. The experience, I believe, has remained substantially the same for many generations of men; if it has evolved and changed, it has evolved and changed no more than the rest of the higher faculties of man – that is, very little, within the period of recorded history. But the interpretation of the experience has changed. It is over the interpretations of the experience, not over the experience itself, that most of our significant religious controversy rages – over the name, not over the thing.

The religious experience cannot, without risk of misleading oneself and others, be described as an experience of the existence of God. The existence of God is rather a deduction from the religious experience. The religious experience is the primary reality. What a man will deduce from it, how he will interpret it, must obviously depend upon his previous habit of mind. If the concept of a personal God has been an integral part of his life – a necessary hypothesis of his understanding, an instinctive assumption in his conduct – then, evidently, the religious experience will be a first-hand confirmation of his conscious thoughts and instinctive assumptions concerning the existence of a personal God. But if these conscious thoughts and instinctive assumptions are absent, if his mind has become a *tabula rasa* on the question of God, then the religious experience will remain primary; it will itself prescribe the limits beyond which interpretation and deduction must not go.

If we wish to discover for ourselves the reality of religion, it is right that our minds should be such a *tabula rasa*: for when we examine the history of religions, we find that their traditions consist of ritual, which is a time-approved method of making the human mind susceptible to the religious experience, and theology, which is a system of deductions from the religious experience. One is a practical, the other a theoretical, organization of the religious experience. Both alike derive their force and virtue from the experience; both alike beg the question when they seek to prescribe the occasion and define the significance of the experience. It is the

223

experience, not they, which is primary and ultimate. It is the religious experience, simple, single, uncontaminated by preconception or interpretation, that must be examined if we are to come near to the reality of religion.

But at this point grave difficulties arise: for most men who have some acquaintance with the religious experience have reached it through precisely these preconceptions, so that their religious experience and their previous religious conceptions are inextricably confused. On the other hand, most of those who profess to conduct an unbiased examination into religious experience – the professional psychologists – do not know what the religious experience is. They are looking for something which they could not recognize if they found it. So they go to the peculiar and abnormal phenomena of religious experience – such as mystical trance and ecstasy – simply because these are well marked: they fail to see that precisely this abnormality renders these mystical phenomena of singularly little value for the valuation of religious experience.

For the religious experience is not, in the usual sense of the word, abnormal. The two greatest religious innovators of whom we know – Jesus and the Buddha – are bewildering chiefly by their sanity. Even to call them mystics is to misrepresent them. The religious experience which determined their lives was plainly much more in the nature of a strangely direct and simple realization of some obvious yet universally forgotten fact of life than of a blinding and catastrophic revelation. From their teaching we should unhesitatingly conclude that the religious experience which was decisive with them was abnormal only by its infrequence, not by its nature.

The religious experience is really a very simple thing. Like all other simple things it is exceedingly difficult to describe, and quite impossible to define. Actually, it is the experience of the creation of a new self, together with an (also experienced) consequence or corollary – an immense simplification of life. It is the coming of a moment to a man who has done his utmost to open his heart and mind faithfully to all experience when he realizes that all his bitterest sufferings, his defeats and dismays, have been for a purpose. He sees, quite simply, that there is an order and a harmony in the world, and he is become a conscious part of it. Therefore, he is what he was not; and in comparison with his new being, his former being seems merely a kind of non-existence. Then his consciousness of self was almost wholly a consciousness of discord; now it has become a consciousness of harmony. It is as though the weary, wind-battered plant had miraculously put forth a flower.

A small thing, it may seem, from which to deduce the tremendous assertion that God exists. A small thing, no doubt, and yet it may be doubted whether the greatest men of God have really had more to go upon. A grain of mustard seed is very potent, as the parable says. The question rather is whether a seed so small, yet so potentially vast, can be kept true to its own nature, and prevented from running riot into the strange luxuriance of ritual and theology.

There is no answering the question. Humanity shows no visible sign of having outgrown its morbid appetite for knowledge of the unknowable; men are only a little less credulous than they were five hundred years ago. And even those who can scarcely be taxed with credulity seem equally far from having learned the humane wisdom of not seeking to know too much. There is a point of focus for the understanding of things: if we come short of it the distance is vague and blurred, if we go beyond it, we cannot see what is in front of our noses. And we can only know the point by finding it. Once we have found it, all goes well.

Such a point of focus is given by the primary religious

experience, so long as it is maintained in its purity, and does not suffer 'a sea-change into something rich and strange.' Its real richness is in its simplicity; it has nothing to gain and everything to lose by putting on purple and fine linen. To be convinced, once for all by immediate and irrefragable experience, by experience which is not solitary and abnormal but can be renewed at every moment of every day, that life is not in vain, is enough. Those who have it would not exchange their seed of certainty against more glorious consolations. The more glorious consolations are meaningless to them; their simple one means much.

Nor do they regret those gorgeous consolations. Desire of them vanished long ago. They banished them because of their imperious need to harmonize experience. For they belong to a sort of men who cannot live in a condition wherein their right hand must ignore the doings of their left. They were born with the belief that experience must be harmonious. A strange belief to be born with, for life seemed busy from the first in teaching them that it was discordant. Still the dim faith endured: somehow the discords could be, somehow they must be, resolved. And the only possible way by which a resolution might be found was by loyalty to experience. Only experience would harmonize experience. A loving and a personal God, to accord with whom these glorious consolations were imagined, was denied by experience. Therefore he was banished, never to return. And he will not return to them. The purpose of which they are conscious is not the purpose of a loving and a personal God. With such metaphors they would 'do him wrong, being so majestical.'

They understand the metaphors, and the necessity of them in times past; but they need them no longer. If 'the love of God passeth all understanding,' as it does, let it not be called love any more, even for the sake of fellowship.

Much may be justly sacrificed for the commonweal; but not so much as this. The possible, the inevitable misunderstandings are too great. For some the love of God was manifest in the death in agony of Jesus, with his last hope extinguished; for others it needs the addition of a vicarious atonement and a glorious resurrection, to make the life of Jesus a revelation of God's love. The abysm between these two conceptions must not be bridged – much less should it be bridged by a single word. That is to make a mockery of unity and truth alike.

The only record of the nature of God is history – the things that were and are. The inscrutable process of the universe, this is He; and man, in whom the great process knows itself for a moment, can know it is not in vain. Little enough indeed, yet enough, and more than enough. To know that there is a purpose, yet not to know the purpose – that is blessedness indeed. To see but a tiny inch into the million miles of the unknown future – this is not forlorn and despairing, as orthodoxy would persuade us, but an authentic *sursum* to the soul. To know the future – what utter weariness!

Pantheism is the religion of humanity that has learned to love its limitations; it is a name for the illumination that supervenes upon acceptance of experience. Because it is the religion that is created by the operation of the things that are upon our human nature, it is the only religion that can suffer that things should be quite simply what they are. But it is not, as it is so often said to be, a religion of the intellect, a mere philosophy. The intellect cannot harmonize experience. Harmony is a thing created, and the intellect cannot create. Plant a conviction of harmony in the human soul, and the intellect can elucidate it; but it cannot create the harmony. The intellect is for ever in the grip of a thousand insoluble antinomies; it is impotent before the simple facts of growth and change. Either it denies them, or it denies itself in accepting them.

Growth and change are ultimate, primary realities. If we know them, and we do know them, we know them first in ourselves: we are growing and changing things, and that strange self-knowledge by virtue of which we assert (what is incomprehensible to the intellect) our own identity is but the conscious concomitant of the growth and change with us. Our power to grow, our power to change – or, lest we be presumptuous, the power of growth and change that holds us life-long in its grasp, is beyond our deliberate scrutiny. It is, and it is ourselves. It alone can harmonize experience; it has created us to be creators of harmony. For we live just in so far as we do harmonize experience, and when we cease to harmonize experience we die. Yet it is not we who harmonize experience; we merely suffer the unknown power to harmonize experience through us. But we have the choice (even though it may be years before we realize that the choice is ours): we can suffer the process to be accomplished through us hardly and ignorantly, or we can suffer it consciously and gladly. We can be compelled like slaves, or we can co-operate like free-men.

For the growth and change which is life consists in nothing else than the harmonization of experience. So long as we live, it goes on, whether we will or no. We may with our consciousness deny it; it does not matter. Life is contemptuous of our mental braggadocio: that our cocksure intellects make of us contumacious and unprofitable servants is our loss, not hers. If we refuse to acknowledge that we know her lesson, though we repeat it by rote every day, ours is the blame, not hers. Yet men go on refusing, and justify their refusal in the name of that harmony of experience to which she points the way. They too want harmony – none want it so much as they – but on their own terms: it must be a harmony achieved and comprehended by the intellect. Nothing else will do. And they sing doleful songs because it is denied them.

Why go on asking for the impossible? For it has its danger. The danger is that if you go on asking for the impossible, one day you may get it, and find yourself chanting like Tertullian: *Certum est quia impossibile*. Better take the unruly faculty of belief in hand betimes, before it asserts itself violently against starvation and rushes you into intellectual suicide. Give it something to feed on; let it browse, in contemplation, upon a baby or an apple-tree. These are of the same kind as human beings, and, fortunately, they cannot talk: therefore they will tell you no lies. You will find that they harmonize their experience admirably well. After a little while you will be inoculated against the extravagances of Tertullian. For you will find that it is more exciting and far more salutary to believe in the possible than in the impossible, in the actual than in the absurd. And that, I think, is Pantheism.

TO BE OR NOT TO BE?

A LITTLE time ago a writer – I believe, Mr. Leonard Woolf – drew our attention to the curious abuse of quotations from Shakespeare which prevails not only among the ignorant, but also among those who should, and very likely do, know better. For one instance, 'the play's the thing,' whereas in fact the play was only 'the thing wherein' Hamlet would 'catch the conscience of the king.' And for another, perhaps more remarkable, there is the sentimental interpretation of

'One touch of nature makes the whole world kin,'

which is, really, a very cynical observation, for the one touch of nature is

'That all with one consent praise new-born gauds,
Though they are made and moulded of things past,
And give to dust that is a little gilt
More laud than gilt o'er-dusted.'

A truth which has singularly little to do with the sympathetic concentration of a whole railway carriage upon a new baby.

More striking even than this strange phenomenon is the invincible misinterpretation of one of the famous and hackneyed passages in Shakespeare. I suppose that the most familiar speech in all Shakespeare is Hamlet's soliloquy: 'To be or not to be.' One might say that everybody knows it, and that everybody knows what it means: and everybody knows wrong. Of course, that 'everybody' is an exaggeration; it must be. But it is the fact that I have never discussed the speech with any person, however educated, however familiar with Shakespeare, without finding that he was convinced that 'To be or not to be' means 'To live or not to live,' and that the whole soliloquy is a debate upon the pros and cons of suicide.

Yet the fact is plain. 'To be or not to be' cannot mean 'To live or not to live.' The words which follow make such an interpretation quite impossible.

> 'To be or not to be: that is the question:
> Whether 'tis nobler in the mind to suffer
> The slings and arrows of outrageous fortune,
> Or to take arms against a sea of troubles
> And by opposing end them.'

What is 'to be or not to be' is not Hamlet, but Hamlet's attempt upon the King's life. Which is nobler? To suffer in patient silence his evil fortunes, or to take arms and act against them? To endure his troubles, or to make an end of them, not by suicide, but by opposing them?

Then comes the thought that, by killing the King, he will himself be killed; and he muses on death. It is not the death of a suicide, but the death of a rebel in arms, on which he muses.

> 'To die, to sleep;
> No more; and by a sleep to say we end
> The heart-ache and the thousand natural shocks
> That flesh is heir to, 'tis a consummation
> Devoutly to be wished.'

The thought is clear: if death were annihilation, he would rush to meet it. But –

> 'To die, to sleep;
> To sleep, perchance to dream: ay, there's the rub;
> For in that sleep of death what dreams may come
> When we have shuffled off this mortal coil
> Must give us pause: there's the respect
> That makes calamity of so long life.'

It is the thought that death may not be a total end that forces men to endure, and thus to prolong, their miseries.

> 'For who would bear the whips and scorns of time,
> The oppressor's wrong, the proud man's contumely,
> The pangs of despised love, the law's delay,
> The insolence of office, and the spurns
> That patient merit of the unworthy takes. . . .'

These are the calamities of life. Who would endure them?

> 'When he himself might his quiet us make
> With a bare bodkin?'

There for the first time the thought of suicide enters the soliloquy. It is a meditation on Death, and suicide enters simply as one means to death. It enters only to disappear again.

> 'Who would fardels bear,
> To grunt and sweat under a weary life,
> But that the dread of something after death,
> The undiscovered country from whose bourn
> No traveller returns, puzzles the will
> And makes us rather bear those ills we have
> Than fly to others that we know not of?'

Hamlet has now returned to his first question: 'To act (and die) or not to act (and live)?' And the answer is plain. Not the thought of death, which will be the inevitable consequence of his act,[1] but the dread of something after death,

---

[1] The question *why* Hamlet is certain that any attempt to kill the King will involve his own death is interesting. Shakespeare seems to have taken it for granted, for the necessity is not apparent in the play as we have it. The possible solutions are two: (1) psychological and subjective, namely, that Hamlet was a thorough-going pessimist; (2) 'historical' and objective, namely, that in the

paralyses his will to act and kill the king. And this conclusion is enforced and made manifest.

> 'Thus conscience does make cowards of us all;
> And thus the native hue of resolution
> Is sicklied o'er with the pale cast of thought,
> And enterprises of great pitch and moment
> In this regard their currents turn awry
> And lose the name of action.'

Not even Hamlet regards suicide as 'an enterprise of great pitch and moment.' The theme of the soliloquy from first to last is: action or inactivity? The specific act which Hamlet has to undertake – namely, the killing of the king – involves, Hamlet feels certain, his own death. From the horror of an after-life, he shrinks away.

It occurs to me that the word 'conscience' in the line

> 'Thus conscience doth make cowards of us all,'

may have been largely responsible for the traditional misinterpretation of the speech. Conscience there means simply consciousness. But those who read it, as most men naturally would, in the modern sense of 'moral scruple,' could hardly help connecting the speech with Hamlet's first soliloquy (I, ii. 129): –

> 'O that this too too solid flesh would melt,
> Thaw, and resolve itself into a dew!
> Or that the Everlasting had not fix'd
> His canon 'gainst self-slaughter!'

There, undeniably, the thought of suicide is in Hamlet's

old play, which very probably lies behind our 'Hamlet,' the King was so strongly guarded that an attempt on his life was certain death to his assailant. Such at least are the conditions in the old forms of the legend. Of the two solutions we strongly incline to (2).

mind: but that is before he has seen the Ghost. After the Ghost has spoken to him, before he can think of death for himself, he must act and kill the king. In the 'To be' soliloquy, there is nowhere any thought of suicide as a solution for Hamlet himself. Suicide enters solely as part of a general meditation upon death; and the whole argument of the soliloquy can be quite simply summarized.

'Shall I kill him or not? Which is nobler; to endure in silence, or to act and die? To die! If death were the end, I would die gladly. But if it is not the end – that is the fear that makes us endure our miseries. Who would bear them, if he knew he could make a final end by suicide? But the fear that there may be something after death, worse than the miseries we know, stays our hands. So, with this thought of what may follow death, our brave resolves grow pale, and our arduous enterprises, wherein death must be risked, dissolve before they become acts at all.'

There is another point of interest in the speech, which has often been remarked, but from which the natural conclusions are seldom drawn. Hamlet positively declares that from the bourn of death 'no traveller returns.' Yet the whole play depends upon the fact that Hamlet recognizes that one traveller at least *has* returned. The Hamlet of 'To be or not to be' has done an incredible thing: he has forgotten the Ghost. It might be urged that immediately before he had been feeling doubtful about the Ghost.

'The spirit that I have seen
May be the devil: and the devil hath power
To assume a pleasing shape; yea, and perhaps
Out of my weakness and my melancholy
Abuses me to damn me.' (II, ii. 627.)

But to be doubtful of the Ghost's intentions and to deny his existence are different, *toto cœlo*. Hamlet could not deny the Ghost; but Shakespeare could.

In other words, there is convincing internal evidence that Hamlet's meditation on death prepresents Shakespeare's own personal thinking. For a moment he utters himself not through a mask, but in person. That is interesting. It becomes more interesting still when we reflect on the nature of his thought. Annihilation – that were welcome; but the thought of something after death – that is intolerable.

Precisely the same meditation occurs in *Measure for Measure* (Act III), where it is divided between two characters – the Duke and Claudio. The Duke tries to reconcile Claudio to death, by insisting upon the miseries of life:

> 'The best of rest is sleep,
> And that thou oft provokest; yet grossly fear'st
> Thy death, which is no more.'

Strange argument, one reflects, for a supposed friar to use. But it shows how completely alien the Catholic and orthodox view of life was to Shakespeare. He gives to a friar the argument of Hamlet – 'To die: to sleep: No more.' And for the moment he persuades Claudio thus to be absolute for death. 'If I must die,' says Claudio to Isabel,

> 'I will encounter darkness as a bride
> And hug it in my arms.'

But when a ray of hope breaks through that darkness, when the bare possibility of life offers itself, the second theme of Hamlet's thought breaks down his resolution.

'*Claud.*   O Isabel!
Isab. What says my brother?
Claud.   Death is a fearful thing.
Isab. And shamed life a hateful.

Claud. Ay, but to die, and go we know not where;
To lie in cold obstruction and to rot;
This sensible warm motion to become
A kneaded clod; and the delighted spirit
To bathe in fiery floods, or to reside
In thrilling region of thick-ribbed ice;
To be imprisoned in the viewless winds
And blown with restless violence round about
The pendent world; or to be worse than worst
Of those that lawless and uncertain thought
Imagines howling: 'tis too horrible.
The weariest and most loathed worldly life
That age, ache, penury and imprisonment
Can lay on nature is a paradise
To what we fear of death.'

What seems to me most remarkable about this meditation of Shakespeare's upon death is that it is almost totally alien to a modern mind. It is the prospect of annihilation, which Shakespeare at this period of his life so eagerly desired, that chills the modern man. The possibility that a future existence should be worse than this has been practically banished from men's minds. Yet it was precisely that possibility which weighed upon Shakespeare, as though out of Catholic orthodoxy he had rejected all thought of Heaven and retained only the thought of Hell. On any showing neither Hamlet nor Claudio were bad men: they had as good a right as most to a place in Paradise. But the thought of an after-life better than this one seems not to have existed at this time for Shakespeare: the alternatives were simply annihilation, or an after-life worse than this.

This attitude has completely changed. The spiritual revolution (for it is nothing less) is astonishing to contemplate. The horror of something after death about which

Shakespeare's thought beat so wildly and despairingly at one moment in his life has softly and silently vanished away from the modern consciousness. Hell, for the modern mind, is here and now – in the blank and forlorn despair of an aimless universe. And, I do not think that, in this opinion, I am making the mistake of generalizing from the minds most familiar to my own; even in the straitest circles of Christian orthodoxy, even in the Roman Catholic Church itself, the old belief in Hell seems to have been mitigated almost to nothingness. There are profound traces of it, no doubt, in the work of an Irishman of Catholic education like Mr. James Joyce; but that, I imagine, is due to the peculiar backwardness of Catholic education in Ireland. I find no such traces in the literary work of continental Catholics. The terror of Hell beyond the grave has been overthrown; the horror of Hell on earth seems to have begun its reign.

This all but imperceptible revolution in man's instinctive thought is but one aspect of an even larger revolution in our beliefs concerning God. We are not afraid of God; what we are afraid of is that He does not exist. This is to put the case bluntly, in terms that are not really apt to the condition. The possibility of a personal God (in any non-casuistic sense of the word 'personal') has disappeared from educated minds: they do not want a personal God, for the simple reason that to attribute to a person the conduct of the universe would be intolerable. That is not to say the universe is conducted damnably, but that it is conducted with a fine and complete disregard of our deepest and most personal feelings. We cannot possibly put the responsibility for it on to a person.

The educated modern man, therefore, does not want a personal God: for that would be to seek for a God in order to hate and despise him. What it wants, where it wants anything of this order at all, is an assurance that, in some sense or other, all is well. And such an assurance cannot be reached by reason. It can be reached, I believe, and validly reached; but not by reason: unless a clear sight of the limitations of reason can reasonably be called reason. On the other hand, it cannot be reached by a denial of reason. Rather the method must be to push reason to the extremest extent of its power, and by so doing to realize how impotent it is to grasp the primary realities.

The universe of Shakespeare was always a universe without a personal God. He had a profound and delicate sympathy with the emotional side of Christianity; he carried on him pretty deep marks of the Catholic metaphysic. But, to speak broadly, in his early period he was too full of the lust of the eye and the pride of life to think about a personal God, and in his later periods he quite palpably disbelieved in such a thing. At one time, death filled his thought: but the main question which afflicted him was the question which afflicts us. Is the whole affair aimless or not? And I believe that he established to his own satisfaction that it was not.

The progress through Macbeth's –

> 'It is a tale
> Told by an idiot full of sound and fury
> Signifying nothing. . . .'

through Edgar's –

> 'We must endure
> Our going hence, even as our coming hither:
> Ripeness is all.'

to Prospero's –

> 'We are such stuff
> As dreams are made on, and our little life
> Is rounded by a sleep –'

the progress, though indefinable, is palpable. That last utterance of Prospero cries to be related to Hamlet's soliloquy. It is no longer we who 'sleep – perchance to dream'; we are the dreams of a great Sleeper. To some, to many, a thought so intangible and evanescent is empty and barren. I find it supremely satisfying; it says nothing, but it says nothing in such a tone that nothing becomes everything; it is the speech of silence. Those who say more cheat themselves, and us if we listen to them; but only those seek to say more, who do not know how to say such things.

I think of Shakespeare much as I think of old Cephalus at the beginning of Plato's *Republic*, when he leaves the younger generation to their mighty debate; and I feel that since Shakespeare made way for others the debate has gone on for three centuries, yet none have gone so far as he. I think of our Clissolds, and they seem to me fussily futile in comparison; and, thinking of them, I can almost persuade myself that I understand why Shakespeare at the end was troubled so little even by the last infirmity of noble mind that it was left to the spontaneous piety of two fellow-actors to rescue more than half his work from the ruin of oblivion.

THE METHOD OF MICHAEL FARADAY

I wonder how many others have found themselves at Christmas reading an old school-prize. There must be many; for it is a natural, almost an inevitable occupation. You go home after many months, it may be years, for more than a few hours' visit; in the quiet intervals you rummage in the bookshelves to see if the old Pickwick and Robinson Crusoe still exist; and there you are bound to find some of those gilt and mottled volumes with which you were once rewarded. They have been piously preserved; they have never been read. Whoever heard of a prize-boy reading his prize? Prizes are not meant to be read by the winners of them. You were presented with two slabs of tree-calf with what was once a book between: you were never allowed to choose the meat in the sandwich. You did not want to read it; and if you had, the thing is so constructed that it cannot be opened except by the main force of two hands. You have never read it yourself, and nobody else would have been allowed to. It has gleamed benevolent and undisturbed, save by the gentlest caress of the drawing-room duster, for more years than you care to contemplate. After so many years it becomes almost exciting to open it. The rest of the books in the house you know, and know by heart: but this is strange.

So I began to read the Life of Faraday. I had forgotten that such a book had ever belonged to me, just as I had forgotten that I was ever rewarded 'For Good Work in Science.' It is indeed scarcely credible. But the Life of Faraday suited me well on the dusky Christmas afternoon. I glanced at the title-page to make sure it was not written by Samuel Smiles. Thank Heaven, Sylvanus Thompson. Better and

240

better! I settled down in the arm-chair. My mind was on tip-toe.

For I really wanted to know something about Michael Faraday: I had read, perhaps in the words of Einstein himself, that Einstein's scientific pedigree ran thus: Faraday – Clerk Maxwell – Einstein. Now a direct approach to the Einstein theory is closed to me. I have tried the frontal attack, I have thought I had a glimpse over the wall; but nothing has remained. Mr. Thomas Hardy once told me that he used Relativity Theory to meditate on when he was threatened with a sleepless night. I have adopted the suggestion and found meditation on Einstein an admirable soporific. But I have also discovered, in other realms, that nothing so helps you to understand a man as to understand his origins. The method might, I thought, work even in the case of Einstein. I think it did. But there was another reason why I wanted to know about Faraday.

Einstein has told us that he finds a deep *ethical satisfaction* in reading Dostoevsky: so do I. He thinks that this is the supreme satisfaction to be derived from literature: so do I. Clerk Maxwell was, to put it mildly, something of mystic: so am I. Now what might Faraday have been? Would the sequence be completed?

I am not suggesting either that I am a scientific genius who took the wrong turning, or that Dostoevsky and true mysticism and the supreme scientific mind have an element in common that I can formulate. I have often suspected that there is a connection between these things. But I am (in spite of my 'Good Work in Science' twenty-five years ago) quite incompetent to make plain the nature and grounds of this suspicion, which after my reading of the life of Faraday has become a real belief.

For the sequence was, most unmistakably, completed. All his life long Faraday was a Sandemanian. You do not know what a Sandemanian is? Neither did I, until I read the chapter which Sylvanus Thompson, who knew that important things are important, devoted to Faraday's religious life and convictions. Sandemanians are the followers of a man named Sandeman, who was in his turn a follower of a dissident minister of the Scottish Kirk named John Glas. Somewhere about 1730 John Glas preached a restoration of primitive Christianity in these remarkable terms:

'He held that the formal establishment by any nation of a professed religion was the subversion of true Christianity; that Christ did not come to establish any worldly authority, but to give a hope of eternal life; that the Bible was the sole and sufficient guide for each individual in all times and all circumstances; that faith in the divinity and work of Christ is the gift of God, and that the evidence of this faith is obedience to the commandment of Christ.'

The message of John Glas was preached by Sandeman who, when he died in the 1770's in America, had these stirring words engraved upon his tomb:

'He boldly contended for the ancient faith that the bare death of Jesus Christ, without a deed or thought on the part of man, is sufficient to present the chief of sinners spotless before God.'

That is a noble faith, albeit a mystical one. And the followers of these two remarkable men lived up to it. They did actually follow the commandment of Christ; they had all things in common; they broke bread together on the Sabbath; they took no thought for the morrow. Naturally, they became a despised and rejected sect.

Of this despised and rejected sect Michael Faraday was an elder. Every penny of his superfluity he gave away in charity to the brethren; he did not save a farthing. He did not believe – how could a follower of Sandeman believe such a thing? – that only through his sect could salvation come; what he did believe, and he had solid ground for his belief, was that 'Christ is with us.' To this simple faith and the austere loveliness of living that it demanded, Faraday was loyal to his life's end.

Sylvanus Thompson found it hard to understand that this great master, perhaps the supreme genius of experimental physics, should have lived his life, as it were, in two halves. But was it lived in two halves? Does not the language beg the question? Faraday was the great experimentalist in natural science – so runs the unspoken thought – why was he not a free experimentalist in matters of religion also? But was he not? Did he not perhaps know something that was hidden from Sylvanus Thompson – that the two realms are different in kind, demanding different methods and different faculties for their exploration? His own noble words admit of none but wilful misunderstanding.

'High as man is placed above the creatures around him, there is a higher and far more exalted position within his view; and the ways are infinite in which he occupies his thoughts about the fears or hopes or expectations of a future life. I believe that the truth of that future cannot be brought to his knowledge by any exertion of his mental powers, however exalted they may be; that it is made known to him by other teaching than his own, and is received through simple belief of the testimony given. Let no one suppose for a moment that the self-education I am about to commend, extends to any consideration of the hope set before us, as if man by reasoning could find out God. It would be improper here to enter upon the subject further than to claim an absolute distinction between religious and ordinary belief. I shall be reproached with the weakness of refusing to apply those mental operations, which I think good in respect of high things, to the very highest. I am content to bear the reproach.'

And yet, perhaps, for all his manifest sincerity, Faraday was not facing the real question. Granted his unshakable conviction that 'man cannot by reasoning find out God,' the next question should have been: 'Was it by reasoning that I, Michael Faraday, found out the laws of electro-magnetism'? But it is unfair to expect Faraday to have asked himself that question. The faculty by which he did what he did in experimental physics was native and simple to him. He could no more help looking at physical things in his curious way than he could help being a Sandemanian. He called one faculty belief and the other reasoning. The distinction was not so clear to his contemporaries. Tyndall, at any rate, who should have come nearer to understanding Faraday than most men, said of Faraday's electro-magnetic speculations: 'Amid much that is entangled and dark, we have flashes of wondrous insight, which appear less the product of reasoning than of revelation.' Strange words for one physicist to use of another. What was 'reasoning' to Faraday appeared quite otherwise to others.

What if, after all, he *was* applying those mental operations which he thought good in respect of the very highest things, to the high ones also?

To me, indeed, there is a manifest connection between Faraday's mystical religious belief and the quality of his scientific vision, that was, most probably, not apparent to Faraday himself. His scientific vision was different in *kind* from that of his contemporaries: Tyndall described it well as a faculty of 'lateral vision.' Faraday could see not merely straight in front of him, but sideways also. And no one could really understand what he was talking about. He used words in curious senses, he talked about 'lines of force,' he seemed to see before his bodily eye some simple and beautiful harmony in the workings of the physical universe; for him some at least of the veils interposed by the secular assumptions of the human mind were as though non-existent. Listen to this: it is at the end of a letter describing one of his experiments in electro-magnetic induction.

'It is quite comfortable to me to find that experiment need not quail before mathematics, but is quite competent to rival it in discovery; and I am amused to find that what the high mathematicians have announced as the *essential condition* to the rotation – namely, that *time is required* – has so little foundation that if time could by possibility be anticipated instead of being required – *i.e.*, if the currents could be found *before* the magnet came over the place instead of *after* – the effect would equally ensue.'

It was not altogether unnatural that his contemporaries, mathematicians or not, should be uneasy about a man who wrote that sort of thing. With a simple gesture he abolishes time: and shows himself perfectly capable of envisaging all the phenomena of the physical universe as a vast simultaneity which we are compelled to perceive as a time-sequence simply because of the limitations of our minds.

Faraday's 'lines of magnetic force' are really a conception of the same order: that is to say that they are not a *conception* at all. Faraday is *seeing something*, and seeing it with some altogether peculiar faculty of direct perception. And what he *saw* was much simpler than what the mathematicians of his day *understood*. Much simpler and much truer. I do not know what the contemporary mathematicians thought of him in fact: that it was nothing to his credit is obvious from his own confessed 'pique' against them. But I should guess that they wavered between thinking him a simple naif and a dangerous visionary – an attitude not unlike that of the Scribes and Pharisees towards Faraday's Master. Even Tyndall, in many respects Faraday's follower, could never quite make up his mind about him.

'It sometimes strikes me that Faraday clearly saw the play of fluids and ethers and atoms, though his previous training did not enable him to resolve what he saw into its constituents, or describe it in a manner satisfactory to a mind versed in mechanics. And then again occur, I confess, dark sayings, difficult to be understood, which disturb my confidence in this conclusion.'

Nobody really understood him. He gained a tremendous reputation because he was always, so to speak, producing the rabbit out of the hat: he made marvellous machines and contrived astonishing experiments. But his real interest was in the why and how of rabbit-production, and his speculations on the why and how were understood by none, until Lord Kelvin (not yet a lord) began to have a glimpse of what he was driving at. Kelvin set Clerk Maxwell on the study of Faraday's 'Experimental Researches.'

Then in very truth Faraday had found his disciple. To Clerk Maxwell all that Faraday had said was perfectly simple and beautiful and true. The manner of his reception of Faraday's work recalls Rousseau's memorable phrase concerning other words of the deepest wisdom: 'They act only at the level of the source' – a casually stated law of spiritual dynamics. Clerk Maxwell found that 'Faraday's method of conceiving the phenomena was also a mathematical one, though not exhibited in the conventional form of mathematical symbols.' Not a little lies hid within that seemingly transparent phrase. It was, indeed, not so simple as all that. After all, it took a Clerk Maxwell to see that Faraday's method *was* 'mathematical,' and when Clerk Maxwell had expressed it in mathematical symbols he had caused a mathematical revolution. Where Clerk Maxwell and Faraday met was not in mathematics, but in the quality of their minds. They had the same way of looking at reality. I do not think it would be altogether fanciful to call it the Sandemanian method in physics.

ON READING NOVELS

THE charming girl was a great reader of novels: I am not,
nor do I often meet with charming girls who are. So I was
eager to make the most of my chance.

'Have you read the C – N –?' I asked.

She had, and she had been disappointed.

I pricked up my ears; she wrinkled her brows.

'It was the last but one,' she said. 'But I can't remember
what it was about. Let me see – there was a large family.
No! I can't remember. You see, I'm always reading a novel,
and the one I'm reading always makes me forget the one I
read before.'

That is one attitude, and at all events an honest one,
towards novels: they are a kill-time, like most games and
diversions. And that it should divert is the demand made
by ninety-nine people out of a hundred on a novel; some
say that it is made even by the hundredth also, though he
may be more particular about the way in which he is
diverted, and in support of their argument they point to
the dictum of Wordsworth, who declared that the proper
aim, even of poetry, is to give pleasure. Nevertheless,
even if it is true, it is not a very valuable sort of truth:
it is too onesided, or too indiscriminate. Not pleasure, but
the thing which shall give pleasure, is the object of most
men's search. And the more serious among mankind
find themselves discarding one source of pleasure after
another because it has ceased to have the power to please;
and very often it ceases to please precisely because it is
a diversion. As a man really grows, he learns that diversion and pleasure are not identical, and that mere diversions, for the most part, begin to leave a remorseful taste

behind. There is not so very much time, and it is a pity to waste it.

Then he begins to demand that the literature he reads shall be worth while. That is the point at which criticism begins, and the troubles and perplexities of criticism. For what is worth while in a book? Quite a number of things. It is, for instance, obviously worth while on occasion to be simply and frankly amused — to be, in short, diverted. 'I have discovered,' said Pascal, 'that all man's misery comes from one single thing, and that is not knowing how to stay quiet, in a room.' And certainly the man who has learned how to stay quiet, in a room, has not much to fear from destiny. But most of us are only apprentices to that wisdom; we find it easier to stay quiet in a room, than in a railway carriage, which is still a room within the purposes of Pascal's act; or easier to stay quiet when we are not nervously exhausted than when we are. When we are both nervously exhausted *and* in a railway carriage, then W. W. Jacobs is a god-send.

But, to make use of Pascal's pregnant saying again, though the worthwhileness of a book is conditional upon our condition, it would be true to say that a book approached more nearly to an absolute worthwhileness, the more nearly our own condition, in which it appears worth while, approaches the blessed state of being able to stay quiet, in a room. For Pascal's phrase is almost a translation, and a very good and vivid translation, of Aristotle's phrase concerning 'the energy of motionlessness,' which was for him the condition of true wisdom. The book that fits best with this state of contemplation is the best book: and the book that fits best with it is the book that gives rise to it. Pascal, who was a great Christian, indeed one of the greatest, would have said the New Testament. I agree: but there are others, and the finest novels are among them.

This surely is the absolute worthwhileness in literature:

the power to awaken in the reader an intense and understanding contemplation of all that is. To create such a condition is, I should say, the final purpose of the art of literature. Yet few critics really have a hold of this truth. They ask that novels shall be worth while, and not as mere diversion; but they generally ask of them a worthwhileness far inferior to that absolute worthwhileness which a representation of life may have. I will try to show, in a single instance, what I mean.

One of the most serious and most interesting critics of novels now writing is Mr. John Franklin of *The New Statesman*. He is always asking that a novel shall be worth while; and, since he is an honest critic, as befits his name, he is frequently at some pains to show what it is in a novel that he considers worth while. I have gathered that he makes, chiefly, two demands: first, that the novelist should show that he is aware of the seriousness of marriage, or, if you like, of the relation between a man and a woman; and, secondly, that he should show himself aware of 'the overriding imperiousness of a higher order of experience,' that is, of the importance of that kind of experience which can vaguely be called mystical, though contact can be made by other channels than the narrowly religious.

Now, at first sight, these two desiderata seem admirable. If any two things are important in this life of ours, it is these: if any two things are important for us to recognize, it is these. Therefore, surely, in that creative representation of life which is the novel, it is important that they should be recognized too. So Mr. Franklin argues, so he judges. His argument seems good: not so his judgments. That is not to say his views are not interesting: they are. But they are interesting as dissertations on these two perennial themes. The novels are a mere text for these excellent sermons: they are never regarded in and for themselves.

It is a queer impasse. Somehow, as a literary critic, Mr. Franklin is always missing the mark. It is as though he put important, very important questions to the novelist, but the one right and proper question he forgot, or did not know how, to ask. Let us examine the conclusion to his lengthy review of Mr. Sinclair Lewis's new novel, *Martin Arrowsmith*. He congratulates Mr. Lewis on having at last made explicit his own belief in 'higher' experience by representing for his hero a man of science, of whose pursuit it is said in the story: 'It is a tangle of very complicated emotions, like mysticism, or wanting to write poetry. . . . The scientist is intensely religious.' There is a genial and generous confusion in those words. 'Wanting to write poetry' *is* a tangle of complicated emotions, mysticism is not. Still, these things *can* be lumped together with religion vaguely under the name of 'higher' experience: and we know what Mr. Lewis is driving at. Mr. Franklin goes on:

'I believe that the excellence of Mr. Lewis's work has always depended upon his tapping, however unconsciously, this region of experience which I have vaguely called "higher," in contrast to the normal conventional framework that determines most of our emotions, acts, and perceptions, nay, even our discursive thoughts. But to develop this would take me too far afield. I must end by pointing out that of the three channels through which this experience finds expression – the religious, the artistic, and the scientific – only the first two have hitherto been used as the immediate subject-matter of novels . . . Who before Mr. Lewis has brought out the real inwardness of what it means to be a man of science? . . . This should be very welcome to all who wish to take literature seriously, because it removes from the novel the reproach of partial sterility. It was anomalous that the novel, as the only living form of literature to-day, should leave on one side the only living spiritual force which the modern world more or less recognizes for what it is, and which we all agree in respecting even when we do not serve it in our lives. It was more than anomalous, it was dangerous. The place of the scientific spirit in our life is such that the novel could not much longer remain emotionally blind to it, without degenerating into a kindergarten.'

In all this there is a serious, even a dangerous, confusion of thought – two of them, indeed. In the first place, Mr. Franklin is a victim, on a 'higher' plane, of the old fallacy, that the truth to life of a representative fiction depends upon the inclusiveness of its subject-matter. If I write a novel of London life (he is saying in effect) which does not include the operations of the Stock Exchange, or the workings of a 'circulation' newspaper, my novel is untrue, because it omits an important province of the life of this great city. It is a wrong and exploded idea; the truth and comprehensiveness of a fiction does not depend upon the truth and comprehensiveness of the subject-matter. Mr. Franklin would not embrace the fallacy in this crude form; but he transplants it to a 'higher' plane, and embraces it there. The important things in modern life, he says, are spiritual. Therefore a novel of modern life to be itself important must represent them. It is the same old fallacy speciously disguised. Before committing himself Mr. Franklin should have looked back a generation. Is *Robert Elsmere* a better novel, a truer novel, than *Treasure Island* or *Kim*? Yet it dealt seriously with religious experience, and they completely ignored it.

The real cause of this dangerous confusion is, first, a general confusion in Mr. Franklin's mind as to the nature of the art of literature, and, second, a particular confusion. Whether the excellence of Mr. Lewis's work has always depended on 'his tapping this region of experience, which

Mr. Franklin calls 'higher,' I do not know, because I do not know whether Mr. Lewis's work is excellent. If it is, then I agree that its excellence does depend on this 'tapping.' The excellent literary artist always does tap it, simply because he is an excellent artist. The excellence of his art directly depends upon his capacity to do this; he is an excellent artist by virtue of this capacity. *But this capacity has nothing whatever to do with the fact that he chooses this 'higher' experience for his subject-matter; and in reality it is a suspicious circumstance if he does choose it.* The artist's comprehension is, in itself, a 'higher' comprehension, and the purer it is the less will it need to advertise itself as such by the choice of a 'higher' subject-matter. What more powerfully religious books have been written in our time than Mr. Hardy's novels? Do they deal with religion for their subject-matter? No, the religion is in the writer's glance of pity and wonder which he casts upon human destinies. What are more profoundly spiritual, more evidently suffused with a higher understanding, than Tchehov's stories? Do they deal with the experience of artist, the saint, or the scientist? Is *Othello*, or *Macbeth*, or *Lear*, or *Antony* concerned with 'higher' thought? The 'higher' thought was in the mind of Shakespeare himself, and because it was there, it was manifested not through the thoughts, but through the created being of all his characters.

To me, I confess, this absolute distinction is as clear as day: yet it is continually lost. People who want to take literature seriously are for ever taking it seriously in the wrong way; and the serious critics, like Mr. Franklin, are the most dangerous offenders, because there is a confused conviction behind their words which is impressive. But, however high the plane on which their confusion is made, it is always the same old confusion. The writer is a villain because he represents a villain; or he is spiritual because he portrays spiritual things. It is about time we had grown out of this, once for all. The spirituality of the artist resides in the *way* he represents what he represents, not in *what* he represents. 'The excellence of every art is its intensity capable of making all disagreeables evaporate from their being in close relationship with beauty and truth.' Every critic who desires to become worth his salt should repeat those words to himself when he goes to bed and when he gets up in the morning, with a prayer that he may one day understand what they mean.

Mr. Franklin is mystically inclined. Therefore I will add a few words for his private instruction. The true artist is always a good deal of a mystic: it lies in the nature of creative literature that he should be so, because, as Baudelaire said, 'La première condition nécessaire pour faire un art sain est la croyance à l'unité intégrale.' Without that unconscious belief no epithet is organic, no sentence truly revealing: it is all a more or less clever intellectual game. The great artist, however, is a great deal of a mystic, but on his own terms and in his own way. The comprehension of the great artist is achieved by a process analogous to that by which the comprehension of the great saint is achieved. He comes to write out of a reborn soul. And, I think, Meister Eckhart told as much of the secret as can be told, when he said:

'Thy face is turned so full towards this birth, no matter what thou dost see and hear, thou receivest nothing save this birth in anything. All things are simply God to thee who seest only God in all things. Like one who looks long at the sun, he encounters the sun in whatever he afterwards looks at. If this is lacking, this looking for and seeing God in all and sundry, then thou lackest this birth.'

'God in *all* things,' said the great mystic, not in the seekers

254

after God. 'I have loved the principle of beauty in *all* things,' said the great poet, not in the makers of beauty. And, I suppose the great scientist would say, 'Truth in *all* things,' not in the seekers of truth.

ON BEING A CLASSIC

I HAD often wondered what it would mean to be a classic. If Shakespeare were alive to-day – and who knows? (I said to myself) he may be somewhere about, smiling at the mess we have made of things since his time, cutting his lawn with a blunt mower of an evening, and waiting patiently for the day when he can write another play with a chance of getting it produced.

At all events, after that sentence, he was alive enough for me to ask him what he makes out of it.

'Enough to rub along with, thank you,' said Shakespeare. 'About a thousand a year.'

'That's very little, you think? You forget: my plays don't run for very long in England. I suppose they aren't such good plays as I thought them.'

'The world's great playwright? Is that so? That's very kind of them. I have heard that I do rather better abroad. I remember some of our fellows made a fair thing out of a tour in Holland and Germany. But I don't get anything out of that. You forget there was no Continental copyright in my day.'

'Mr. S. – makes twenty thousand? What a lot of money! But you forget. I am a classic: he is not. You mustn't judge my income by non-classical standards. I assure you I do very well. A thousand a year – it's a great deal of money. And I don't pay income-tax.'

'Why ever not? Not for want of trying, I assure you. But when the income-tax came in – that's rather before your time, I imagine – I wrote on the form: *William Shakespeare, gentleman, player and playwright*, and the inspector sent me another and said I was liable for a fine of £20 for giving false information. I filled up the other: *William Shaxper, armiger, histrio et fabulator*. He sent me another, saying I was liable to a fine of £30 for using a foreign language. I filled up the third, *William Shakespeare, author of "Hamlet."* (You have heard of it, I dare say. It always went well: I don't know why.) The inspector did not trouble me again. Things have changed since my time --

> "the insolence of office and the spurns
> That patient merit of the unworthy takes."

I could *write*: don't you think?'

'Oh, you're one of the Shakespeariolaters, are you? And that's why you think I should have more than £1,000 a year. Bless you, boy. It's kind of you to think that. And you are one of those who write kind things about me, I'm sure. People are very kind: but I sometimes wish they would read me before writing about me. But I suppose it shows a good heart.'

'A million! Good heavens, boy -- forgive me, but you are a good deal younger than I, aren't you? -- what on earth should I do with a million? I am independent, and a gentleman. I never asked for more.'

'You think it strange I should have asked so much? I suppose I had to prove to myself the word was not a dream -- not altogether. But I say that, now, looking back. I did not think like that when I began. I had to pull myself out of the gutter, the veritable gutter. So you've heard the story of my holding horses for twopence? It's true. "Put money in thy purse." Money! It's terribly important. It gives a man whereon to stand. Money enough to stand on -- no more -- but that I slaved for. They can't understand that? I'm afraid they don't understand many things even now. They don't understand that there is a difference in kind between the man who has known poverty, and the man who has never known it. They're like Lazarus and Dives on the painted cloth: between me and thee is a great gulf fixed, so that they which would pass from hence to you cannot; neither can they pass to us that would come from thence.'

'They call me a snob? I think the people who call me that belong to Dives' company. When you are in the gutter, you fight your way out of it, or you die. A good many of our fellows died. Hardly a snob, I fancy. I don't like well-to-do writers. A writer must never lose sight of the gutter, never forget that how thin is the ground on which he treads.'

'Yes, they come to see me sometimes. I like the young ones best – Keats and Chatterton are my favourites. I think they're happy in the garden here, above all in the evening.'

'What do we talk about? Oh, nothing much. When you grow older, when you've learned a little more, you'll understand that at the last there's nothing much to *say*. We dream and hope and believe. There are a great many flowers in the garden here, you know, sweet-smelling evening flowers. Sometimes a nightingale sings. I'm glad of that, for Keats's sake. One evening he told me a poem, as though it had been a dream. Oh, you know it? I'm glad of that. Even I never wrote a poem like that one. Have you ever thought what it meant that a *boy* should have written that? Terrible, terrible; but wonderful, wonderful. You have? Well, I am glad. So you do really think about us sometimes. Love us? Ah, that is the word. But don't waste it on me, boy. Love them. They suffered much for you. And yet – perhaps your love of me is not wholly wasted. No true love is. It keeps your own heart sweet, if nothing more.'

'That's hard? There is nothing harder, boy: nor anything more precious. A sweet heart alone can know that it is not all in vain.'

'You would like to come and listen? You are truly young

you still think there is a secret somewhere that we might speak and you might hear? No, no! All that we could *say*, we have said, even the youngest of us. You would be disappointed, boy, – you are young – to hear us say: "These are good apples," or "The sky is red to-night." '

You are still looking for a sign. You remember: An evil and adulterous generation seeketh after a sign, and no sign shall be given it. Oh, no; I did not mean it for you. But there's a tinge of the old Adam still, isn't there? It's the hardest thing of all to learn: that there are no signs, because everything is a sign.

Prospero? Was I Prospero? No, you shouldn't ask such questions; you should know that I cannot answer them. Not that I would not, but simply that I cannot. Shall I say 'Yes,' when I made Prospero? Can I say 'No,' when he was of my making?

You love Miranda? Well, so did I. You knew it, did you? Why not? I couldn't keep it out – 'The fringèd curtains of thine eyes advance, And say what thou seest yond.' You know what those words have in them. And Perdita. I made things lovely for her to see:

'O Proserpina,
For the flowers now that frighted thou let'st fall
From Dis's waggon! Daffodils
That came before the swallow dares and take
The winds of March with beauty; violets dim
But sweeter than the lids of Juno's eyes
Or Cytherea's breath; pale primroses,
That die unmarried, ere they can behold
Bright Phœbus in his strength – a malady
Most incident to maids. . . .'

Yes, that is lovely. 'Behold, I make all things new.' Perdita, the lost one; Miranda, the one to be wondered at.

Why did I make a new woman, and not a new man? Boy, you press your questions home. Why? I wonder. It happened so. I loved women. And the new man must be *born*. The woman who should see loveliness, her I knew: but the man who shall do loveliness, he is yet to come.

'Take these,' he said suddenly, filling my pockets with apples from a dish. 'These are good apples.' And he smiled.

I understood his meaning, and went my way.

CONCERNING ANGELS

ON the whole, I have never cared much for angels. They have suffered in my estimation from a certain lack of reality. But in some moods of the Western world they have been real enough. The angels concerning whom St. Thomas Aquinas sought to determine how many could be accommodated on the point of a needle were real: too real, indeed, to be angelic, for they were something of the nature of atoms and electrons. God himself, for the great Thomas, came perilously near to being the universal substance, towards which in a rigorously intellectualized religion he is bound to tend. Fra Angelico's angels, on the other hand, were both real and angelic. You have but to look at them to know that angels could be quite certain inhabitants of a mediæval painter's world. But the Renaissance put salt on their tails. Shakespeare's angels are but ejaculations – 'Angels and ministers of grace defend us!' – or metaphors: lovely and profound metaphors sometimes. 'Reverence, that angel of the world,' says something which, without the conception of the angel, could not be said so perfectly. And out of such a phrase, with a memory of a Fra Angelico picture to make the vision substantial, we can extract (even if we cannot define) some quintessence of the spiritual truth that was embodied in the vision and the thought of angels.

But when I think of angels, I think first of them as fallen. Lucifer has more substantiality than any of his uncorrupted brothers: and Lamb's description of Coleridge as 'an archangel a little damaged' gives me a curiously exact idea of that divine and all-too-human poet. No other description of Coleridge comes near to it for cogency and precision. Which is, on the face of it, strange. For Lamb's phrase is, palpably,

a definition *ignoti per ignotius*: of the unknown by means of
the more unknown. Yet it tells me something essential;
through it I know more about Coleridge than pages of description – even of masterly description like Hazlitt's – can
tell me.

So it is clear that, though I do not care for them, I do
know something about angels. Though I am utterly ignorant, and utterly sceptical, of them as substantial beings, and
bother no more about them than I do about ghosts; yet when
they are used as symbols to articulate and define that aspect
of reality which we call the spiritual world, I understand
them immediately. More than that, I feel that I am a positive expert in angels. 'I am the best of them that speak this
language, were I but where 'tis spoken.'

Yes, angels turn out (upon examination) to be very necessary and very familiar things: for they are the personification of that more perfect condition to which we cannot help
relating the quotidian existence of this world. *Omnia exeunt
in mysterium.* To the contemplative eye man is always a
torso, an uncompleted statue which we cannot comprehend
save by referring him to some unrealized perfection. The
seemingly simple question whether the statue is broken, or
unfinished, or both, is one of the fundamental issues which,
without men's knowing it, divide the world of men.

Anyhow, for the moment let it stand that angels are the
personification of man's unrealized perfection. When we are
told that some one is like a fallen angel, or Coleridge an archangel a little damaged, we instantly understand that there is
in him still the visible potentiality of some more than ordinary human condition. And when we first think in this
spiritual category we find ourselves gliding easily from time
to the timeless. We hardly know, and at first we hardly
care, whether our former angel was once perfect in this life
and has declined from his zenith; or whether the fall was

simply an effect of mortality itself, due to the mere entry into mundane existence. We are at first content with a vague feeling that perhaps we all come trailing clouds of glory; but only those who keep some wisps hanging round them pretty late in life come under notice as having had something angelic in their composition. The rest are wiser, and quicker to conceal these treacherous indications that they have seen better days.

But these nebulous possibilities are only the beginnings of the angelic science. It is easy to see that much depends upon how the properties of angels are determined. Were we all angels once, and changed our nature for the worse by being born? Or is heaven, indeed, still about us in our infancy? Trivial questions, you may think, and scarcely distinguishable. Yet for centuries the whole gulf between Heaven and Hell has yawned between them: for the first is the great classical and Catholic dogma of original sin, and the second the great Romantic dogma of men being born equal and perfect. God alone knows how many of his creatures have endured a lingering death by fire and sword and boiling oil for giving the wrong answer to the question: When do men cease to be angels? At conception, or at fourteen?

I, as my readers should know by this time, am a Romantic. Therefore I hold, almost violently, to the latter date. The words 'Conceived in sin' in the service of baptism stick in my gizzard. After all, it is nonsense: rather sublime nonsense, in its grandiose denial of life *ab ovo*, nonsense with a spiritual significance, as most of St. Paul's nonsense was — yet still nonsense, and what is more, dangerous and pestilent nonsense. This Christian condemnation of life in and through the body which derives from Paul, with his everlasting thorn in the flesh, led straight to the fabrication of those pious legends concerning the birth of Jesus, and ultimately to the priggish and repulsive dogma of the immaculate conception: than which nothing more anti-Christian (in the exact sense) can be imagined. The most monstrous errors of the Christian Church really arose out of the fact that Paul knew nothing about children. He could not see life straight.

Jesus could. Being a wise man, he also knew all about the reality of sin. But he did not, he could not, make the truly terrible mistake (from which Christianity has not yet been freed) of identifying sin with the body. Had he lived to hear Paul speak of 'the body of this death' he would have groaned in spirit. Jesus had a sense of reality: therefore he had a sense of humour, which Paul never had. He knew that in the days when he had called across the market-place in the dusk to the other little boys: 'We piped unto you, and you did not dance,' there was nothing particularly wrong with him. Dean Inge is more doubtful on the point, but Jesus was certain that children had heaven about them in their infancy. He looked on children not as sin-stained products of sin, but as glorious creations of life. Therefore, without demanding that they, any more than he himself, should have been immaculately conceived (*Ach Gott!* what a phrase!) he simply declared that the kingdom of God belonged to them. And when he had to tell people how to get into the kingdom (which is still the most difficult and the most important thing in life) he could only say: 'Except ye become as little children ye shall in no wise enter into it.'

Here we come back, though indeed we have never left it, to the subject of angels. For little children and angels were closely connected in Jesus' mind: they were almost identical. When he warned people against offending one of these little ones he told them that 'their angels do always behold the face of my Father which is heaven.' He did not mean that they had little duplicates up above; but something at once more simple and more difficult, namely, that the spiritual part of them was in perpetual contact and communion with God himself. Now this for Jesus was the all-important thing: that the soul or spirit of man should be in perpetual contact with God. That, nothing less and nothing more, was to be a member of the kingdom. You had the choice: you could either achieve it now, or wait till afterwards. By waiting you took the hell of a risk. (How Jesus tried to reduce that risk to a minimum is another story, the greatest story in the world.)

Jesus believed in – was he not himself baptized for the remission of his sins? – the reality of sin. Only a man who knows nothing about himself or anything else does not believe in the reality of sin. So the three ages of man were simple to him. There was the child who had this perpetual contact with God by nature, and therefore possessed his angel; there was the man, in whom inevitably the contact was broken, and who lost his angel; there was the reborn man, who re-established the contact and regained his angel. If you were born again, you once more became a member of the kingdom and a son of God, as you had been in the days of innocency. You were different, of course, for no grown man can ever, ought ever, become a child. But the reborn man was whole as the child had been whole. The interval between the wholeness of the child and the regained wholeness of the reborn man was the epoch of the divided consciousness.

Against such exquisite and absolute spiritual truth, the coarse and clumsy approximation of 'original sin' and the downright flummery of 'immaculate conception' make an ugly show indeed. Yes, they are *ugly*: there is no other word. Life is more wonderful than that. Romanticism is truer than classicism; though it is harder to manage. Romanticism walks as it were on a razor's edge, as Jesus did. What wonder that it takes a great man to be a Romantic and not fall into the chasm? But its triumphs are supreme. 'Conceived in sin': 'their angels do always behold the face of my Father.' It doesn't take a genius to decide, *pace* Freud and the rest of them, on which side lies the spiritual truth.

Little children, for Jesus, had angels, in the sense I have described. There came the time when the child lost his angel, he grew up, and grew up into that strain of the divided consciousness (if he remained spiritually alive at all) which poor old Paul could never overcome. Paul was a great man, but Jesus would never have allowed that he had been properly born again, any more than he allowed it in the case of John the Baptist. 'I have fought the good fight' is glorious, but it is not the voice of a member of the kingdom. The strain, the tension, are too evident. Paul never regained his wholeness, never quite got back his angel; and Christianity has suffered for his failure ever since. If he had been properly re-born, he would have had a sense of humour.

The re-born man gets back his angel. Of course, not the same one that he had before: he grows a new one. When the Sadducees put to Jesus their silly question – silly, as put to Jesus: sound as ever, if put to nine Christians out of ten – about the wife with seven husbands, he said they were far astray, 'not knowing the Scriptures *or the power of God*. For in the resurrection of the dead men neither marry nor are married, but are as the angels in heaven.' That, incidentally, puts the final nail in the belief in the resurrection of the body, at all events as a belief ever held by Jesus. If the Christian Church chooses to cling to the crudity of the Sadducees without the Sadducees' sense of its absurdity, that is its own affair. To be 'as the angels' did not mean for Jesus going about with an awkward pair of wings like Charlie Chaplin in 'The Kid': it meant to have one's spiritual part, the whole of one's eternality, eternally alive. You could have that this side of the grave, if you cared to have it. You could regain your angel. And when you had regained him, and had learned what he meant and was, you would not worry about immortality or the rest of it: you would know that all those vexing problems are born of the feverish attempts of those who will not take the pains to get their angel back again to secure themselves against the loss of things that are not worth keeping.

PAULINES AND GALILEANS

OBJECTION has been taken to my remarks concerning St. Paul. My critics do not make clear what it is they object to; but they object. There is no doubt about that. The mere fact that their objection is inarticulate, so far from absolving me from the duty of reply, makes reply more urgent. Because I believe that the criticisms most worth taking seriously are those which are inarticulate. These often proceed from profound, instinctive reactions. If these can be dragged to the light, knowledge may be gained.

I am certain that this vague sense of objection was not due to any apparent lack of respect in my references to Paul. For it was quite obvious that my judgment upon Paul was relative and not absolute. I was comparing Paul's teaching, which I believe to be profound, with the teaching of Jesus, which I believe to be profounder. To suggest that Paul is a small man beside Jesus, is not to suggest that he is a small man by any other comparison. The standard of reference – the character and teaching of Jesus – was plainly declared throughout my essay. For any one of good faith misunderstanding was impossible.

I am sure of the good faith of my critics, and sure also that what they really object to is *any* criticism of St. Paul, not the imaginary flippancy of mine. When I spoke of his 'sublime nonsense,' I meant it; when I said 'Poor old Paul!' I meant it; when I said he was 'a great man,' I meant it. I stand by every word of the essay, because I believe it to be true. Those who find flippancy in it are those who cannot distinguish between seriousness and solemnity. They find it hard to believe that there is a seriousness beyond solemnity.

What these criticisms have made clear to me is that the opposition is not really between my conception of Paul and theirs, but between two psychological or spiritual types: let us call them the Pauline and (to avoid the question-begging ambiguity of 'Christian') the Galilean. The Pauline instinctively resents any criticism of Paul, because he feels, consciously or unconsciously, it is directed against himself.

And this opposition of spiritual types is extremely interesting. If we could establish their existence and define their qualities we should have accomplished something of value. It is of course connected with Dr. Jung's investigation into psychological types, and his great distinction between the extrovert and the introvert. But that distinction has always seemed to me quite unworkable in criticism: it is far too *coarse*. It may be useful for the purposes of ordinary clinical work: I do not know. But it is practically valueless for the more delicate work of psychological criticism.

The opposition between the Pauline and the Galilean types seems to me, on the other hand, distinctly suggestive. Not only has it recurred throughout the history of Christianity, but it is obviously repeated in so striking an antithesis as that between Milton and Shakespeare, and less certainly later in the relation between Shelley and Keats. It is, moreover, a well-observed fact that those who highly appreciate Milton find it hard to abandon themselves to Shakespeare (*e.g.* the Poet Laureate), and those who greatly enjoy Shelley find Keats much less satisfying (*e.g.* the late Dr. Garnett). *Vice versâ*, I, who have a passion for Shakespeare and Keats, find it difficult to be altogether just to Milton and Shelley.

But perhaps I am going too quickly; it may not be so obvious to others as it is to me that Shakespeare is Galilean, while Milton is Pauline. It is, of course, strictly impossible to *demonstrate* this identity; but if we look a little into the antithesis between Paul and Jesus, the affinity may become plain.

My charge against Paul, it may be remembered, was that he denied life. There are many ways of denying life, but I should say that every one of them can be found in Paul. First, he denied sex. Marriage was essentially a remedy for incontinence. It inevitably followed, first, that he regarded woman as an inferior, and children as born in sin. No one who reads the magnificent first epistle to the Corinthians can fail to see how inordinately difficult it was for Paul to admit woman's right to existence. (The affinity with Milton here, at least, leaps to the eye.) Thus, Paul regarded the life of the Christian as one incessant struggle against temptation. There never came a time when the struggle was over: the man was divided against himself for ever. He was born in sin, he was full of sin; but he was redeemed.

So, quite inevitably, the Kingdom of God and eternal life were not to be attained in this world at all. These were the reward after death for the Christian who had fought the good fight. Essentially the Christian was one who renounced life in this world in order to get it hereafter. The guarantee of this life after death was the resurrection of Christ.

The Galilean attitude, on the other hand, is one of life-acceptance. The teaching of Jesus must be kept completely free of Pauline accretions. And this is not easy to do, because to every phase in the teaching of Jesus corresponds a phase in the teaching of Paul. Both teachings are profound, both are complete. The difference between them is scarcely capable of intellectual statement. Yet it is obvious. Perhaps it can be most clearly seen in the two conceptions of rebirth.

Both Jesus and Paul taught the necessity of a re-birth. Those who have no belief at all in the reality of the process are necessarily precluded from understanding either of them. But the two re-births were remarkably different: in Paul's teaching there was a birth of the spiritual man who was the enemy of the fleshly man. What really happened was that the balance of power was shifted. Whereas the fleshly man formerly held the preponderance, it suddenly passed over to the spiritual man. The spiritual man was henceforward supreme. But the opposing forces were still there; the distribution of forces alone had changed.

The re-birth that Jesus taught was quite different. It took place secretly and swiftly, but not in the least catastrophically. Suddenly you had a glimpse of the meaning of the Kingdom of God, and the glimpse swiftly grew into knowledge. If you knew the mystery of the Kingdom of God you were re-born; you knew that you and all men were quite simply not subjects but sons of God; you saw the divine and ineffable beauty of creation, and you yourself were subdued by it; you became spontaneous as a child once more: life simply uttered itself through you. The time of effort and struggle was over. You, a conscious man, became reintegrated into that wholeness of life from which consciousness had driven you forth. For the re-born man sin was a sheer impossibility: he simply *was* God.

To describe the condition is really impossible. It was one of wholeness, and life-acceptance:

'I tell you, love your enemies and pray for those who persecute you that you may be sons of your Father in heaven: for he makes his sun to rise upon the evil and the good, and sends rain upon the just and the unjust.'

The *whole* of creation is a divine creation, known as such by its beauty. Once you know that, you love your enemy because you cannot help it; you forgive, in Tchehov's words, because it would be strange not to forgive.

Joyful acceptance of the whole creation, and of one's own part in it: rejection of nothing – 'Behold a gluttonous man and winebibber, the friend of publicans and sinners' – such was the condition of re-birth in Jesus' teaching and experience. It was startlingly different from Paul's.

Now there is no doubt that the majority of spiritually minded men are Pauline rather than Galilean. Their highest conception is that of doing their duty, and they accomplish miracles in doing it. But it is an incessant struggle for them, and they are inclined to resent the idea that a man may be good without a struggle. On the other hand, the Galilean type does not find it very easy to get on with the Pauline: for it seems to him that the Pauline drags the fulfilment of duty into places where its presence is a sacrilege, and thus shows himself lacking in fineness of discrimination. The notion of doing one's duty to one's wife is, for instance, repellent to him. He would say that a man's attitude to his wife should be spontaneous. If that is impossible for him, why did he marry her? Thus it is that the Pauline makes a good and conscientious, but scarcely a thrilling husband.

This is but a simple instance of the curious and fundamental contrast. The Galilean type is happy only when acting spontaneously: he cannot rest in a condition of inward divorce between his intellect and his emotions, or between his body and his soul. The tension of these divisions is as the breath of life to the Pauline. That, indeed, *is* life to him. To the Galilean it is death. As Keats said of Milton: 'Life to him would be death to me.'

I don't know what is to be done about it; for it seems very hard, if not absolutely impossible, for a Pauline to become a Galilean, and quite out of the question that a Galilean should become a Pauline. And the trouble is complicated by the fact that it is comparatively easy for the Galilean to accept the Pauline – he does it, so to speak, *ex hypothesi* – but excessively difficult for the Pauline to accept the Galilean.

PATRIOTISM

I LATELY read a volume of English poems by a Hindu, who was sent to this country at the age of seven, and educated at St. Paul's and Christ Church. Not till he was twenty-five did he return to his own country, and then it was to serve as a Professor of English literature in an Indian university. At such a task he died.

The poems perplexed me. Their author's command of the English language was notable; his emotional sincerity obvious: yet never for one moment could I be lulled into the belief that they were good poems. Something was lacking. What was it? Though I thought over the question for long, I could find no pat and positive answer; but I came to certain conclusions about the poems.

What troubled me, I concluded, was a constant hiatus that I felt between the language and the thought, between the expression and the experience. The poet was using English words to convey what English words never could convey. It was not that other English words than those he used would have done the work better: on the contrary, his diction was surprisingly felicitous. The truth was that no English words could possibly convey what he wanted them to convey, and no doubt supposed that they did convey.

It might be asked: How did I know what he wanted to convey, seeing that I had only his words to inform me? A fair logical objection; but, fortunately (for otherwise literature would be unnecessary) logic is not sovereign in literature. It is true that, if I took an isolated verse, or an isolated sequence of verses, I could not pronounce positively that he meant something other than he said: I could merely register an indefinable dissatisfaction. But the cumulative effect of many pages was not to be mistaken. A thousand approximate expressions of a thought will make a thought distinct even though no individual expression be exact. So with the Indian poet: though no one of his poems really expressed his thought or his feeling, and therefore no one of them was a true poem, yet all together conveyed to me a fairly distinct impression of his habit of thought and feeling. And I am confident that such a habit of thought and feeling cannot be expressed in the English language.

The problems that arise out of that fact are innumerable. The one which immediately concerns me is the impossibility of describing that mind and sensibility in English words. I cannot use the epithets that suggest themselves – weak, cloying, backboneless (this last is most insistent) – for the reason that these adjectives are derogatory. Not only have I no desire to be derogatory; but, far more important, it would be untrue to the facts to use these biased epithets. For it is an essential part of the impression that this mind and sensibility made upon me that it is valid in itself. In its own context, so to speak, it is neither weak nor cloying nor backboneless. If I call a man backboneless, I insult him; but if I call a snake backboneless I ascribe to it its proper virtue. (I am not speaking scientifically: a backboneless man has vertebræ; and so has a snake, for all I know.) The backbonelessness of the Indian poet is positive, like the snake's. It is a truth and a virtue; yet it repels me. What has happened is that I have been brought up against a racial otherness. Between the Indian poet's consciousness and mine there is an abyss.

In the practical world, this backbonelessness of the Indian consciousness is the excuse for the English Raj. We are there to supply the backbone; and on the whole we supply it – Dyerisms apart – efficiently and economically. But let us not get into the way of expecting gratitude for these services. They do not deserve gratitude. The Indian does not ask for backbone. A backboneless existence is natural to him, and he prefers it. It is simply one way of life against another; and the differentiations go back to a timeless Aryan past. Why should the Indian be grateful to us for supplying him with something of which he feels no instinctive need? The chaos and lawlessness, the despotism and cruelty, from which we save him is not an intolerable evil to him. We are intellectual fools if we expect from him a moral emotion in response to what to him is not a moral act.

But neither is it, as our sentimental radicals would have it, an immoral act. Educated Bengalis may pour their grievances into the vernacular Press; but their grievances are borrowed. They do not belong to them: they belong to the English consciousness, which is not theirs. What does, what can, self-government or liberty *mean* to the Indian? To the illiterate nothing at all; to the educated nothing profound. To neither, for certain, a necessary condition of existence. The English Raj is the last of many despotisms in a country that expects despotism. It is worse than its predecessors in that it is alien; it is better in that it is benevolent. Plus and minus cancel out. Our mission in India (if we may call it a mission) is to be like Stalky's headmaster – 'a beast, but a just beast,' and not to expect the gratitude we do not deserve.

As for the 'mission,' it is simply that if we do not do it, some one else will. No one will do better, it is true. But that is not the reason why we do it. In spite of our professions we English are not altruists – we look like it (to ourselves alone) because we have learned in long experience a good deal of practical wisdom as a ruling race. But the reason why we hold India is simply that we are a ruling race. We *bagged* India in the days when the world was yet 'mine oyster'; and, let us hope, we intend to keep it. For when we begin seriously to entertain the notion of 'educating India into self-government,' then we shall be revealed, not as moral heroes, but as intellectual fools.

I did not intend to divagate into politics. But this fact of the existence of a racial consciousness fundamentally alien to our own is seldom realized, and if realized, generally misunderstood. For, if we do realize the existence of an alien racial consciousness, the first impulse is to a kind of scepticism – intellectual, moral, political. Here is a culture and a civilization which is to the eye of eternity as valid as our own. Why, then, our truth, our good, our right, are not absolute. That seems terrible; and, after the shock of shipwreck, we generally try to scrape together some sort of raft from the wreckage, and indulge ourselves with 'omnihuman' ideals. Or we attempt some feeble religious syncretism, taking 'the best' of Buddhism, of Vishnuism, of Christianity, and imagine that we have attained a sort of universality thereby. It is all in vain, for it is all wrong. Just as in art – the microcosm of the profoundest human problems and potentialities – the only true universal is the truly particular, so with men and nations. We shall not reach whatever is to be reached of a world-unity by suppressing our idiosyncrasies, but only by obeying them. Each race, each nation, and each man has his own possible perfection, which it is his mission to attain: that particular perfection is universal, with the only kind of universality that is real and not a mere abstraction. Between such separate perfections there is spiritual equality. Whatever I may be, I cannot be better than the agricultural labourer who has learned the wisdom of the earth and sky, and is bound by the same secret loyalty to his craft as I to mine. I respect him, he me; it is true he calls me 'Sir,' while I call him 'Roper': that is part of the rules, and since he is as good a man as I, and knows it, and knows that I know it, he is content to obey the rules. We should gain nothing, but lose much, were we to call each other 'Comrade': for, when there is true mutual respect, the forms of courtesy themselves have meaning. We play the rules, because we know that rules must be.

This spiritual equality between particular perfections seems to me to be the salt of life. We think too much, we talk too much, of understanding and of sympathy. Sympathy, in the best-compounded man, is short-lived: the anguish of an hour must yield before the work of the day. If we build the future on sympathy, we build on sand: we cannot bind fast with a rope of tears. Nor will understanding take us far. There are too many things, too many men, we do not and cannot understand. I cannot understand an Indian, or a miner, or a Roman Catholic, even a good many writers that I could name. But what we cannot understand, we can sometimes respect; and respect it not in ignorance. For there is a sixth sense that tells us when respect is due: that here is something alien to us, yet pure and valid in its own right. And the same sense tells us when respect is due to ourselves. When we are, for a moment, wholly what we are – sincere, in the old sense, *sine cera*, without a veneer of wax to conceal the holes in our surface – then we are worthy of respect. Nor do I doubt that this wholeness, this integrity, will win respect from others: they cannot understand it, but they respond.

Respect seems a cold word to some; but it is better to build with than some warmer words, which, like vapours, when they cool, shrink into nothingness. Love is a warm word, but it does not accomplish much. Not because the thing is weak, but because the thing is wanting. Love is not an easy business: it is so much easier, as Dostoevsky said, to love humanity than men – much easier, much more frequent, and a waste of breath. Far better than to delude ourselves with the idea that we possess impossible virtues, is to set ourselves to attain a possible one – to become capable of

278

respect and worthy of it. So, to take a present example, with this long and bitter struggle in the coal-mines, we need not concern ourselves with the violent and foolish words of the men, or the cold insolence of the masters, but simply remember that we owe it to ourselves as a nation that no class of men in this country should be compelled to work under damnable conditions for a starvation wage. The question is one of *noblesse oblige*. As the noble Bishop of Durham said, Christianity does not enter into it at all; but not, as the noble Bishop thought, because it ought not, but because it cannot. How *can* Christianity enter into a struggle for possessions? But what should enter in is the sense that it is beneath our national dignity to have a running sore in the commonwealth; and that if economic law commands that this running sore must be, we had better put things to the proof and face the outcome of a conflict between our national dignity and economic law. Economic law! Economic law commanded that slave-labour should continue in the plantations; that a man should be hanged for stealing a sheep; that little children of six should work thirteen hours in the cotton mills. Yet the heavens did not drop blood when these economic laws were broken; nor was Manchester less rich than it had been.

Justice is not something which we owe to others, but to ourselves. If England must jettison her national pride to keep afloat, far better that she should sink now, quickly, with honour; for sink she assuredly will. She cannot make port (whatever that final haven may be) unless Englishmen believe in her. And Englishmen cannot believe in an England which turns her face from the light. For this light of hers is not blinding-white and transcendental, but homely; warm, and shaded – a simple instinct to do the decent thing, a quality so utterly peculiar to ourselves that it cannot be described save in these commonplace terms. This is *our* differentiation, not better perhaps than anybody else's, certainly not to be expected of anybody save ourselves, but the finest grain of our nature, and our sole sure star.

I am amazed, with a sweet amazement, when I suddenly look into my heart and discover the depth of my love for this country of mine. 'Patriotism is not enough,' said Edith Cavell, and we know what she meant, and it is true: so true that its simple opposite is true. 'Patriotism *is* enough.' For patriotism, when purified and strengthened by doubt, is the knowledge that this country has its own part to bear in the universal harmony; and what that part is, how subtle, how lovely, how majestic, we can learn from our great ones. When I think that it is our birthright, as Englishmen, to speak the tongue that Shakespeare spoke; to listen to his faintest modulation and catch his lightest breath of meaning, as no man of another speech can ever listen and comprehend; to have his voice, and the voices of the long succession of our great ones, from Chaucer to Hardy, for ever sounding in our ears, touching our souls, with the reminder of what it means, what it demands, what it bestows, to be an Englishman – how rich, how delicate, how generous, how strong, how beautiful, the secret spirit of this country is – how terrible to fail it, and how glorious to be found not wanting – when I think of these things, then I am thrilled with the wonder of our privilege and our destiny.

But then it is, also, that I know most deeply the wonder and the privilege of the destiny of other nations than my own: for they, too, have their secret voices, which our ears cannot distinguish, their holy of holies our minds cannot penetrate, their light we cannot see.

A DIVAGATION ON POLITICS

MR. CHARLES WHIBLEY has, not for the first time, written an excellent book. His life of *Lord John Manners and his Friends* [1] is not merely, to use the common cliché, 'a valuable contribution to the social and political history of the nineteenth century'; it is something which is as much more important as it is more rare – to wit, a *book*. The narrative flows equably, never turbid, never stagnant, from its source to the sea; so that no one who combines a moderate amount of interest in doings of man as a political animal, with a sense of the amenities of literary locomotion, can fail to be delighted by this smooth progress through the Victorian scene.

Lord John Manners was born in 1818 and died, Duke of Rutland, in 1906. He had been a Cabinet Minister for a greater length of time than any of his contemporaries, chiefly in minor offices, though he refused not a few great ones. But the interest of his career, for one who takes little stock of either aristocracy or cabinet ministering for their own sakes, is that he was in the 'forties a leading member of that Young England Party, whose memory is kept a rather vivid green by Disraeli's *Coningsby*.

The romantic Toryism of Young England is a curious phenomenon, and it is appropriate that its history should be chronicled, with rather more restraint than Disraeli would have found congenial, by Mr. Charles Whibley, who forms, together with Professor Saintsbury, the Tory Party in England to-day. For himself he probably would like to decline the name 'romantic,' though his admiration for Lord John Manners would hamper the customary vigour of his gesture

[1] Blackwood. 2 vols. 30s. net.

of refusal; and, in any case, to be a Tory to-day is to be romantic indeed.

I have neither the desire nor the ability to discourse upon the politics of 'Victoria's middle time'; but I should like to muse for a moment on that bewildering confusion of principles from which the ideas of Young England were born, and which took visible form in the elevation of the brilliant and rococo Disraeli to the Delphic oracle of Toryism. Surely only England – delightful, preposterous England – could have conceived and begotten the Primrose League.

Toryism: it is a pleasant word. I should like to be a Tory, for the sound of the thing. I dare say I am; at all events, if I were to claim to be one no one could say me nay, since nobody knows what a Tory is. He is one who elects to stand on the old ways – *stare super antiquas vias*. But which old ways? Those of ten years, or a hundred, or a thousand years ago? Rousseau chose to stand on the ways of the state of nature. That was going a long way back. He ought, by all the rules, to have been a very crusted Tory indeed: but he was a revolutionary. Again, in the matter of the Christian religion those who desire to go as far back as they can are generally called heretics.

The good old ways, if they are old enough, are the damnable new ones. Lord John Manners, when young, was all for 'the Patriot King' and dancing on the village green: but, instead of stopping discreetly at the Elizabethan era, in his youthful enthusiasm he went back further, to pre-Reformation days, when the Church was still one and indivisible. He dallied with extreme Tractarianism, and he was promptly turned out of Parliament on the good old 'No Popery!' cry. Up to a dozen years ago 'No Popery!' was still a sound plank in the Tory platform: perhaps times have changed since then. But I do not think so. English Toryism is a post-Reformation affair. Naturally: for how many of our 'old nobility' received their acres as their share of the plunder of the monasteries! Toryism, as a political creed, has but a relatively short period in which to seek its principles: a period bounded on the one side by the Reformation and on the other by the Whig Revolution of 1688. And it is not easy to see what practical principles it can get out of it. The divine right of kings is scarcely adapted to an age which has endured a European war through an inspired Hohenzollern. Mr. Baldwin (of Baldwin's, Ltd.) no doubt considers the King a kindly and honourable gentleman to whom devoir is due; but I imagine that neither his majesty nor he are under any illusions concerning the divine right of royalty. It is a dream, fatal to those who dream it.

The fact is that Toryism is not a practical creed, but a romantic velleity. The sole principle which might be excogitated for it is a refusal of democracy. But, for an Englishman that is hardly possible. He may mistrust democracy, he may believe that in practice it is pernicious, but if he wishes to refuse it he must leave this tight little island and take himself off to Russia or the parts about Cyrene. And, of course, this is what Disraeli, the political realist, clearly saw, when he invented Tory Democracy – a conception nearly as hybrid as Disraeli himself, but not sterile as most hybrids are: the first parent of Joseph Chamberlain's radical Imperialism.

Disraeli's political creed was as good as most, better than many. It had at least a germ of imagination in it, a vision of something beyond the mere ledger loyalty of the narrow Cobdenite persuasion. In his own rococo way Disraeli had a grasp of one aspect of the truth that man does not live by bread alone, as the Manchester school believed. The question: What besides bread man needs, has been answered in many ways. Disraeli thought, with the Romans, that it was circuses. Young England had faith in the maypole. But circuses (in politics) are as likely to turn out nice little wars as morris-dances. And then Little England found its opportunity.

The see-saw of Victorian politics is mildly interesting, but it belongs with last year's snow. The wealthy manufacturer now stands with the landowner; the agricultural and the commercial interests have had to sink their differences long ago in the recognition that the real political battle is to be fought over the question of private property. That is a real issue, and, one would have thought, a pretty straightforward one. Unfortunately it is continually confused with an issue of another kind – the equality of men. That all men are equal is the fundamental doctrine of Christianity, which should, by its title-deed, find more joy in one sinner that repenteth than in the ninety and nine which need not repentance. But this equality is a spiritual equality which all men share by virtue of their having an immortal soul, if they can find it. This spiritual equality has consequences in the material realm, but it is not included in those consequences that men should be equal in material things. The real corollary of the spiritual equality of men is that in all the affairs of life one man should regard another as an individual being, that he should love his neighbour as himself: which does not mean that he should share all his property with him. Doubtless there is a condition, which some men have reached in the past, and which humanity as a whole may one day attain, wherein men may become supremely indifferent to possessions and find it beneath their dignity to take thought for the morrow. But that condition is far away; nor is it in virtue of that ideal that the equality of man is proclaimed as a political principle to-day.

The equality of man that is demanded and proclaimed to-day is equality of possessions. There is no reason in earth or heaven why men's possessions should be equal. And this is so evident that more often the naked 'principle' is discreetly disguised as 'equality of opportunity.' It is utterly impossible that men's opportunities should be equal, for opportunity is not a tangible and divisible thing like a barrel of apples; it is a happy conjuncture of the man and the moment, and no amount of care in preparing the moment can assure the capacity of the man. The grain of solid truth in these specious catch-words is that it is an injustice, and a remediable one, that a child, who is not yet fit to battle with circumstance, should be deprived of the opportunity to become the best man he is capable of becoming. Nearly all that Governments can do in the way of remedying that injustice has already been done: most of the rest depends upon mothers and fathers.

But even if the time comes when they will do their part, neither possessions nor opportunities nor men will be equal. It would be a nightmare world if they were. But there is no danger of it. As far as we can see there will always be masters and men in the world. What is to be desired, and what is demanded by the true principle of equality (which, being spiritual, can have no material *equivalent*) is that they should be good masters and good men – a simple demand, in truth, but one that is still far from being satisfied by the one side or the other.

Equality is, as a political principle, pure bunkum; while to declare that the present distribution of rewards is just, is pure hypocrisy. It is unjust that anyone should possess a million pounds, for no man's work for the world is worth that share of the world's goods; it is unjust that a bad mechanic should be paid the same wage as a good one. It is just that a man should get his deserts, good or bad; it happens once in a thousand times. The real question is why on earth men should go on making all this fuss about justice. It is not a thing to ask for too insistently: one might be disconcerted if justice were really given. Again, there is no danger. There is no one to dispense it. 'One would need to see with the eye of God to decide who is good and bad,' as Tchehov said.

But, of course, the justice for which men clamour is not justice at all. They want happiness, which is a very different thing, and they have an extraordinary conviction that they are entitled to it; and an equally astonishing notion that they will get it by possessing some concrete thing which they do not possess already.

Every grown man knows that happiness does not depend upon a change of material conditions; yet, because few men are grown, the old will o' the wisp still allures. Capitalism will be abolished, and the golden age will begin. Just as men say 'opportunity,' not 'possessions,' they say 'capitalism,' not 'property,' for they thereby conceal from themselves the fact that they are simply asking for what belongs to other people; if they were to say that property must be abolished, they might realize that they themselves would have to make sacrifices for their own ideal. And the abolition of property is an ideal, and a high one, so high that we may be fairly certain, that when men get so far they will be content to abolish their own property, and not be concerned to abolish other people's. Then they will regard with pity the man who is so far behind them in development that he cannot be scornful of possessions; but the last thing they will wish to do is to convert him by violence. So long as they do, we may be sure that their motive is not the high spiritual ideal of renunciation, but the common and fallacious desire to acquire happiness by riches, or the eternal grudge of the have-nots against the haves.

It is very easy to confuse spiritual ideals with base desires; and the confusions are plausible. The communism of to-day is glibly identified with the communism of the early Christians; from which it differs by the whole breadth of heaven and not a few miles of hell. On the other hand, those who expose the fallacy, lie often and justly under the suspicion that they are magniloquently defending an order of things by which they profit. They would be heard more gladly if they were to show, by their behaviour and their lives, that the spiritual equality of men was a reality for them. It is not enough simply to denounce the wild-fire word of Rousseau: 'Man is born free, he is everywhere in chains' as a lie. A mere lie never becomes a wild-fire word. Rousseau's word is part truth, part falsehood; and only he can convincingly point the falsehood who shows himself responsive to its truth. Man is born to freedom, but the chains which prevent him from it are chiefly of his own making: and not only is the servant in bondage, but the master also, until the one can recognize that he can be free in service, and the other understand that only a free man's service is worth having.

Doubtless this also is an ideal, but it has the advantage of being an ideal that has sometimes been attained. It is not on record that the first thing the noble Roman convert to Christianity did was to free his slaves; he entered upon a new relation with them, by which they both recognized the necessity of the temporal relation of master and man, and both recognized the spiritual obligation of one free man to another. The thing is still being achieved, in innumerable corners of England; but it is harder to attain now that the master is so often depersonalized into a company, and the man into a member of a trade union. Had the masters lived up to their responsibilities in the good old days of *laissez-faire*, there would have been less bitterness in the hearts of the men, and less of the stubborn desire to do no more than they can be compelled to do.

But there is no going back. Trades Unions and limited companies have come to stay. The true-blue Tory may regret times past and claim that he, or his ancestors, did recognize a relation of mutual obligation between master and man; and that it was the soulless manufacturers who first regarded men and women and children as mere units of power to be ruthlessly used and ruthlessly discarded. There may be a grain of truth in it, but not more. The agricultural labourer of the 'forties fared hardly better than the slave of the factory. His cottage was, as often as not, a picturesque and pestilent hovel; and one of the few agricultural labourers I know well – a man of eighty odd years – has told me that his father, a farm-labourer likewise, and on a noble earl's estate, had to bring up eight children on nine shillings a week. They had nothing but bread soaked in water from one week-end to another. Six of them died. I am afraid there was very little to choose between the Manchester manufacturers and the Tory squires, in bulk. The good old days always turn out, on closer knowledge, to have been the bad old days.

Pat to my purpose, as I write these words, comes the *Times Literary Supplement* (April 30, 1925) with a leading article on 'Life in the Eighteenth Century,' reviewing two books by authors who have devoted themselves to investigation, unbiased either by Tory romanticism or by the Socialistic *arrière pensée*, of the conditions in London and the country prior to that industrial revolution which is continually paraded as the source of all our discontents.[1]

'Our brief survey (says Professor Bowden) has sufficed to reveal conditions of pauperism, helplessness and degradation, from which the older economic society seemed to offer

---

[1] *London Life in the Eighteenth Century.* By M. Dorothy George. (Kegan Paul. 21s. net.)

Industrial Society in England Towards the End of the Eighteenth Century. By Wilt Bowden. (Macmillan. 15s. net.)

no way of escape. To multitudes long hopeless, the new system of production offered promise of deliverance. . . . Historical veracity demands the blotting-out of the idyllic pictures that have been painted of working-class conditions in agriculture and the older industries preceding the great economic change; it necessitates a modification of the judgment that the status of the workers in the new industrial centres was inherently, inevitably inferior. . . . During the earlier stages of industrialization, the new industries ameliorated rather than rendered harsher the conditions of life for the workers.'

The truth is that the industrial revolution was one result of an awakening of the national intelligence. Another result was that men began to be ashamed of the beastly conditions in which the poorer classes lived, whether the servants of citizens or noblemen. What had really happened was not that conditions had deteriorated, but that the general conscience had improved. But it seemed to men that things were worse, not themselves a little better; and they put the blame for a degradation which had not occurred upon the great visible change in the country's economy which had. At the touch of the facts the Tory romanticism of Young England vanishes into thin air.

Toryism is a queer amalgam of a dream of the past and a dream of the future; in other words, it is only another variety of Rousseauism. The Tory is a romantic in silk stockings, the Socialist a romantic *sans culotte*. These facile romanticisms are equally futile. There is a profound and eternal verity in a true romanticism, but it lies at the core and will not be found in these superficial transpositions of the creed. True romanticism does not dream; it is an unrelenting pursuit of the *reality* of the individual, just as a true classicism is a faithful pursuit of the verity of the external world. Let that be grasped, and it is obvious that true Romanticism and true Classicism make the best of bedfellows: they do not conflict with, they complement each other. Romanticism is not revolutionary, neither is classicism conservative. Both seek the truth, and each is aware that it does not possess all the truth.

'Why tempt ye me? Bring me a penny that I may see it. And they brought it. And he saith unto them: Whose is this image and superscription? And they said unto Him, Cæsar's. And Jesus, answering, said unto them, Render to Cæsar the things that are Cæsar's, and to God the things that are God's.

So we come, as ever, back to fundamentals.

People have a way of resenting being brought down to bed-rock. It is necessary and salutary, for it is abhorrent to human dignity that a man's left hand should be ignorant of the behaviour of his right. That is no true belief which does not insist upon being squared with all a man's thoughts and actions; and it seems to me that a true connection between religious belief and political creeds can only be established if we think less in terms of 'rights' and more in terms of 'obligations.' In the old phrase of the catechism, it is 'my duty towards my neighbour' that chiefly matters, and, if the conception were real to us, it would take us a good deal nearer the millennium than the rights of man, or the rights of property. *Noblesse oblige*, if you like, provided you remember that noblesse is the privilege of any man who cares to make it his.

And the Socialists should give up dreaming of the golden age to be; and the Tories give up dreaming of the golden age that was. The present days are better, even though they may seem dark; and the future lies not with that country which expropriates or exterminates its masters, or with that which most swiftly forces its men to work on the old terms, but with that which can push through the present universal deadlock of capital and labour to a more widespread sense of the responsibility of each man for his neighbour.

Let us hope that country will be England. It has been in the van of Western progress too long for any true-bred Englishman not to feel instinctively that England will yet show the way out of the confusion that has fallen upon the West. But whether England, which was the first to plunge into the unknown of the industrial system, will be the first to emerge from it, or whether English industrialism will speed onwards to new and extreme developments of which we do not dream, – these things are hidden. But there is a compass by which we may steer across the uncharted ocean of the future; and that is a true individualism. If every man would strive for the possession of his own self, he would reach a point at which he knows that all manner of things which seemed important, are not important at all: that wealth does not produce happiness, and that happiness itself is not a thing to be aimed at, that circumstance is as it must be, that the only change worth having will be a change in men's attitude to circumstance, and therefore to their fellows, that in so far as this change comes to pass (and each man must do it for himself) men will be content to do as well as they can the work they have it in them to do, and not falsely dream that, if outward things were otherwise, they might be otherwise also.

THE LORD'S HOUSEKEEPER

THE other day I took a holiday and wandered into the National Portrait Gallery. Being in holiday mood, I found myself quite without interest in literary (or any other) celebrities, and began to browse among the unfamiliar faces. Being a man, I looked chiefly among the women – for some one wholly unknown and wholly delightful. It was as though I had entered invisible into a room full of women, with privilege to choose whom I would for my companion. She must charm me first – that was the rule of the game – then I would get my introduction to her.

Down in the darkest corner of one of the rooms, as though deliberately placed in obscurity, is a pencil drawing of a woman whom one would guess to be fifty years old. She wears a great white Dolly Varden hat, and a white bodice, and a book is open in her hands. Some kindly Quakeress she might be, but for that merry open look in her eyes. Yet merry is perhaps too strong a word – smiling, rather, with a very human kindness: the motherly landlady of one's dreams. If Heaven really did exist, she would be in charge of one of the mansions, with 'Come unto me all ye that are weary' written on a door-plate of gold. And she would have some trouble to prevent her lodgers from falling in love with her. For arched above her smiling eyes are two of the most delicate eyebrows an artist's pencil ever trembled over. Dark curls peep from under her great bonnet; there is a touch of apple colour in her cheeks; and her small mouth is firm and red. She is a woman with the amazing gift of growing beautifully old. At fifty she is enchanting, no less. Till you saw her, you did not know how enchanting fifty could be. Your heart flutters. Who is she? Who will introduce you? Do not despair: I am here for the purpose.

That lady, who by the way is not fifty but sixty-two, is Mistress Joanna Southcott, 'fanatic,' as she is curtly described in the *Dictionary of National Biography*. You may have heard of her; you may have seen in recent years, bills posted in the Underground railway stations, calling upon the Bishops to open Joanna Southcott's box. Evidently, she has still her followers: and I am not surprised. She may have been a fanatic, but it is certain she was no deceiver.

The portrait was taken by William Sharpe, the famous engraver, who was one of her disciples, in January, 1812. Less than three years later Joanna was dead. In those three years strange things happened.

Joanna was born in 1750, a simple Devonshire girl, the daughter of a small farmer. From her earliest girlhood she was given to the things of God. The language of her prophecies shows that her mind was saturated in the Bible, and to some purpose, for though the prophecies are sometimes inconsequent, they are beautifully limpid – the outpourings of a soul whose natural language is the Bible. Like the more famous Joan, she was virgin all her life. That was to be pathetically established by the surgeon's knife.

'Your maidens shall dream dreams.' When Joanna began to dream them is uncertain; but by the age of forty-two the prophetic spirit had descended irresistibly upon her. God, in the person of Christ, told her of a great famine that would come upon the land. She confided the revelation in her sister, who laughed at it. But Joanna was unconvinced; she began to write her prophecies, and to seal them with a seal she had found while sweeping the floor of the haberdasher's shop where she was employed. Her prophecies had a trick of coming true – enough of them, at least, to attract the attention of the religious-minded of her neighbourhood.

Apart from her prophecies of events the essence of her message was the old Christian promise – that an epoch of universal love would soon be miraculously inaugurated.

She began to gain followers – three clergymen of the diocese of Exeter among the first. And it is clear from the constancy of her disciples that they were attracted chiefly by the pure simplicity of her nature. She made repeated challenges to the Bishops to investigate her claims to be inspired by the spirit of God: if they rejected them she promised that she would renounce her mission, and condemn herself as deluded. The Bishops were wary. It has always been a difficult business for Bishops (or any one else) to pronounce whether the spirit, when it actually begins to work, is of God or the Devil. Like Gamaliel, they left Joanna alone.

But they were not faithful to the principles of that wise Jew. When Joanna's following grew, and it grew very rapidly, one of them was rash enough to denounce her. This was Joanna's response: she was simple, but no simpleton:

'Though the Bishops are silent to the request made of them, and the warning given to them, that they will come forth to support the work, if it be of God, or to confute it, if not; yet I am informed that one of the Bishops hath said that I have done more mischief than ever an individual had done before.

'I can scarcely credit the report to be true, that a Bishop should see it in this light, and not use his authority to stop the "mischief," when the power is put into his hands.

'I shall answer such Bishops, as the King's Jester once answered them. When a nobleman sent a petition to his majesty to crave his pardon for a third murder he had committed, the king said to his jester, "I know not what to do concerning this man: he hath killed two men before, which I pardoned him for, and now he hath killed the third." The jester answered, "No, he has not killed three men; he has killed but one." His majesty asked him how he could make out that. The jester said, "If thou hadst had him hanged for the first man, he would never have killed another; so thou hast killed the other two." '

Joanna was more than a prophetess; she was a prophetess with a sense of humour. 'Fanatic' is not the name for her at all. Which of her Bishops could have written so cogent a reply as hers? My eye detects a touch of genius in those lucid sentences. John Bunyan hardly did better.

A little later she began to 'seal' 144,000 of the elect against the advent of the Lamb. They were given little certificates of salvation in envelopes, sealed with the seal she had used for her prophecies: I.C. and two stars. Joanna interpreted I.C. as a sign of her mystical marriage with Christ; and at about this time (1804) it was revealed to her that she was 'the wife of the Lamb,' in a singularly vivid vision of Christ rising from bed with her, his flaxen hair damp with sweat, dripping as though he had emerged from a river, which, she supposed, had come from his having to sleep tight-pressed between herself and her faithful female body-servant, Anne Towneley.

Not till nine years later did her visions culminate in the promise that she should conceive and bear a child – Shiloh, the second incarnation of Christ. She published the revelation; and shut herself away from all society. This was her account of the miraculous conception:

'On the 14th October, 1813, I was ordered to sit up all night in a room by myself, which I did. Many extraordinary things were revealed to me, why Christ took man's nature upon him, and what he suffered for man's sake; that I should keep that night in everlasting remembrance, and not forget the giver of the blessings I enjoyed. About twelve o'clock I looked at the candle; there appeared something like a large bowl behind it, with a point towards the candle; the candle was flaming very bright and there appeared a ring as red as scarlet, circled about the middle of the flame; immediately there appeared a hand as white as snow, which came out between the bowl and the candle, and pointed towards me. I trembled to see it, but was answered – "FEAR NOT: IT IS I." I was then ordered to put on my glasses, and the hand appeared *the second time*, more brilliant than before; but then the flame of the candle seemed parted in two, and looked in a different manner from the first, but burnt very bright. The hand was pointed towards me the second time, as white as snow, and a red cuff was on the wrist.'

Six months later, in March, 1814, she fell ill, and shortly after began to manifest all the outward signs of pregnancy. She was pathetically anxious not to delude herself or others. She was examined first by a jury of matrons, then by a number of medical men: of whom the majority (six of nine, to be precise) pronounced that her symptoms were such that in a younger woman – she was now sixty-five – they would certainly have indicated pregnancy. One of them, a Dr. Richard Reece, was bolder; he announced his verdict to the world that she was pregnant. Her own statement, made in October, 1814, is the most interesting:

'I have felt life increasing more and more from the sixteenth of May to this day; but never having had a child in my life, I leave it to the judgment of mothers of children who attend me, who give their decided opinion, that it is perfectly like a woman who is pregnant. Then now, I say, it remains to be proved whether my feelings and their judgments be right or wrong; whether it is a child or not; which a few months must decide: or the grave must decide for me; for I could not live to the end of this year, with the increasing growth I have felt within me in so short a space, without a deliverance.

'I have assigned my reasons why I believed, and had faith to publish to the world that such an event would take place; and I am truly convinced that wondrous events must take place to fulfil the Scriptures before men can be brought to the knowledge of the Lord as spoken by the prophets, or the fulfilment of the Gospel be accomplished. But, however, men have mocked my folly and faith in believing what I have published; yet I plainly see that I should be mocked much more, had I concealed it from the world till this present time; for then there would be room for the world to mock as to my being a prophetess, and such an event not to be foretold, to make it known, that men might believe.'

There speaks a heart innocent of guile. Though the world jeered, her adherents were wildy excited. A great house for a public accouchement was advertised for; a magnificent cot, costing £200, was prepared for the little Shiloh. Innumerable rich gifts for the blessed babe flowed in, which Joanna caused to be carefully kept, and the names and addresses of the senders recorded in a book, that in case the child was not born they could be returned. For Joanna was not certain, nor did she ever pretend to be. Never was woman less of an impostor. It had been revealed to her that she would conceive and bear the miraculous child; and she had had the courage to make public her revelation. Now something was happening inside her physical body, such that all the women, and two-thirds of the doctors who examined her, pronounced her symptoms to be the symptoms of pregnancy. What was she to believe? Nothing but what she actually did believe – namely, that she would either bear a child, or die, or do both at once.

On November 19, Dr. Reece, who had assured her and the public that she was indeed pregnant, was summoned. Reece, who cuts a very poor figure in the whole affair, gave this account of the interview:

'She appeared much exhausted, low and dejected, and unable to speak her mind. Finding herself, she said, *gradually dying*, she could not but consider her inspiration and prophecies as *delusion*. As my opinion of her situation had been *publicly expressed* and *stated*, she thought it her duty that the task of opening her body should also be confided to me. This examination, she observed, would clear me in the eyes of the public, and that consideration alone induced her to give her consent, for against it she had otherwise extreme horror. . . .

'You will, she again strongly repeated, find *something alive* in me, and which will prove to my friends that I am not that impostor I am represented to be. . . .'

Characteristically, Joanna's sole thought was for the Doctor's reputation. He did not deserve the consideration. He goes on to tell that he asked her whether he should not make an effort to save the life of the child by operating. She answered: 'If it is the work of the Lord, he will deliver me, and if it is not, it is fit it should die with me.' After shedding tears, she had her disciples called to her, and said to them:

' "My friends, some of you have known me nearly twenty-five years, and all of you not less than twenty. When you have heard me speak of my prophecies, you have sometimes heard me say that I *doubted* my inspiration. But at the same time you would not let me despair. When I have been alone it has often appeared *delusion*, but when the communications were made to me, I did not in the least doubt. Feeling, as I now do feel, that my dissolution is drawing nigh, and

298

that a day or two may terminate my life, it all appears *delusion*." She was by this exertion quite exhausted and wept bitterly. On reviving in a little time she observed that it was very extraordinary, that after spending all her life investigating the Bible, it should please the Lord to lay this heavy burden upon her.'

At Reece's next visit, on December 6, she had regained a modest confidence in her mission. If she was not (she said) the favoured woman to produce the Prince of Peace she was at least an instrument in the hands of God to produce some good.

On December 27 she died. Her body was kept warm, by her instructions, for four days. Then the body was examined, by Reece and a number of other doctors. The result of the *post-mortem* examination was mysterious: for no cause was found for her previous appearance of pregnancy.

Reece was disconcerted. His professional reputation was in jeopardy. Had an internal tumour been discovered, there would have been some explanation of his mistaken diagnosis. In fact, all the doctors had been equally mistaken, even Dr. Sims, who had pronounced definitely against pregnancy and for a disease of the womb. There was neither disease, nor child, nor anything whatever to account for the physical symptoms which no one had denied.

Reece, to extricate himself, wrote an unworthy pamphlet, accusing her of a deliberate and carefully planned imposture. The pamphlet is a childish piece of self-contradiction. Dr. Sims, who had been peremptory against pregnancy, was equally peremptory for Joanna's good faith. No sober student of the strange story can doubt it.

Probably the explanation is to be sought in the unexplored realms of psycho-physiology. By the fervour of her faith, the physical symptoms of pregnancy had come to her. It was a supreme effort of the spirit to bend the body to its will. Under the effort Joanna died. She was a remarkable, and a beautiful, woman; nor am I surprised that her disciples should have remained faithful to her after the disaster to her hopes and theirs. As Reece records with chagrin and astonishment, 'they all believed that, though she was dead (which, they said, had been foretold twenty years before) there would be a child. None condemned her as an impostor. One declared he would ever revere her memory and once a month visit the spot where she was laid with pious and reverential awe.' I like that man. On a loyalty like his, Christianity was built.

What was the explanation eventually given by the disciples, I do not know. I do not know whether the church still exists as a church; and I am ignorant of its doctrines. But I should guess that the orthodox explanation would be that Joanna was indeed with child, but that the Almighty changed his plans, and Shiloh was taken back whence he came.

A strange destiny for the woman of that comely face, drawn but a few months before the last incredible revelation came to her; yet not discordant with her loveliness, for surely there is great beauty as well as pathos in Joanna's story. If she was not to be as she (like other saints) had dreamed – the bride of Christ – I cannot help thinking she will find her place as his heavenly housekeeper.

THE DIVINE PLAIN FACE

IN the National Portrait Gallery, among the portraits of female Victorian celebrities, from George Eliot to Harriet Martineau, is a pencil drawing of a lovely face – a wild woodland gleam amid the rigours of high seriousness. You look and look; looking is enough, but it brings no word. For there is singularly little to be *said* about that face. Its charm lies in some exquisite perfection of ordinariness, which belies the emphasis of adjectives. This loveliness is immune from the caprice of fashion, unruffled by the breath of any *Zeitgeist*. Were it met to-morrow, or a hundred years hence, it would be recognized straightway for what it was; as some one met it more than a hundred years ago, and fell in love, and found the perfect phrase.

For this is Charles Lamb's Fanny Kelly, of Drury Lane, and 'the divine plain face'; and this is, as near as may be, the face as it was when its glimpses haunted him at his desk in East India House. There is nothing on the drawing to tell you that it is veritably she; in her company of female celebrities she has taken on a protective colouring and become Frances Maria Kelly (1790–1882). The drawing was taken in 1822, when she was thirty-two. Three years before, Charles Lamb had proposed to her and been rejected. She lived to be ninety-two, and never married.

The story is no secret; yet not so familiar that it will not bear retelling. It contains, I fancy, more of the elusive essence of Charles Lamb than any other single episode of that well-mastered life.

When Charles Lamb's admiration of Fanny Kelly first began there is no saying. She was on the stage of Drury Lane at seven years old; at eleven she was playing Prince

Arthur to Mrs. Siddons's Constance, and feeling the great actress's tears (real tears!) drop warm upon her neck. The first sign made by Charles Lamb was in 1813, in the first dramatic criticism he wrote for a newspaper, Leigh Hunt's *Examiner*. In his article he contrasted the old acting and the new, of course to the advantage of the old. The new school was tainted with the vice of playing to the audience, not the play: but there was one bright exception:

'I am sure that the very absence of this fault in Miss Kelly and her judicious attention to her part, with little or no reference to the spectators, is one cause why her varied excellencies, though they are beginning to be perceived, have yet found their way more slowly to the approbation of the public than they have deserved.'

Probably at this time – when Fanny was twenty-three and Lamb thirty-eight – was written the poetic version of the same sentiment which appeared in the *Works* of 1818 as a sonnet:

'To Miss Kelly.

You are not, Kelly, of the common strain,
That stoop their pride and female honour down
To please that many-headed beast, *the town*,
And vend their lavish smiles and tricks for gain;
By fortune thrown amid the actor's train,
You keep your native dignity of thought;
The plaudits that attend you come unsought,
As tributes due unto your natural vein.
Your tears have passion in them, and a grace
Of genuine freshness, which our hearts avow;

302

THE DIVINE PLAIN FACE

Your smiles are winds whose ways we cannot trace,
That vanish and return we know not how –
And please the better from a pensive face
And thoughtful eye, and a reflecting brow.'

Soon after 1813, I imagine, they became acquainted. For, though it is not till October, 1817, that her name appears in his letters, the habit of talking to her in the green-room was by that time of old standing. 'Have you' (he writes to the Kenneys in France) 'any plays and green-rooms, and Fanny Kellys to chat to?' A little later (in February, 1818) he writes to Wordsworth as though his admiration for Fanny Kelly were familiar to his friends, with a confession of 'the darling thoughts all his own' that might occupy his mind at his ledgers, were it not for the interruptions of 'a set of amateurs of the Belles Lettres – a faint memory of some passage in a Book – or the tone of an absent friend's voice – a snatch of Miss Burrell's singing – a gleam of Fanny Kelly's divine plain face.'

In December, 1818, he published an anonymous note in the *Examiner* complaining that Miss Kelly was not in the new comedy at Drury Lane: he had seen her sitting among the spectators. What was the reason? Was there a cabal against her among the managers? I fancy that this little note was 'inspired,' and that it was with Charles Lamb that Fanny Kelly was sitting in the theatre. Next month, January, 1819, he published the following unsigned comparison of Fanny Kelly with her famous predecessor:

'Mrs. Jordan's was the carelessness of a child . . . she seemed one whom care could not come near. . . . Hence, if we had more unmixed pleasure from her performances, we had perhaps less sympathy with them than with those of her successor. The latter lady's is the joy of a freed spirit,

303

escaping from care, as a bird that has been limed: her smiles, if I may use the expression, seem saved out of the fire, relics which a good and innocent heart had snatched up as most portable; her contents are visitors, not inmates; she can lay them by altogether, and when she does so I am not sure that she is not greatest. . . .

'I do not know whether I am not speaking it to her honour, that she does not succeed in what are called fine lady parts. Our friend C. once observed that no man of genius ever figured as a gentleman.'

In this the *personal* preoccupation is manifest. Lamb is not merely considering Fanny Kelly as an actress; but he is evidently bent on separating the woman from the actress to the uttermost, driving, indeed, with all his delicate strength, a wedge between them. Fanny Kelly's function, for him, is to be herself. When her part permits it he is satisfied; when it does not he is malcontent.

By July he is still further advanced in admiration, and goes one further in his criticism. He writes on Fanny Kelly's appearance in Brome's *Jovial Crew*:

'The Princess of Mumpers was *she* that played Rachel. Her gabbling, lachrymose petitions; her tones such as we have heard by the side of old woods when an irresistible face has come peeping on one on a sudden: with the full black locks, and a *voice* – how shall we describe it? – a voice that was by nature meant to convey nothing but truth and good-ness, but warped by circumstance into an assurance that she is telling us a lie . . . her jeers, which, we had rather stand, than be caressed by other ladies' compliments, a summer's day long – her face, with a wild out-of-doors grace upon it. . . . No less than the "Beggar Maid" whom "King Cophetua wooed." '

' "What a lass that were," said a stranger who sate beside us, speaking of Miss Kelly as *Rachel*, "to go a gipseying through the world with!" '

Charles Lamb's stranger, without a doubt, bore the same name as he. Nothing more nearly resembling a proposal of marriage ever did, or ever will, masquerade as a dramatic criticism. As far as man could he had prepared the way: it remained only for him to take the plunge *in propria persona*. Another fortnight, and it was done. On July 20th he wrote to Fanny Kelly:

'Dear Miss Kelly, – We had the pleasure, *pain* I might better call it, of seeing you last night in the new Play. It was a most consummate piece of Acting, but what a task for you to undergo! at a time when your heart is sore from real sorrow! It has given rise to a train of thinking, which I cannot suppress.

'Would to God you were released from this way of life; that you could bring your mind to consent to share your lot with us, and throw off for ever the whole burden of your Profession. I neither expect nor wish you to take notice of this which I am writing in your present over-occupied & hurried state. – But to think of it at your leisure. I have quite income enough, if that were all, to justify for me making such a proposal, with what I may call even a handsome provision for my survivor. What you possess of your own would naturally be appropriated to those, for whose sakes chiefly you have made such sacrifices. I am not so foolish as not to know that I am a most unworthy match for such a one as you, but you have for years been a principal object in my mind. In many a sweet assumed character I have learned to love you, but simply as F. M. Kelly I love you better than them all. Can you quit these shadows of existence, & come & be a reality to us? Can you leave off harassing yourself to please a thankless multitude, who know nothing of you, & begin at laſt to live to yourself & your friends.

'As plainly & frankly as I have seen you give or refuse assent in some feigned scene, so frankly do me the juſtice to answer me. It is impossible I should feel injured or aggrieved by your telling me at once, that the proposal does not suit you. It is impossible that I should ever think of moleſting you with idle importunity and persecution after your mind once fairly spoken – but happier, far happier, could I have leave to hope a time might come, when our friends might be your friends, our intereſts, yours; our book-knowledge, if in that inconsiderable particular we have any advantage, might impart something to you, which you would every day have it in your power ten thousand fold to repay by the added cheerfulness and joy which you could not fail to bring as a dowry into whatever family should have the honor and happiness of receiving *you*, the moſt welcome accession that could be made to it.

'In haſte, but with entire respeсt and deepeſt affeсtion, I subscribe myself

'C. LAMB.'

Prompt indeed came the reply:

'Henrietta St., July 20, 1819.

'An early & deeply-rooted attachment has fixed my heart on one from whom no worldly prospeсt can well induce me to withdraw it, but while I thus *frankly* & decidedly decline your proposal, believe me, I am not insensible to the high honour which the preference of such a mind as yours confers upon me – let me, however, hope that all thought upon this subjeсt will end with this letter, & that you will henceforth encourage no sentiment towards me than eſteem in my private charaсter and a continuance of that approbation of my humble talents which you have already expressed so much & so often to my advantage and gratification.

'Believe me I feel proud to acknowledge myself

'Your obliged friend

'F. M. KELLY.'

It is almost a model of the common form of the period: 'How to decline an offer of Marriage.' I wonder whether the myriad lovely ladies who made use of it – 'Let me, however, hope that all thought upon this subject will end, etc.' – really expected, or really desired, that their commands should be obeyed. If they did, women have changed in a hundred years; for I am told, on excellent authority, that the women of to-day find no small pleasure in the knowledge that they are the objects of a secret and fruitless passion.

Lamb, however, played the game according to the rules; and characteristically went one better. Still on the same day, July 20th, he replied:

'Dear Miss Kelly, – *Your injunctions shall be obeyed to a tittle.* I feel myself in a lackadaisical no-how-ish kind of a humour. I believe it is the rain, or something. I had thought to have written seriously, but I fancy I succeed best in epistles of mere fun; puns & *that* nonsense. You will be good friends with us, will you not? let what has past 'break no bones' between us.[1] You will not refuse us them next time we send for them?

'Yours very truly,

'C. L.

'Do you observe the delicacy of not signing my full name?

'N.B. – Do not paste that last letter of mine into your Book.'

---

[1] This is a punning reference to the little bone discs which were given to the 'dead-heads.'

I would give much to know precisely how Fanny Kelly felt on receiving that. Was she hurt? Or sad? Or did she merely feel that there was no accounting for Charles Lamb? And what did she feel when, a fortnight later, she read the epilogue to this little love-story in print in the *Examiner*? Charles Lamb wrote of her performance in *The Hypocrite*:

'Miss Kelly is not quite at home in *Charlotte*; she is too good for such parts. Her cue is to be natural; she cannot put on the modes of artificial life, and play the coquet as it is expected to be played. There is a frankness in her tones which defeats her purposes. . . . She is in truth not framed to tease or torment even in jest, but to utter a hearty *Yes* or *No*; to yield or refuse assent with a noble sincerity. We have not the pleasure of being acquainted with her, but we have been told she carries the same cordial manners into private life.'

That was the end of Lamb's brief career as a dramatic critic. Since every one of his newspaper criticisms was concerned with Fanny Kelly, and since they end promptly with his proposal and rejection, we may conclude not only that he originally embraced the career for the sole purpose of singing Fanny Kelly's praises, but that, perhaps unconsciously, it was to him a means of preparing the way to his offer of marriage. In fact, it was Charles Lamb's peculiar method of courtship. Once he was refused the courtship ceased.

But it is not easy to get a real glimpse of Fanny Kelly through Charles Lamb's rose-coloured spectacles. One feels that here for once his good-humoured and whimsical faculty for seeing things as they are had failed him a little. There is that in the tone of a part of his truly charming letter of proposal which makes me suspect that he had misconceived the situation, by imputing to Fanny Kelly herself his own sense that the theatre was a bondage (and a little even of a degradation) to her. That was what Lamb felt; the feeling peeps out plainly in his criticisms. And, no doubt, Fanny Kelly herself in conversation lent substance to Lamb's eager imagination. Artists of all kinds are prone to talk to the admiring and sympathetic listener of the burden of their lives; but it does not mean they want to change them. Lamb would have understood this well enough of any other person; but of Fanny Kelly he was only too willing to believe that she felt herself as a caged bird behind the footlights – a fine spirit, like Ariel, waiting for the word of freedom.

How Lamb was inclined to romanticize Fanny Kelly appears plainly from his story of 'Barbara S–' which was avowedly based on an incident of Fanny's childhood. In that story, you may remember, the little actress Barbara, aged eleven, goes to draw her weekly half-guinea, on which her family wholly depended. By mistake the Treasurer pops into her hand a whole guinea. Not till she reaches the first landing of the stairs does she notice it; the struggle in her mind whether to return or no carries her to the second. Then virtue triumphs, and she returns. In her old age Fanny Kelly told the true story, and told it extraordinarily well – better, I think, than Lamb had done. At least, I find nothing in Lamb's story so moving and so real as the anxious question put to little Fanny as she returns from the pay-box by a grown woman of the company: 'Is it full pay, my dear?' That is the real accent of behind the scenes in the old days.

The true story, as Fanny Kelly told it in 1875, was of a mistake between a one-pound and a two-pound note. The two-pound note, given her by mistake, had been torn and joined again with a thick strip of gummed paper.

'Now observe (she wrote) in what small matters Fanny

and Barbara were to a marked degree different characters. Barbara, at eleven years of age, was some time before she felt the different size of a guinea to a half-guinea, *held tight in her hand*. I, at nine years old, was not so untaught, or innocent. I was a woman of the world. I took *nothing* for granted. I had a deep respect for Mr. Peake, but the join might have disfigured the note – destroyed its currency; and it was my business to see all safe. So I carefully opened it.'

There is surely a sub-acid flavour in the comment: 'I was a woman of the world.' Probably, all through her friendship with Charles Lamb she was a little more of the woman of the world than he wanted to, or did, believe. In her later life she confessed that the reason why she did not accept his proposal was her fear of the strain of madness in the family. Perhaps, also, £600 a year was rather less in her eyes than it was in his: for when she retired from the stage in 1835, she retired with a competence of £13,000. To be sure, she lost it not long after, by building a small theatre, where she opened an academy of dramatic art, which failed. The theatre is now the Royalty in Dean Street.

Fanny Kelly was assuredly none the worse for being 'a woman of the world': it was her business to be. In her face one discovers a sense of realities; it is a frank and open face, but not a dreamer's; the charm is open and above-board, the charm of a charming friend. And a friend of the Lamb's she remained. The next year Mary Lamb was teaching her Latin; and it was then, I imagine, that little Mary Novello, who was also being taught Latin by Mary Lamb in Lamb's rooms in Russell Street, saw a lady come in who appeared to her strikingly intellectual-looking, and still young: she was surprised, therefore, to hear the lady say, in the course of conversation, 'Oh, as for me, my dear Miss Lamb, I'm nothing now but a stocking-mending old woman.' It was

Fanny Kelly. Mary Novello records having seen her twice again – once, elegantly dressed, drinking porter out of a tankard with Charles and Mary Lamb on a bench before an inn near Enfield, and, for the laſt time, when the Lambs were dead and gone, during the rehearsals of the famous performance of 'The Merry Wives' which Dickens arranged in 1848. Fanny Kelly was coaching the company of amateurs, Mary Novello – then Mary Cowden Clarke – among them. 'Keep your eyes on the people in the upper row of boxes, my dear,' said Fanny. 'Then your under eyelids will save you from the glare of the footlights.' Good, sound professional advice, no doubt; but Charles Lamb's shade may have winced a little to hear it.

APPENDIX

I REPRODUCE Goethe's poem and Huxley's comment as they appeared in the first number of *Nature*, on November 4, 1869:

'Nature! We are surrounded and embraced by her: powerless to separate ourselves from her, and powerless to penetrate beyond her.

'Without asking, or warning, she snatches us up into her circling dance, and whirls us on until we are tired, and drop from her arms.

'She is ever shaping new forms: what is, has never yet been; what has been, comes not again. Everything is new, and yet nought but the old.

'We live in her midst and know her not. She is incessantly speaking to us, but betrays not her secret. We constantly act upon her, and yet have no power over her.

'The one thing she seems to aim at is Individuality; yet she cares nothing for individuals. She is always building up and destroying; but her workshop is inaccessible.

'Her life is in her children; but where is the mother? She is the only artist; working up the most uniform material into utter opposites; arriving, without a trace of effort, at perfection at the most exact precision, though always veiled under a certain softness.

'Each of her works has an essence of its own; each of her phenomena a special characterization: and yet their diversity is in unity.

'She performs a play; we know not whether she sees it herself, and yet she acts for us, the lookers-on.

'Incessant life, development, and movement are in her, but she advances not. She changes for ever and ever, and rests not a moment. Quietude is inconceivable to her, and she has laid her curse upon rest. She is firm. Her steps are measured, her exceptions rare, her laws unchangeable.

'She has always thought, and always thinks; though not as a man, but as Nature. She broods over an all-comprehending idea, which no searching can find out.

'Mankind dwell in her and she in them. With all men she plays a game for love, and rejoices the more they win. With many her moves are so hidden that the game is over before they know it.

'That which is most unnatural is still Nature; the stupidest philistinism has a touch of her genius. Whoso cannot see her everywhere, sees her nowhere rightly.

'She loves herself, and her innumerable eyes and affections are fixed upon herself. She has divided herself that she may be her own delight. She causes an endless succession of new capacities for enjoyment to spring up, that her insatiable sympathy may be assuaged.

'She rejoices in illusion. Whoso destroys it in himself and others, him she punishes with the sternest tyranny. Whoso follows her in faith, him she takes as a child to her bosom.

'Her children are numberless. To none is she altogether miserly; but she has her favourites, on whom she squanders much, and for whom she makes great sacrifices. Over greatness she spreads her shield.

'She tosses her creatures out of nothingness, and tells them not whence they came, nor whither they go. It is their business to run, she knows the road.

'Her mechanism has few springs – but they never wear out, are always active and manifold.

'The spectacle of Nature is always new, for she is always renewing the spectators. Life is her most exquisite invention; and death her expert contrivance to get plenty of life.

'She wraps man in darkness, and makes him for ever long

for light. She creates him dependent upon the earth, dull and heavy; and yet is always shaking him until he attempts to soar above it.

'She creates needs because she loves action. Wondrous! that she produces all this action so easily. Every need is a benefit, swiftly satisfied, swiftly renewed. – Every fresh want is a new source of pleasure, but she soon reaches an equilibrium.

'Every instant she commences an immense journey, and every instant she has reached her goal.

'She is vanity of vanities; but not to us, to whom she has made herself of the greatest importance. She allows every child to play tricks with her; every fool to have judgment upon her; thousands to walk stupidly over her and see nothing; and takes her pleasure and finds her account in them all.

'We obey her laws even when we rebel against them; we work with her even when we desire to work against her.

'She makes every gift a benefit by causing us to want it. She delays, that we may desire her; she hastens, that we may not weary of her.

'She has neither language nor discourse; but she creates tongues and hearts, by which she feels and speaks.

'Her crown is love. Through love alone dare we come near her. She separates all existences, and all tend to intermingle. She has isolated all things in order that all may approach one another. She holds a couple of draughts from the cup of love to be fair payment for the pains of a lifetime.

'She is all things. She rewards herself and punishes herself; is her own joy and her own misery. She is rough and tender, lovely and hateful, powerless and omnipotent. She is an eternal present. Past and future are unknown to her. The present is her eternity. She is beneficent. I praise her and all her works. She is silent and wise.

'No explanation is wrung from her; no present won from

her, which she does not give freely. She is cunning, but for good ends, and it is best not to notice her tricks.

'She is complete, but never finished. As she works now, so can she always work. Every one sees her in his own fashion. She hides under a thousand names and phrases, and is always the same. She has brought me here and will also lead me away. I trust her. She may scold me, but she will not hate her work. It was not I who spoke of her. No! What is false and what is true, she has spoken it all. The fault, the merit, is all hers.'

So far Goethe.

When my friend, the Editor of *Nature*, asked me to write an opening article for his first number, there came into my mind this wonderful rhapsody on 'Nature,' which has been a delight to me from my youth up. It seemed to me that no more fitting preface could be put before a Journal, which aims to mirror the progress of that fashioning by Nature of a picture of herself, in the mind of man, which we call the progress of Science.

A translation, to be worth anything, should reproduce the words, the sense, and the form of the original. But when that original is Goethe's it is hard indeed to obtain this ideal; harder still, perhaps, to know whether one has reached it, or only added another to the long list of those who have tried to put the great German poet into English, and failed.

Supposing, however, that critical judges are satisfied with the translation as such, there lies beyond them the chance of another reckoning with the British public, who dislike what they call 'Pantheism' almost as much as I do, and who will certainly find this essay of the poet's terribly Pantheistic. In fact, Goethe himself almost admits that it is so. In a curious explanatory letter, addressed to Chancellor von Müller, under date May 26th, 1828, he writes:

APPENDIX

'This essay was sent to me a short time ago from amongst the papers of the ever-honoured Duchess Anna Amelia; it is written by a well-known hand, of which I was accustomed to avail myself in my affairs, in the year 1780, or thereabouts.

'I do not exactly remember having written these reflections, but they very well agree with the ideas which had at that time become developed in my mind. I might term the degree of insight which I had then attained, a comparative one, which was trying to express its tendency towards a not yet attained superlative.

'There is an obvious inclination to a sort of Pantheism, to the conception of an unfathomable, unconditional, humorously self-contradictory Being, underlying the phenomena of Nature; and it may pass as a jest, with a bitter truth in it.'

Goethe says that about the date of this composition of 'Nature' he was chiefly occupied with comparative anatomy; and, in 1786, he gave himself incredible trouble to get other people to take an interest in his discovery, that man has an intermaxillary bone. After that he went on to the metamorphosis of plants, and to the theory of the skull; and at length, had the pleasure of seeing his work taken up by the German naturalists. The letter ends thus:

'If we consider the high achievements by which all the phenomena of Nature have been linked together in the human mind; and then, once more, thoughtfully peruse the above essay, from which we started, we shall, not without a smile, compare that comparative, as I called it, with the superlative we have now reached, and rejoice in the progress of fifty years.'

Forty years have passed since these words were written, and we look again, 'not without a smile,' on Goethe's superlative. But the road which led from his comparative to his superlative, has been diligently followed, until the notions which represented Goethe's superlative are now the commonplaces of science – and we have a super-superlative of our own.

When another half-century has passed, curious readers of the back numbers of *Nature* will probably look on *our* best, 'not without a smile'; and it may be that long after the theories of the philosophers whose achievements are recorded in these pages are obsolete, the vision of the poet will remain as a truthful and efficient symbol of the wonder and mystery of Nature.

T. H. HUXLEY.